PRAISE FOR
A FAMOUS DOG'S LIFE

"This book is more than just a fascinating look at the tale behind a twelve-pound pop-culture icon. Rather, this heartwarming story celebrates the bond between people and their canine best friends. *A Famous Dog's Life* is a must read for any dog lover."

—*New York Times* bestselling author Jen Lancaster

"This wonderful book tells the charming story of Gidget, a special little dog. It'll make you pant with pleasure."

—*New York Times* bestselling author Rita Mae Brown

"As an animal-safety rep for the American Humane Association's Film and Television Unit—the only organization in the world authorized to protect the welfare of animals in the entertainment industry and sanctioned to award the famous 'No Animals Were Harmed' end credit—I act as the voice and the advocate for all the animals on set. In this book, Sue has given a voice to Gidget as well as all the animals she has had the opportunity to train and bring through her doors. What a great tribute to Gidget, who was a star among animal actors. And Sue is a star among Hollywood animal trainers."

—Netta Bank, senior certified animal safety representative,
American Humane Association, Film & TV Unit

"This is my favorite kind of story: one that proves that with hard work, a great attitude, a lovable personality and large glorious ears, you can accomplish anything."

—Bret Witter, coauthor of the #1 *New York Times* bestseller *Dewey*
and *Dewey's Nine Lives*

A
FAMOUS
DOG'S LIFE

The Story of Gidget,
America's Most Beloved Chihuahua

Sue Chipperton
and
Rennie Dyball

 NEW AMERICAN LIBRARY

NEW AMERICAN LIBRARY
Published by New American Library, a division of
Penguin Group (USA) Inc., 375 Hudson Street,
New York, New York 10014, USA
Penguin Group (Canada), 90 Eglinton Avenue East, Suite 700, Toronto,
Ontario M4P 2Y3, Canada (a division of Pearson Penguin Canada Inc.)
Penguin Books Ltd., 80 Strand, London WC2R 0RL, England
Penguin Ireland, 25 St. Stephen's Green, Dublin 2,
Ireland (a division of Penguin Books Ltd.)
Penguin Group (Australia), 250 Camberwell Road, Camberwell, Victoria 3124,
Australia (a division of Pearson Australia Group Pty. Ltd.)
Penguin Books India Pvt. Ltd., 11 Community Centre, Panchsheel Park,
New Delhi - 110 017, India
Penguin Group (NZ), 67 Apollo Drive, Rosedale, Auckland 0632,
New Zealand (a division of Pearson New Zealand Ltd.)
Penguin Books (South Africa) (Pty.) Ltd., 24 Sturdee Avenue,
Rosebank, Johannesburg 2196, South Africa

Penguin Books Ltd., Registered Offices:
80 Strand, London WC2R 0RL, England

First published by New American Library,
a division of Penguin Group (USA) Inc.

First Printing, May 2011
10 9 8 7 6 5 4 3 2 1

Copyright © Sue Chipperton and Rennie Dyball, 2011
Foreword copyright © Reese Witherspoon, 2011
All rights reserved

Front cover photo of Gidget by Vern Evans Photography. Back cover photo of Sue Chipperton and
Gidget by Ron Galella, Ltd. Cover design by Mary E. O'Boyle.

   REGISTERED TRADEMARK—MARCA REGISTRADA

LIBRARY OF CONGRESS CATALOGING-IN-PUBLICATION DATA:

Chipperton, Sue.
    A famous dog's life: the story of Gidget, America's most beloved Chihuahua/Sue Chipperton and
Rennie Dyball.
        p. cm.
    ISBN 978-0-451-23309-7 (pbk.)
    1. Gidget (Dog)   2. Chihuahua (Dog breed)—United States—Biography.   3. Dogs—United
States—Biography.   4. Show dogs—United States—Biography.   I. Dyball, Rennie.   II. Title.
    SF429.C45C47 2011
    636.76—dc22   2010053452

Set in ITC Berkeley Oldstyle Std
Designed by Ginger Legato

Printed in the United States of America

PUBLISHER'S NOTE
Penguin is committed to publishing works of quality and integrity. In that spirit, we are proud to offer
this book to our readers; however the story, the experiences, and the words are the authors' alone.
    While the authors have made every effort to provide accurate telephone numbers and Internet
addresses at the time of publication, neither the publisher nor the authors assume any responsibility
for errors, or for changes that occur after publication. Further, publisher does not have any control over
and does not assume any responsibility for author or third-party Web sites or their content.

CONTENTS

"I hope if dogs ever take over the world and they choose a king, they don't just go by size, because I bet there are some Chihuahuas with some good ideas."

—Jack Handey

FOREWORD

When someone walks up to you with a dog, the whole energy of your encounter changes. Immediately, everyone smiles. And everyone draws closer to one another in relating to the dog. I feel blessed to have had many wonderful animals in my life—and some of the most extraordinary ones I've met through my job.

I remember when I first read the script for *Legally Blonde*, I thought, *Oh, my gosh, my costar is a canine. I hope he's awesome!* I had worked with Rhodesian ridgebacks on a movie I did in Africa, and it was a really positive experience. But the dog in this script had *character*. He had action scenes, visual jokes, and the two of us practically had dialogue. For the movie to work, we had to have an incredible animal trainer and an amazing dog.

When I heard that our trainer on the movie, Sue Chipperton, had also trained the Chihuahua in the Taco Bell commercials, I got really excited. My family and I loved those commercials. They were just so clever and hysterical. And when Sue introduced me to Moonie, who played Bruiser, I knew we were going to have a blast. He was this very, very tiny, *very* high-energy boy who was incredibly smart, well trained, and ready to go.

Certain dogs just *love* to work. They're natural performers. They're focused, and they love the attention and the focus that's on them. Moonie was that kind of dog.

And so was Gidget, the Taco Bell Chihuahua herself, who also worked on *Legally Blonde*. She was bigger than Moonie and *all* ears—she literally had gigantic satellites for ears! She was also gentler than Moonie, and incredibly special. Whenever she came on set, everyone would end up gathered around her. Gidget was just magical.

All of my experiences with animals on movies have been uniquely rewarding. In 2010, I shot a movie called *Water for Elephants*, and I got to work with an elephant named Ty. There was so much fascinating, nonverbal communication that went on between him and his trainer. It really reminded me of the way Sue works.

Every animal trainer I've encountered has a lot of respect for Sue because she's so loving and she manages to bring out the best in her animals through praise and positive reinforcement. She has a beautiful, intuitive communication with her dogs, and a huge respect and care for them. It's a pleasure to work with her, because she lets other people love her animals too. She encourages you to connect with them.

Anyone who chooses to work with animals for a living is doing something really special, in my opinion. It's a big commitment to train an animal every day of your life, almost like raising a child. And animal trainers in Hollywood have to be in constant communication with the filmmakers to make sure they get what they need to tell the story, while at the same time respecting the needs of the animals and bringing out their best performances. We're talking about a degree of patience that supersedes the normal person's capacity!

Sue would spend hours working with and encouraging Moonie, and as a result he had tons of tricks—which we were really able to take advantage of in *Legally Blonde 2*. He was given a big character arc, and the audience even finds out that he's gay! In developing the script, I sometimes wondered whether that moment would be hysterically funny or ridiculously absurd. But in the end, it worked, because Moonie had enough personality to support an entire story line that revolved around him.

Before Gidget or Moonie or any dog hits the big time, they have to be "discovered," so to speak. That's where animal trainers like Sue come in. She has a knack for picking extraordinary animals. She can go through a group of dogs and sense immediately which ones will be the best workers and performers.

The dogs who make it in the business are driven. And they're charismatic. When I watch the Westminster dog show, I always think you can tell which dogs have that extra sparkle. They're little stars. Hollywood dogs are the same way. They're such special spirits, it's been my huge privilege to work with them, and with Sue.

—Reese Witherspoon

A
FAMOUS
DOG'S LIFE

A young Gidget on the beach

CHAPTER 1

Finding a Star

Studio dogs know that they can do amazing things. They have this air about them—they carry themselves in a certain way. They're attentive and they're very open to learning. Gidget was all of that and more. In fact, she was a celebrity. When she was on set, there was a ripple effect amongst the cast and crew. She would sit up on a chair and hold court for the day because she was the Taco Bell dog. As for Sue, well, Sue is like Dr. Doolittle. From ducks to cats to dogs, she makes them do impossible things. She just has a way with animals and talks to them in a language that perhaps you and I don't understand. Her animals only have eyes for her. A Hollywood soundstage is a large and noisy place—I've seen dogs fall apart in that environment. But with Sue's animals, there's this intense focus on her. She's the only thing that exists in the room, and that's a fascinating bond that they have. It's a very stealthy process, watching a trainer and an animal work together. There's a lot of whispering and signaling that goes on. I was expecting "Sit! Down!" and shouting, but it's not like that. It's a very intimate little exchange that they do, and I've watched Sue guard the space she has between the animal and herself. It's a very hallowed space.

—Robert Luketic, director, *Legally Blonde,*
Monster-in-Law, and *The Ugly Truth*

'd love to say that on the day I found Gidget, the future Taco Bell dog, I instantly knew that she would be the biggest star I'd ever train. It would be fun to tell people that, at the moment I met the little three-pound Chihuahua, an array of fireworks exploded over my head and I spontaneously broke into song, knowing I had found the next great four-legged celebrity—a dog who would become an iconic piece of American pop culture.

But the truth is, I just thought she was really cute.

It was February 13, 1995, and Chihuahua puppies were just about the farthest thing from my mind. I had been a studio animal trainer in southern California for almost a year, and on that particular day I was scouting for West Highland terrier puppies (better known as Westies) for a pet-food commercial.

There's actually a whole lot more to being a trainer for the studios than the actual training part. One of the biggest aspects of the job is casting for commercials, TV shows, and films, which is very similar to casting a human actor for a project. You need just the right actor for the job. And for this ad, we needed just the right Westie.

At times, I could hardly believe that I'd landed this job in the first place. It was the perfect blend of two of my favorite things: animals and working on set. Not that it had been so easy to get here. I grew up dreaming of working on sets when my sister Pamela, who worked as a photographic assistant in picture publicity, would take me to visit her at the BBC. I always loved visiting the old BBC buildings in the center of London. There was such history. On occasion, we would head over to a different part of London where they filmed all the BBC TV shows and sitcoms and visit her husband, who was a BBC photographer. While he worked, we got to watch many different shows rehearse. We would sit there all day long and I'd be positively riveted. She'd be bored out of her mind, asking me at many an opportunity, "Do you want to leave yet?" But I'd always say no, even if we'd been there for a solid six hours, watching the same thing over and over. My other budding interest was animals. We'd had a number of family dogs by the time I was a teenager, and I loved the idea of working with them so much that I even tried to be a Royal Air Force dog trainer after school. But back in the early 1980s, they didn't hire women to be trainers. It's funny to think about what would have happened if they did—my life might have taken an entirely different turn.

When I was about nineteen years old, I moved from my native England, where I had spent about half my life living in the countryside of Buckinghamshire and then lived outside of London. I relocated to Fort Lauderdale, Florida, armed with not much more than a dream: to train dolphins at Ocean World, a smaller, now-defunct version of SeaWorld. I was first hired as a fish cutter and assistant to the trainers, so I spent my time dragging bait around all day, hauling forty-pound blocks of frozen fish, thawing them, cutting them up, and carrying the weighed portions to the different show areas. There was no formal training involved—it was a learning-on-the-job situation where I picked up my skills by assisting other trainers and studying what they did. Eventually, I worked my way up to becoming a trainer, then head trainer, and I got to do all the shows with the dolphins, which—believe me—is every bit as much fun as it looks.

After three years at Ocean World, I decided to head out to California to pursue a bigger paycheck. No one really gets into dolphin training for the money to begin with—it's not exactly a lucrative field. Dolphin trainers do it because they love it. As much as I enjoyed working with marine mammals, I needed a bit of a pay hike. Seeing as I'd started at four dollars an hour and had worked my way only up to seven, I clearly wasn't going to accomplish that with dolphins. I'd heard that trainers in California made closer to twenty an hour (a much more livable paycheck in the late eighties) doing something called studio work. So I made my move out west, the first step toward what would end up being my career for seventeen years—and counting. And all it took was a phone call to Studio Animal Services, asking if they were hiring. They took me on as a volunteer and I learned on the job there too, assisting other trainers on set and learning the ropes as I went.

For our pet-food commercial search that February morning in 1995, my fellow trainer Deb and I set out on a trek through the Valley to a breeder's house to see if one of her Westie puppies might work for the job. As Deb and I drove along, we chatted about the new behaviors we'd been working on with our animals. After graduating from a two-year exotic-animal training program at a southern California college (there are many roads to an animal training job—some people have formal training while others, like myself, do not), Deb started as a trainer at Studio Animal Services at the same time as me as well as another girl named Charity. I felt like I was learning the ropes pretty well, but whenever I had a green moment in my work, it was nice to have my girls to rely on for help and support.

Our "office" is located in Valencia, California, buried amid the orange groves and oil fields that dot the southern California landscape. About three miles north of the massive roller coasters at Six Flags Magic Mountain, through the rows of avocados and the corn and pepper fields, lies a deserted, winding canyon road. About two miles up from there, you'll find the eight-acre home of about a hundred dogs, a hundred cats, and other small animals who all belong to the company Studio Animal Services—better known among the trainers as simply "the ranch."

Hitting the road to look for new animals was nothing new to me, even with only a year at the company. As a trainer, if you're at an animal shelter, you're always on the lookout for new dogs and cats. Sometimes we just take a couple of days and cruise around and hit a slew of them, plus a bunch of breeders and breed rescues in the area too. But on a day like this, when we have a specific type of dog to go out and find, it's because we've exhausted all our usual options.

The basic process goes like this: Whenever a client asks us for a certain type of animal, we look at our own first, but if we don't have just the right one to meet the client's needs, we'll canvass the other animal companies in the L.A. area. All of the trainers know one another, and we're constantly calling the other companies to fulfill client requests—an easy, fairly regular occurrence. Technically, you could say we're competitors, but we're all part of such a specific niche of show business that the "if you can't beat 'em, join 'em" mentality tends to reign supreme. Many of us are quite friendly.

"I've got a client who wants an Australian shepherd who can catch a Frisbee," I might tell a trainer from another company. "Do you have any of those?"

When that doesn't work, we'll occasionally go to private owners, but this is one of the least attractive options, because the owner, naturally, will want to tag along with us to watch his or her dog work. We try to avoid that. It's not that we're doing anything we don't want them to see, but we've found that having an owner present is a huge distraction to a dog.

I once worked on another dog-food commercial where the production office used all of their own animals, so we had ten privately owned pets to work with. We were promised that one jumped up and down in place, one played tug-of-war, and one chased its tail. When it came time to shoot, however, none of those dogs did those behaviors in front of the camera. At any point. They all just stood there staring at us.

"I don't understand it!" the agency director told me. "I mean, these dogs come to our office every day and they do their tricks until the cows come home!"

People don't really understand the difference between their dog doing tricks in a comfortable environment, and on a set with lights and strange people. Not to mention being asked to do the required action twenty times in a row and in the exact same spot the director wants. It's like saying your two-year-old will do this really cute dance in your living room and then yanking her out of her comfort zone and plunking her down in front of twenty strangers. It can be a bit intimidating if she's never done it before—and the moments before film rolls through the camera is not the time to learn. So we often head out to breeders and shelters to find just the animal we need, like we were doing on Mission: Westie.

The breeder, a middle-aged woman named Doris, lived smack in the middle of the Valley. As we followed the quiet, treelined residential road to her house, I gazed out the window as we passed a home that played host to a German shepherd rescue organization and then one that served as a boxer rescue. To call it a dog-friendly neighborhood would be an understatement—this was Dog Valley. And I felt right at home.

I've loved dogs for as long as I can remember. My family always had them while I was growing up. My parents got a black poodle mix named Cindy about four years before I was born, so we pretty much grew up together. She was almost completely blind by the time I was four or five, and I remember coming home from school and going on hikes through the woods with her and my mom. Despite her disability, she trusted my mom completely, and my mom had trained her to do quite an amazing behavior. On our walks, Cindy would run full-speed through the woods with all the happy abandon of a dog who had her sight. If she were headed toward a tree, my mom would yell, "Cindy, tree! Stop!" and our little dog would skid to a halt before my mom repositioned her in a safe direction. At the time, this was no big deal to me. It was a common occurrence—"Cindy! Tree! Stop!"—but now, when I look back, I wonder if I inherited my training skills from my mom.

A short time after Cindy passed away, we got a black-and-white English cocker spaniel we named Tessa. I remember going to pick her out from the breeder's farm and laughing about her full name written on her pedigree: Grizelda of Sunnybrook Farm. To me, it sounded like the name of a princess in a children's book or something, which was fun, of course, but Tessa suited her much better. The poor thing, sweet and kind as she was, would occasionally suffer the degradation of being forced to play dress-up with my friends and me. My mom had trained Tessa not to go upstairs at our house, but if my parents were entertaining or having a party I was allowed to take her upstairs when I went to bed. I always looked forward to those nights with great anticipation.

Years later, living in the East Sussex countryside, we were surrounded by fields and farms, so I would seek out horse owners who needed help exercising their animals and ride my bicycle to their farms after school. It was a great way to ride for free. Nothing made me happier than being on horseback in the country—except having dogs, of course. There were foxhunting clubs in the area, and the riders would take hounds out with them on their hunts. One afternoon when I was a teenager, I remember coming across one of the hounds in the woods near my home. Tessa had passed away by this point, so I took it upon myself to tie a piece of rope around this poor hound's neck and I dragged him home alongside me as I pedaled my bike home. I'd get a new pet one way or another! I didn't have the hound home for more than a few hours before my mom pointed out that he belonged to the hunt, and she called them to come pick him up.

Over the years that followed, I had many dogs of my own. Still, it was always fun going out looking for new dogs on casting calls, even if we didn't keep them much longer than I'd kept that hound from the hunt. Doris, like many of the breeders in the neighborhood, worked out of her home, and she had several kennels on her property for the dogs she breeds and those whom she rescues. She's also got dozens of stray cats who live on her property, several of whom were milling about the driveway, sunning themselves and batting around bits of gravel as we pulled up.

"And how are you ladies today?" Doris asked, rising from a lawn chair where she'd been busy whittling a new hole in an old dog collar.

"We're good," Deb answered cheerfully as one of the stray cats walked a languid figure eight through my legs.

"Puppies are in the back," said Doris, leading us into her house. We walked down the dim hallway toward the back room, which she used mainly as an office and a room to house supplies. Whenever she had a litter of puppies or a group of dogs to show to prospective buyers, the room doubled as a puppy motel.

We crossed through the doorway and I glanced down at the puppy pen, a group of metal gates arranged into a rectangle and placed a few feet away from a space heater to cut through the February chill—fifty degrees is quite nippy for California. As Deb and Doris began chatting about the puppies, something in the back of the room caught my eye. Between the slats of the puppy pen was a tiny fawn-colored puppy bouncing up and down like a little rubber ball, desperately trying to catch our attention.

"The male seems to be real outgoing—the bravest of the litter," I heard Doris say about the Westies, but in all honesty, I was only halfway paying attention at this point. I squatted down with Deb to interact with the little white dogs—adorable in their own right—but I kept stealing glances at the back of the room. When there was a break in conversation, I piped up.

"What's back there?" I asked Doris curiously, gesturing to the far puppy pen. I could make out a tail wagging furiously in response to my pointing in that direction.

"Oh, I've got a couple Chihuahua puppies in the back," Doris said casually, clearly not picking up on how interested I'd already become.

"They're *so* cute," I said, edging toward them.

"Go ahead," said Deb, nodding toward the back room as the male Westie eagerly licked her palm. "I'll check these guys out."

I walked to the rear of the room to find two small Chihuahua puppies in the pen. The male puppy sat and lifted a paw at me like a stoic little greeting, while the female puppy wiggled and jumped and flirted shamelessly, winning me over with each passing second. As the smaller, wilder of the two, she propped her feet up on the gate and then pranced around for my attention.

Look at me! Look at me! Hey, hey! *You aren't looking at me! Now you are, hooray! You're looking at me!*

I was totally smitten.

"Oh, my, that is the cutest little puppy! What's the deal with this one here?" I asked Doris, hoping she'd be available.

Doris told me that the puppies were brother and sister, eight weeks old, born right around Christmas. As I took in the information from Doris, the smaller puppy kept up her happy, exuberant little dance. In addition to making me want to snatch her up and take her right home for her sheer cuteness, that kind of outgoing personality also happens to be exactly what I look for in a dog that I will eventually train for studio work.

"Deb!" I said with such urgency that she and the Westie puppy both jumped a bit. "This is a little brown dog. We don't have any little brown dogs! And aren't we always saying we should get the types of dogs we don't already have?"

Deb stifled a grin, clearly bemused with how taken I was with this little pup, who was now eagerly looking in Deb's direction as well.

"Seriously," I added, trying to level my tone. "We don't have any Chihuahuas. Or anything this small. We really could use one."

"Let's call Paul and Karin," she said.

Paul and Karin are the owners of Studio Animal Services as well as the owners of all of the company's two hundred–plus animals. That includes a large percentage of the dogs who live day to day with the trainers in their homes, for a variety of reasons. Small dogs, for example, always live with a trainer, since the more delicate types aren't very well suited to living in a kennel environment. So whenever one of us is at a breeder's or a shelter, we put in a call to Paul and Karin for clearance to pick up a new animal, and to pay any fees that come with adopting or buying him or her. It's one of the most fun perks of my job—to be able to walk through a kennel or a breeder's house, spot a cute puppy, and say, "I want that one!"

I put in the call to Karin, and she said we could get the puppy. I was thrilled. Looking back, I wish I had also taken her brother, the quieter guy in the puppy pen. For years we tried to find an appropriate backup for Gidget, but to no avail. It's always helpful to have a backup for a studio dog, one who looks just like her whom you can use in certain scenes to give your main dog a break. And as her littermate, the male puppy obviously looked a whole lot like her. But at the moment, I had eyes only for the girl puppy.

Even though I can't say I knew she'd be a big star, in just the hour that we spent at Doris's, I became more and more convinced that this puppy did have the makings of a studio dog. When it comes to checking out a group of dogs in a puppy pen or kennel, I'm immediately drawn to those outgoing, excitable types. I wouldn't necessarily recommend the most hyper dog in a bunch to the would-be pet owner, but the needs of an animal trainer are different from those of the average person.

For me, the most important quality for a future studio dog is a big personality, even a dog you'd call wild or crazy. I want the dog who isn't afraid to be outgoing in a scary, intimidating place like the local shelter, or the dog who jumps on you when you meet him and thinks that knocking over big, loud metal trash cans is fun. I want the crazy dogs, because I can channel that energy into training. I want that drive and "I'm not gonna quit" attitude. For your pet on your couch, however, this attitude can turn into "I'm not gonna quit until I tear apart each and every couch cushion and throw pillow!"

In my line of work, a high-energy dog who wants to work, wants to learn, and is eager to do anything I ask of him is easier for me to train than a shy, more timid dog who is reluctant to offer natural behaviors. Again, this is what I look for in a *studio* dog—the more laid-back type might be perfect as a pet. That's why we are quite successful at finding great studio dogs in local shelters. People end up not wanting the super-high-energy Lab or the hyper shepherd.

Dogs are always very excited in a shelter environment. There are so many in one area, contained for much of the day in their kennels, and whenever a person walks through, they bark like crazy and get worked up so much that the excitement level can go through the roof. But excitement isn't always a good thing for a dog—it can be stressful. So when we're looking for adult dogs at shelters, one good indication of their personalities is whether they'll take treats from us, since a truly stressed dog won't accept food. But if a dog can focus on you and regulate his stress in that environment, you've got a good chance of his being adaptable to other situations, like shooting a movie with boom mics and dozens of people moving about and a director barking orders on a megaphone.

If a prospective pet owner is looking for a dog in a shelter, an excitable attitude isn't necessarily a red flag. When you walk into a kennel, most of the dogs will be barking as a result of having so many dogs together in a small area. But when you go over to greet a dog, if he stops barking maniacally and starts to interact with you, that's a good sign. If a dog continues to bark for the sake of barking and is less interested in interacting with you, that might be one to pass by. Along the same lines, a dog who doesn't leave his dog bed and doesn't show much interest in befriending you would be an animal to look at more carefully, since that could suggest a variety of problems. He might just be depressed from living in a kennel environment—or the problem could be something more serious. It's also important to consider what you're looking for in a pet. If you want a dog to go hiking with you every day, you may want to bypass the shy one in the shelter. However, if the dog will be staying home all day with your eighty-year-old mother, you may not want to discount that quiet dog. Animal shelters usually have an area where you can take the dogs out to play with them, and that's a good opportunity to see whether the dog perks up and interacts.

When my fellow trainers and I get a new dog from a shelter, we sometimes encounter a scenario where a dog who initially seemed promising doesn't actually do well in studio work. If this is the case with a dog we picked up from a shelter, we never take him or her back there—we always find a loving home for the dog instead. A funny example of a dog who didn't do well on set was Hank, a Weimaraner I'd find several years after getting Gidget.

For the record, I got Hank because I thought he was downright beautiful. I wasn't focused on his personality, even though he did appear friendly and confident in his environment. This is a common mistake that people make in selecting a pet—falling in love with a dog because of his looks without fully considering the personality—and here I was, falling into that very trap! I saw him at a breeder's place just outside of San Diego, when I was in the area searching for dogs for another job. He's a blue Weimaraner, which I'd never seen before, with bright yellow eyes. So I got him as a studio dog, thinking somewhere deep in my subconscious that if he didn't work out, he'd always have a home with me.

Well . . . he didn't work out. It wasn't that Hank wasn't smart—he picked up everything I taught him and responded to all the basic commands—but from the first time I took him to a set, he was completely void of any personality. You'd put him up on the set, armed with his toys and favorite treats, and get *nothing* from him. At this point, most dogs perk up and look at you with their ears pricked, at attention.

Oh, this is fun! I'm working! And there's food!

But Hank would just stand there with this sad look on his face, like someone had beaten him, tail tucked between his legs, head down. Pathetic.

Whaddaya want from me? Can we go home?

Everyone kept asking me what was wrong with him, but I couldn't figure it out! He was totally sweet and fun with me—not the most outgoing dog I've ever met, but definitely not overly timid or scared. So we took him out on other jobs, thinking maybe he was just intimidated by that first set and would move past it. But things didn't change. Even when he met new people, there was just no personality. People would pet him and he would stand there like a bump on a log. Sometimes his tail would move ever so slowly, back and forth, as if he were contemplating every painstaking wag. Deb would joke with me, asking why I even liked this dog. But there was just something about Hank. We had a special connection, and I knew it from the second I saw him. Hank was always happy and jumping and wagging his tail when I came home—he just wasn't the social type, and it sure helps if a studio dog is social. As a pet, though, he's all I could ask for—just a big, sweet, dopey guy.

For TV and film work, we pretty much use all breeds, and usually waste no time working their innate behaviors to our advantage (like training a Labrador retriever to bring back almost anything you ask her to, since she'll enjoy it and do it well). When it comes to pet owners, I think the biggest mistake people make when they decide to get a dog is not considering the dog's breeding and innate qualities. A Dalmatian is a fine choice if you go running for ten miles in the morning and another ten at night. However, thinking that your cute new spotted dog will be happy to just hang out in your big backyard is a devastating mistake that makes for a very sad dog—not to mention a disappointed, frustrated owner who ends up sending his animal back to a shelter.

Back at the breeder's house, after Karin approved of our taking the little brown dog, Deb and I agreed that she'd live at home with me. In addition to all the dogs who live at the ranch, many live with trainers in their homes. The Chihuahua was a no-brainer due to her size, but then you have the opposite end of the spectrum, like Smith and Jones, two yellow Labs I trained from puppyhood. These two would destroy your home before you knew what happened. Luckily, living at the ranch was clearly okay with them. They have their own dog runs at night, and during the day they share an exercise yard with two Shiba Inus, a bunch of toys, and, in warmer temperatures, a doggy pool. And the bike rides they get to share with Karin on cool California evenings are an added bonus.

As Doris left us alone to make our decisions, I smiled—quite thrilled with my find—and Deb decided the male Westie would be a strong option to present to our client. I carried the Chihuahua puppy to the car and sorted through my bin of dog equipment to find a collar that would fit her. My teeniest one could still turn circles around the even smaller neck of the new puppy, but I put it on and off we went.

We told Doris that Karin would be sending her a check for the little brown dog, whom I loaded into a crate in the backseat of the SUV. The tiny pup looked at me with wide eyes and a small shiver that I would come to know quite well from this heat-loving little dog.

Can't I sit in your nice warm lap? (tail wag, tail wag). *I'll just be so cold and lonely back here on my own. . . .*

I looked around the backseat for a sweater in her size—I had a collection of beautiful, hand-knit alpaca dog sweaters designed by my good friend Kim for occasions like these. I chose the smallest one I could find, slipped it over Gidget's head and gently placed her in her travel crate. She let out a little sigh.

Well, I suppose this'll do for now.

With the Chihuahua tucked in for a little snooze, we hopped in our seats and took off.

"So, how will your landlord react to this one?" Deb asked me with a laugh.

I was living in a second-floor apartment two blocks from Venice Beach, and my landlord had a no-dogs policy. Of course, this was Venice—the land of the free-spirited hippie types—so the policy wasn't as strict as, say, a New York City apartment building. I'd been living with Beans, my Australian cattle dog, for about eight months, and I'd reasoned with my landlord that she wasn't just a pet—I took her to work with me every day to train her, so it wasn't like she'd be home all day, barking at every imaginary noise that she heard. My landlord agreed to let me keep Beans, so I figured he wouldn't have much trouble accepting this tiny little three-pound thing.

"It'll be no problem," I told Deb with as much confidence in my tone as I could muster.

As we climbed the hill out of the valley toward the ranch, I watched the sky turn to shades of late-afternoon pale pink, and for just a moment I allowed myself to daydream about the types of jobs this tiny pup might land. So far in my new job, I had seen the smaller breeds like Chihuahuas land only a pretty limited variety of jobs, but either way, I had an adorable new pet to come home with me. It had been a good day.

Puppy Gidget and Beans, lounging at home in 1994

CHAPTER 2

Initiation

I remember "auditioning" dogs for the role of Mom in my series *Oh, Grow Up*. Before Beans and Sue came in to meet me, I was given a copy of the dog's résumé, which informed me that "Beans loves to work." And indeed she did. Throughout the short life of that show, whenever I encountered Beans on the set, I—being the sloppy, dog-loving freak that I am—would drop to the floor and try to engage her in play. She would oblige me (mostly out of deference to my role as executive producer, I'm tempted to think), but I always got the sense her focus was elsewhere; she was too busy eagerly awaiting the next bit of action she would be given to perform. She truly did *love* to work.

—Alan Ball, writer, producer, and director, *Oh, Grow Up,*
Six Feet Under, and *True Blood*

After our Westie puppy expedition in the Valley, I headed toward Venice Beach, eager to get the new Chihuahua home after a quick stop to drop Deb off at her house first. As I crawled along the ever-congested Santa Monica Freeway (which is pretty much just a parking lot for twenty hours out of the day), I took a peek to see how the new puppy was handling her first trip in a crate—let alone her first car ride. Judging by how soundly she was sleeping, I figured she was probably just fine. Nothing like a well-adjusted, adaptable eight-week-old pup. This was a good sign!

Five miles—and thirty minutes—later, I was finally home. I pulled my Ford Bronco into the parking space in front of my apartment building and walked around to the back to collect the little dog, now stretching in her crate, tail eagerly wagging. I lifted her out of the crate and down to the ground so she wouldn't hurt her delicate legs leaping out. Then I took a moment to let her sniff around her new surroundings and do her business (which she got to only after thoroughly inspecting all of my landlord's flower beds). We walked around to the door leading up to my apartment, and I wondered for a moment whether I should carry such a bitty dog—she weighed only three pounds, after all—up the rather steep stairwell. But before I could decide, this teeny little thing hopped up each stair like it was nothing. I grinned and followed her up. She seemed to be as eager to meet Beans as I was to introduce them.

I'd gotten Beans, an Australian cattle dog mix, eight months prior from a local animal shelter just a few miles down the road from Studio Animal Services. I wasn't looking for a specific dog for a job at the time. This was the first opportunity for me to have a dog of my own whom I could take to work with me every day as my pet. She was the first dog I saw, at the first shelter I visited (not necessarily the best way to find the right pet for you, I might note). She was this little four-month-old red-and-white mutt, jumping and happy and totally eager to play. Deb had come along with me—by this point we were already nearing best-friends-forever status—and we brought some treats and a tennis ball with us. We walked through the runs, and all the dogs barked. Some propped their paws up on the fence as they barked at us, while others sat on their dog beds, looking dejected or defeated, and some wagged their tails and sat politely, showing off the skills they'd honed. It's hard not to want to check them all out and try to take them out of there, but you have to be realistic and focus on why you're there. It differs from trainer to trainer, but for me, I'm able to sort of separate from the emotion of it all and act objectively at shelters (and not come home with fifteen new dogs!). So I asked the kennel help to open the meet-the-pet pen so we could get to know one exuberant little red-and-white puppy.

As it turned out, bringing the tennis ball was the best thing we could have done: This dog was tennis-ball *crazy*. She was one of those dogs who just doesn't quit. If you threw that ball for six hours, she'd never refuse to go catch it with as much oomph and gusto as the first time. A huge play drive in a dog is a great sign for him or her to become a studio animal. It's also a good trait for becoming a police dog or search-and-rescue dog, since those animals need to love doing a job, and it's easier to train a dog who is motivated (a tennis ball or tug toy can be a huge motivator). Standing outside in that pen, I thought to myself, *I think I found my dog!* It was as simple as that.

Her name came just as easily as the decision to adopt her. After our rousing game of catch, we paid her adoption fee, loaded her into the car, and went to grab lunch at Del Taco on our way back to work. While thinking about what to name her, I happened to notice bean burritos on the drive-through menu. Being from England, I grew up eating Heinz baked beans on toast, a favorite of mine ever since, so the menu item got my brain working. My new puppy was the color of baked beans—plus she was full of beans, as the expression goes.

"Hey, Deb," I said. "How about Beans?"

Deb turned around and looked at the puppy sitting in the crate. After a moment's consideration, she smiled at the red-and-white dog with the cute pointy ears.

"Hi, Beans."

Funny enough, for the rest of Beans's life—which featured tons of studio work—Deb would tell her the story of the day we picked her up and named her. While on sets over the years, whenever there was a break in the action, Deb would grab Beans by the collar and make the dog look at her, which Beans never seemed entirely keen on doing.

"Beans, I want to tell you a story. Once upon a time . . . Hey, Beans. Beans! Look at me! This is important. Okay, I'm going to tell you the story of the day we found you. Once upon a time, Sue and I went to the animal shelter. . . . Seriously, Beans, are you listening to me? I want to tell you this story! Okay, so we found this beautiful red-and-white dog. . . ."

It was pretty funny to watch: Like a bored child being told the story of his birth for the umpteenth time and plotting to escape the mundane storytelling, Beans would sit there, going, *Oh, no, when is this going to end?* But eventually she would focus on Deb, who told the story the same way each time, from her "once upon a time" opener, to every detail of our time together, and how a fast-food chain inspired her name. When you spend hours on sets, a little bored and waiting for things to get started, you develop some peculiar inside jokes and routines. Beans had probably heard that story about a hundred times in her life, and despite her escape attempts, I think she secretly loved it, because she gave Deb a kiss at the end of every telling of the tale.

Now poised at my front door with a new, as-yet-unnamed puppy, I could hardly wait for Beans to meet the new addition. As I turned the key in the lock, the puppy squirmed at my feet, her rear end wagging in tandem with her tail. I opened the door and the little Chihuahua burst into the living room like she owned the place. Beans looked surprised at first, then curious, then slightly miffed as the new puppy leaped up and down, licking at her face and bounding from side to side, inviting her to play.

Instead of joining in, Beans looked up at me. If dogs could roll their eyes, she would have done just that.

What is this? she seemed to ask.

This, it turned out, was the first day of a very new life that Beans would have to adjust to—a life that included other dogs. Many other dogs. Dogs from work who would live with me full-time, pets I'd acquire, and studio dogs who would stay the night before countless shoots. For eight months, Beans had the luxury of eating up all my attention and training—by this point, I knew that she was incredibly smart and would be a special working dog—and now a feisty three-pound ball of energy had shown up and changed everything. In an instant, the little brown dog had altered life as Beans knew it. In the first few days of living together, Beans just sort of took the puppy in stride, acting fairly indifferent to her hyperactive new roommate. Things would get interesting in the days to come, though.

Right away, the new dog began joining Beans and me each morning as we headed out to work. As her trainer, I was expected to expose the puppy to new things—a huge, key part of the early training of a studio dog, as well as for your average pet. For a new studio dog, exposure comes in many forms, from going to the set and seeing the crazy world of lights, sets, and people dressed in wonderfully strange costumes, to a simple trip to the local coffee shop. There, I like to hand out treats to willing participants so the dog learns that meeting a new person is always fun—and delicious. It's also a good idea to take a new puppy (after they've had all their vaccinations) to stores like PetSmart, PETCO, or Home Depot, or any big, warehouse type of store that allows dogs inside. Those stores are the perfect environment for puppies to meet people and see all sorts of things. The great thing about pet stores is that they are usually filled with dog lovers who don't mind spending an extra few minutes to give your dog a treat.

I also took my time with the new puppy to get her acclimated to her crate. Pretty quickly, she was managing to make it through the night, sleeping peacefully once she understood that this little plastic cave was actually her sanctuary—a home within her home, and a place that she would eventually crave and love.

Crate training is a great way to get a puppy housebroken. Having a puppy sleep in a crate at night and go into the crate when you are unable to watch her (while you're in the shower or talking on the phone, for example) will help prevent housebreaking accidents. It will also keep bad habits, like chewing on the furniture, from forming. Plus, it's helpful to make sure a new puppy is on a feeding and watering schedule. That might sound overly strict, but it's a surefire way to housebreak a puppy, especially small breeds.

Driving the four-lane highway en route to the ranch with

Beans and the puppy in their crates, I passed through a wonderful corridor of orange groves, vegetable fields, and tree farms. Huge trucks full of lemons drive back and forth, while fruit stands decorate the sides of the highway. The route also takes you past Phil's Animal Rentals, a company that owns many of the horses and livestock in the studio industry, including the cows in the California cheese commercials. Phil has all sorts of animals at his place, from birds to emus and even a mountain goat whom you can sometimes see from the road, munching on grass on the side of his hill.

A makeshift avocado stand with a hand-painted sign (and a bargain price—twenty-five cents apiece) sits close to the turnoff for the small, quiet road that leads to the ranch. That last segment of the drive to Studio Animal Services is peaceful and filled with wildlife. The winding canyon road is fairly desolate and filled with small hills that make you feel nearly airborne if you drive over them fast enough.

At first, the property appears pretty unassuming, marked by chain-link fences and a wooden sign with STUDIO ANIMAL SERVICES painted in white. There's a small parking area across from one of the runs where the dogs crowd at the fence, eager to see who might step out of the car. As for me, I was eager to see what trainers might be around to help me with naming the puppy. After a couple of days with me, she was in dire need of a name, and I was starting to wonder if she thought "Hey, c'mere!" was it.

After we parked, I decided to give "C'mere" a little walking tour of the ranch. There are two houses on Studio Animal Services' eight-acre property. The one in the center belongs to one of the owners of the company, Karin, who lives there with her camera-operator husband and their three kids. It's got a big fenced-in yard in front where the retired dogs tend to hang out during the day—the "retirement yard," as we call it. To the right of Karin's house is a single white trailer where one of the employees lives, checking on the animals on nights and weekends. There are also several dog runs and an exercise yard. To the left of Karin's house are the training house and kennels, which stretch back behind the houses as well. There are cat runs in this area of the ranch too, though our cats don't actually run nearly as much as they snuggle up together in baskets perched up in the corners. Back by the cats are some small dog runs and kennels and a short set of stairs where a couple other trainers and I carved our initials before the cement dried. I often wonder who will see our names years down the road, and what animals will live there long after we have all moved on.

We use the training house—which is almost completely empty, except for a couch and a table—to work with the animals when it's cold in the winter, very hot in the summer, or whenever a trainer needs a busy place to work an animal. If a trainer needs her dog's undivided attention while teaching him something new, she'd probably seek out a quiet spot elsewhere on the ranch. But it's usually important to have distractions while you're working, to mimic the environment a dog will face on set. Working in the training house involves plenty of distractions—other people and animals working, a trainer who walks between you and your dog to get to the fridge—these types of things duplicate the hustle and bustle of working on a set quite well. We even have a slightly creepy-looking, life-size dummy called Dan that we've used for training. It's quite funny to watch the occasional cat jump into his lap and curl up as Dan sits motionless on the couch, waiting for his next task.

The living room and the kitchen in the training house are almost completely empty, leaving ample space for training, and one of the bedrooms serves as the office where Karin and Paul have desks and our office manager takes calls. The other bedroom is our crate room, filled with dog and cat crates that come in handy while we're training. If you see a cat in a commercial, TV show, or movie, it's most likely a team of four or five cats who look alike and share the "acting" duties. When we're training a team of cats, we do multiple short sessions a day with each one, working them one at a time in the house while keeping the others in crates with litter boxes. It's easier on all involved when we don't have to go back and forth from the house and up the hill to the cat kennel. This process also gets new cats used to being in their crates. When we work cats on set they travel in crates, and we rotate them into covered pens so they all get a chance to stretch their legs, play with some toys, and soak up the atmosphere of their new working environment.

All of our animals have to get used to the idea that they'll be traveling and hanging out in crates when we're working on set. Pet owners often have trouble bringing their cats to the vet in crates, so it's a good idea to get a cat used to the crate before you absolutely need her to go inside one.

People are generally pretty amazed that you can train a cat to work on set. The number one question that we get is, "Do you train a cat the same way you train a dog?" The short answer is yes, although there are a few key differences. First, a cat works primarily for food (where a dog will work for a toy or a pat on the head in addition to food). We use a cat's favorite treats to motivate him or her, whether it's chicken, tuna, or baby food—a real feline delicacy!—on a long spoon.

We also use positive reinforcement and clicker training with cats, just like with dogs (a clicker is used as a bridge to let the cat know when he is doing something right). So it's really the same concept, but cats are more hands-off than dogs. We don't put a leash or collar on a cat like you would a dog—just a harness, sometimes, if you're working outside and you don't want to risk the cat wandering off, or if you are exposing the cat to a new environment for the first time.

Personally, I'm much more of a dog person than a cat person, so I've focused on dogs in my training career. I've had cats as pets a couple of times in the past, but only when I've lived in a place that doesn't allow dogs. At work, our trainers Chrissie and Deb do the primary training on our cat teams because they enjoy it so much. Then, if I get a job where I'm working cats, I'll take the cat team that's already had basic training and work on the behaviors specific to that job.

Behind the training house on the Studio Animal Services property are the indoor-outdoor dog and cat runs, which are heated in the winter and air-conditioned in the summer so the animals get to spend plenty of time running around. Behind that is a big fenced-off area with a pond for our ducks—many of whom would go on to star in commercials and in the movie *Duck*—and several tall cages where we keep six working squirrels, who scurry up and down their seven-foot-tall walls and jump around when they hear a visitor walking by. There's also a grooming area where we bathe the dogs, and several sheds that hold all of the dog and cat food, tools, and dryers.

As I walked the new dog around the property, I noticed just how big this little girl thought she was. Nothing seemed to faze or scare this three-pound Chihuahua as we toured the grounds, even when our big German shepherds and Labs barked their intimidating greetings. Walking through the house, the rocky paths around the property, or down the street, she just took it all in stride, clearly content to be embarking on a little journey at my side. And if another animal—any animal, even the ducks or squirrels, which she surely had never seen before—were nearby, she would just wag her tail eagerly in greeting.

Hey, how ya doin'? Who are you?

Next, we turned toward the front of the property, where all the company vehicles are parked. We rarely use our personal vehicles to drive to set, so we have several Ford fifteen-passenger vans with all the seats taken out so we can fit all our animals and equipment for a job. We've also got a big horse trailer that's filled with crates in case of a southern California fire evacuation. It doubles as a mobile home for animals we take on jobs—when we have a job with the ducks, we fill it with kiddie pools for them while we travel and while we're camped out on set. (We also used one of them for a Capital One job that we'd later work with a skiing goat—it served as his makeshift barn!)

Surrounding the property, there's nothing but canyons. The land is owned by a company that also owns oil fields, so when we go on hikes with the dogs up the hill, we pass plenty of derricks pumping oil all around us. There are a few homes scattered here and there as well, but the area is basically just trainers and animals amid the canyons. One of my favorite things to do in the winter is to go on a hike in the rain with a pack of muddy dogs at my side. I'd do it year-round, but the southern California summers are too hot for that. In those winter months, though, you just can't beat that down-to-earth combination of mud, cool temperatures, and a bunch of happy, dirty dogs.

By the time we reached the front of the property, I noticed Paul and a group of trainers standing around. There's never any traffic on the road in front of the ranch, so sometimes we'll go out there and train. On this morning, everyone looked to be getting started with the day: Some had dogs out; others were just chatting with one another. But when they saw us, the group perked right up and made a big fuss over the new dog, who I must say was looking especially adorable in her little sweater to fend off the winter chill.

"Oh, my!"

"Who is this?"

"Wow, she's cute!"

"Do you have a name for her yet?"

That last comment was courtesy of Deb, since she knew I was stumped on a name for the puppy. Not that the dog seemed to mind all that much as she greeted several new friends, who stroked her little head as she happily pranced around them, licking their fingers and wiggling in appreciation of all the attention.

"Guys, I just don't know what to name her."

This was more of a problem than you might think. If your average pet owner adopted a puppy and named it, they'd tell other people the name and people would politely say, "Oh, that's cute!" Not so much at Studio Animal Services. We are brutally honest with one another, and no one would be shy about saying, "Um, no, sorry, that name sucks."

"She's so tiny, I want to name her something that plays off of her size," I said, thinking aloud. "I don't know, maybe like Midge or Midget, or something, or . . . wait. How about Gidget?" I suggested.

After all, Sally Field played a character named Gidget, and they were both little and cute.

"Oh, I like Gidget," said one trainer.

"That's a good one," said another.

And with that, the little puppy had a name. As Gidget got older, Deb and I came up with a funny little nickname for her. At first, it was Gidge-a-roo, but ultimately it just got shortened to Roo, as in, "Hey, where's the Roo?" For now, though, she was just Gidget.

As the group dispersed to go about their day, I took the now-shivering puppy into the training house to warm up. There are several dog beds on the floor in the office, so I set one up for Gidget near the office manager so she'd have some company while I went out to work with the dogs on my training list. I started with a pit bull named Brandy.

Since Deb, Charity, and I were the new trainers in the group, Karin would have little training sessions with us from time to time to work on new skills with our dogs. It was nice having two other new trainers at the time that I started, so that I didn't feel like the only one who didn't always know exactly what she was doing. Today, we were working on walking around a dog and training him or her to stay facing forward, without turning around in a circle to follow our movements. Clearly, this isn't something that a pet would need to learn. The behaviors you train a studio dog to perform can be very different from the training you'd do with a pet. In fact, the first thing you do with an average dog—teach him to sit—is one of the last things we train on a studio dog. In any filming situation, whether it's a feature-length movie or a thirty-second commercial, you're going to have times when a dog is needed to stand.

"Just have him stand there, next to the actor," a director will inevitably say. But after a while, a dog who's maybe a bit on the lazy side will eventually end up sitting. This is why we avoid training our dogs to sit for as long as possible. In fact, "on your feet" is a far more useful command when training studio dogs, since a dog often needs to be standing in a scene before he needs to be sitting. The behaviors you train for studio work differ from pet training because trainers often need to teach dogs traditionally "naughty" behaviors. For example, we've had many dogs who are trained to jump up on an actor and, in some cases, even knock them down. So these dogs develop a bit of a jumping habit, which you'd obviously want to discourage in a pet.

After about an hour of work, I took Brandy back to the kennel. We decide whether our dogs will live on the Studio Animal Services property or in someone's home on a canine-by-canine basis. All of the small, more delicate dogs are placed in homes automatically, and with the medium and larger ones, we watch how they do in a kennel environment before deciding whether they'll stay there. For the business to function properly, there have to be dogs on hand, living on the property. However, if an animal isn't doing well living in that kind of environment, we find a home for them with a trainer (we have between eight and ten trainers at any given time at Studio Animal Services), or a friend of a trainer—we've placed dogs in all sorts of situations. The common denominator is that the home where the dog goes to live needs to be close to the ranch.

For instance, we once had a pair of golden retrievers, Ty and Travis, who starred on the TV show *Providence*. They started on that show as puppies, doubled each other for the series' entire run, and basically grew up on the set—Deb trained one and I trained the other. On some jobs, we use two dogs who look alike so that they can double for each other, swapping them out so as to give one dog a break while the other is working and vice versa. It's also nice when you have a team of dogs who have slightly different personalities, so we can utilize them for different scenes. One might be friendlier than another, so we would use the friendly dog for interaction with an actor.

When the show wrapped, we tried Ty and Travis out at the kennel, but they didn't do as well as we'd hoped. They were just these two big, dopey goldens who wanted nothing more than to curl up at your feet rather than run around an exercise yard and play with other dogs all day.

Travis went to live with a family in Valencia who were located just ten minutes from the ranch. The family had three kids and a swimming pool—right up Travis's alley. He was happy as could be. But he still enjoyed working the occasional job, so we were able to keep using him in addition to letting him be a pet. Whenever we needed him for a job, his new family would leave their side gate unlocked and we'd pick him up, take him to the set, and then drop him back off at the end of the day. We found a similar setup for Ty, who went to live with Deb's mom and dad in Agoura, California, and we'd pick him up and drop him back off after jobs as well. It made for the best of both worlds for those dogs.

For the dogs who thrive in a kennel environment, like Brandy, they'll live at Studio Animal Services full-time, with periods of travel and shooting on location providing a good balance. The majority of dogs who live at the ranch all get along, so during the day they get out together in the large exercise yards, where they can play with one another or lie in the sun, or take a dip in the doggy pools we set up in the summer. There are always staff on the property who make sure the dogs are healthy, happy, and well exercised. They start the day early, around six a.m., to begin the morning rotation of feeding, cleaning, and exercising, until the last person leaves around seven p.m., with the trainer who lives on the property keeping watch after that. And when weather permits in the evenings, Karin will take out a whole pack of dogs on those mountain-bike rides through the canyons (she's riding; they're running). It's like doggy nirvana.

As for Gidget, the minute I entered the office after my session with Brandy, she leaped to her feet and ran toward me.

You've been gone so long! Where have you been? And where are we going? I'm ready! Are you ready? Let's go, okay?

I smiled the whole drive home to Venice.

That evening, I encountered an interesting roommate situation back home. While in my bedroom, sorting through some old boxes of photos, I noticed that it had suddenly become very quiet in the living room. Beans and Gidget had been playing and now it was silent. Did they both decide to take a nap at the same time?

My curiosity got the better of me and I put down the photos and went to check on the normally very active dogs. At first glance, it appeared that Beans was gently nuzzling Gidget. *Oh, how cute*, I thought—until I realized that the cute nuzzling was actually Beans twisting Gidget's collar! It took me a moment to realize that the flailing Chihuahua, lying upside down with all four feet in the air, was pretty much helpless as Beans pinned her to the ground, ever so casually, professional wrestler style.

Okay, little dog. You wanna play? Let's play.

Still, bless her heart, as Gidget thrashed around she had this playful, joyous gleam in her eye. Clearly, she wasn't in any grave danger.

This is fun! I can't believe this big dog wants to play with me.

"Beans!" I shouted, and both dogs scrambled to their feet.

"What are you doing?"

Beans just blinked at me.

Me? Nothing. We were just . . . playing.

Beans had a twinkle in her eye as Gidget looked in my direction too, wondering what the interruption was all about.

Yeah! What she said.

With a sideways glance at the dogs, I went back into the bedroom. Five minutes later, it went silent again. I went back into the living room to find that Beans had Gidget pinned down in the same headlock, and Gidget seemed to be enjoying the little game even more. After a few moments she wiggled out of Beans's grasp and hopped up to her feet to face her.

Oh, that was fun! Do it again?

I cleared my throat and gave Beans a stern look. Her gaze lingered in Gidget's direction before she looked at me with what I can only describe as a slightly defeated expression.

Really? It's staying?

When I brought Gidget home the first time, I hadn't given much thought to the introduction process (other than, "Beans, meet Gidget; Gidget, Beans"), since I knew Beans got along with all dogs, big and small. Still, if I had to do it over again, I would introduce a new dog to my household by taking both dogs for a walk. Not walking your dog, by the way, is pretty much the root of all evil in animal ownership. Dogs by nature are meant to get out and walk or run, and they need to be walked for their mental well-being. Many behavioral problems come from dogs who get stuck in backyards instead of taking walks. It's frustrating for a dog to be confined to one area without any mental stimulation, so taking a dog on daily walks is incredibly important.

Now that I know more about doggy intros, when I first bring a new puppy or adult dog home, instead of just opening my front door and letting her barrel inside (potentially surprising or even pissing off the first dog), I'll keep the new dog in a crate in the car and bring my dog into the car and put him in his own crate. Then I'll drive to the end of the road, where there's a great trail, let both dogs out, and we'll immediately head out on a hike through the canyons. This way the dogs are meeting in a neutral environment, and they will get worn-out on the hike, so when they come back to the house, they walk in together with no excessive excitement, no one guarding his or her territory, returning to the house as equals.

In that first introduction, if two or more dogs are moving forward on a walk and no one's just standing around staring at each other, there's less opportunity for conflict. On the other hand, if they're eyeing each other up and down, then you're going to have a potentially dangerous interaction where they could look at each other like, *Who are you? Well, who are you?* But if everyone is walking or running along, there's usually no time or opportunity for that kind of confrontation.

As the two dogs are getting used to each other, I never leave them alone for an extended period of time. I make sure to treat the first dog fairly when spending time with the new one. If your first dog is watching you make a fuss over a new puppy, that dog is going to start to feel left out. It's important to take time out for your first dog on his own, maybe leaving the puppy or new dog in her crate and taking your old friend out to play ball in the yard.

Even though I didn't follow any of those guidelines at this point in my career, Beans and Gidget still ended up becoming friendly. Within another week or two, Beans gave up on her collar-twisting game and seemed to accept that our new addition wasn't going anywhere. The basic training I had started doing with Gidget was going well too. She was not yet three months old, but she already understood where she was welcome to sit in the apartment. Being so tiny and delicate, Gidget could easily hurt herself leaping up and down from the furniture, so I had designated little areas for her—a pillow here, a blanket there—which were "her spots," and I discouraged her from just climbing all over the bed and other furniture at will by correcting her anytime she tried to do so.

Even as a new trainer, I was not a big fan of dogs on the bed or dogs on the couch. And it's really much easier than people think to establish this rule with a new puppy. If you get a puppy and put him on your couch when he's ten weeks old, for the rest of the dog's life, he's going to think, *Well, why* can't *I be on the couch? Why can't I sit as close to you as I possibly can and be stuck to your side like glue?*

So my own personal theory is, for the first six months to a year, it's key to establish the ground rules with a new dog. I sleep here; you sleep there. Years later, I had solid proof that my method worked after keeping Jackson, a Weimaraner who belongs to director Robert Luketic, at my home. From the time Jackson was a puppy, Robert would allow him on the furniture, including the bed and the couch. When Jackson was about six months old, Robert mentioned that he was always on the furniture and never really responded when he asked the dog to get down. I would tell Robert that he'd already established with a young Jackson that it was okay for him to be on the furniture. It's really hard to go back on that when you've allowed it for the first six months of a dog's life. I know that the puppy is supercute on the couch, watching TV with you, but before you know it, you've got a seventy-five-pound dog who won't budge when you ask him to get off your furniture!

As it turned out, Robert actually enjoyed having his dog on the couch or the bed—it's up to the individual dog owner what he wants in the furniture scenario. But what each owner has to realize is that it all goes back to setting up those ground rules early on, so everyone knows where they stand and there's no confusion or battles as the dog gets older. Case in point: I never let Jackson on any of the furniture in my house. And at six months old, he already understood the difference between my house and his own—and that the furniture at my house was completely off-limits. Setting these sorts of boundaries is probably pretty similar to disciplining and raising kids (well, I can only imagine)!

In short, you can spend your dog's whole life telling him to "get down!" or you can sacrifice some cuddle time on the couch at the beginning to teach the dog what he's allowed and not allowed to do. Gidget was never a particularly snuggly dog, so that helped a bit. She was always happier to lie on her dog bed in a patch of sunlight than right in your lap. Plus, she was always cold—typical of a Chihuahua—so a warm spot was always her preference. Of course, there were those times when I needed my dog right next to me. During the 1994 earthquake, before I got Gidget, my whole apartment was shaking and I wanted Beans close by for emotional security, companionship, and, I'd like to think, for safety (I mean, what if the roof fell in?), so Beans and I snuggled on the bed for quite a while that night.

A few days after my dogs' wrestling tournament, I decided to take them out for a romp on the beach. On my way out the door, I made sure to grab my camera to capture them on the beach together. For as long as I can remember, I've been interested in photography. It was my dad's favorite hobby, and he often won amateur photography contests. My favorite thing to do as a child, in fact, was to sit down with my family and watch slide shows of all our wonderful vacations we took every year, visiting different parts of England, Wales, and most of Europe. Seeing our camping trips in the Swiss Alps or our ride in a gondola in Venice, Italy, displayed up on the projector was like reliving it every time.

I loaded the dogs up in their crates in my Bronco, plopped the camera down on the passenger seat, and drove out to a dog-friendly beach just north of Malibu. It's a relatively short stretch of sand, rocks, and surf, accessible from the side of the highway down a long set of stairs. The drive is stunningly beautiful along the coastline, and the dogs get excited for nearly the whole thirty-five-minute drive, since they can smell the ocean. The beach was Beans's favorite place in the entire world. I swore she always knew where we were going as soon as the air started to get salty as we got closer to the coast. The smell just entranced her. She'd always be asleep in the back of the truck, but once we turned onto the Pacific Coast Highway, she jumped up and peered out the window.

When we arrived at the beach and I found a spot on the highway shoulder right up on the bluff, I walked around to the back of my truck to find Beans standing in her crate, looking at me impatiently.

Please *open the crate! We're at the beach. I love the beach. I mean, really, what is taking you so long to open the door?*

I put my camera strap over my shoulder and carefully walked both dogs on leashes down the steep stairs, since they'd probably tumble down with excitement if left to their own devices. I helped them navigate over the rocks to the sand before removing Beans's leash. The second I gave her the go-ahead, Beans was off, a red-and-white blur flying just above the soft sand. She always liked to run just inches above where the surf licks at the shore, so she could soak up the spray of the sea without getting too wet. Within fifteen minutes of our arrival, she had to poop, as always. You could set your watch by this dog's bathroom habits at the beach. She was just so excited that pooping was the only option! And I knew Beans was independent, but whenever I took her to the beach it became even more apparent just how self-sufficient she really was. She'd "check in" with me every now and again, but days at the beach weren't about me and Beans—it was all her. I could see it written all over her face whenever we'd arrive and I'd take her out.

I don't need to be entertained; I'm good! Just let me go run.

Years later, Beans's laps on the beach would come in quite handy when she booked a guest-starring role on *Baywatch*, complete with a run down the beach with Yasmine Bleeth.

On this, Gidget's first trip to the beach, it was clear that she wanted to get in on the action too, and roam around without her leash. So when Beans came trotting in my direction, I unclipped Gidget's leash, and instantly both dogs exploded toward the water. Any misgivings that Beans may have had about the new puppy seemed to have thoroughly melted away. I laughed to myself as I watched Gidget, her tiny legs churning, as she tried to keep up with Beans. And she did! I grabbed my camera and snapped away as the dogs ran their little hearts out. Many years later, I would find myself photographing other people's dogs on the beach as I pursued a side career as a pet photographer. I would let the owner decide whether they wanted their dogs photographed at their homes or on location somewhere, like the beach or the mountains. I used my experience as a dog trainer to get some fun shots, even employing another trainer from work to come along and assist me. Armed with lots of noisemakers and a bag full of treats, and brimming with creativity, we'd work for two or three hours to come up with some really memorable shots for the client.

I also made sure to get lots of shots of Gidget in the sand on her first beach trip, and I snapped plenty of Beans in the water as the sun was setting as well. Ever a fan of sunbathing over actual bathing, Gidget kept her distance from the water and ran alongside Beans farther up in the sand to stay warm and dry. Every now and again, without warning, Beans would stop and change direction, and Gidget kept up with her every time, both dogs running full-out, ears blowing back in the wind, looking as if nothing could stop them.

I'd never seen either one of them so happy.

Gidget posing on a motorcycle

CHAPTER 3

On Your Mark

As a director, there are many times when I dream up what seems to be the impossible shot. I then turn to my production team to execute the impossible. For one specific shot, I needed a duck to run on a treadmill toward the camera against a green screen with a wide-angle lens, so no trainers could be in the shot. I hemmed and hawed over the reality of pulling this off. I called Sue. *Riiiiiing* . . . "Sue? It's Steve. I need a duck running toward the camera. Oh, and he needs to be right in front of the lens with no trainers. And he's in front of a green screen and running on a treadmill." The silence that followed was expected. Sue's response was not. "Do you want him looking camera left, camera right, or right at the lens?"

—Steve Chase, commercial director

About a month into life with Gidget, the little Chihuahua seemed to be adjusting well to living in Venice Beach with me and Beans. Running on the beach together continued to be their very favorite pastime (mine too), and Gidget ran her little heart out every time to keep up with her buddy.

My early training with Gidget was also going well. People always ask me if you need to wait to train puppies until they get older, but it's really something you can start at a very young age, provided you keep the sessions short, fun, and full of positive reinforcement. People are amazed at how much you can teach a twelve-week-old puppy—the little guys you see barking, turning in circles, and scratching in flea-medicine commercials aren't doing it by accident! They've actually learned each of those behaviors and can perform them on command when asked to "circle" or "scratch." At just three months, Gidget was already learning to bark on command, and we were working on her landing on her mark next—one of the most key basics for a studio dog.

Going to and staying on a mark is a starting point for many other behaviors. We start by training dogs to stand on a large object, like a tabletop or a wooden box, and then over time we reduce the size of the object they stand on—maybe to the size of a small rock. Once the dog understands that many different objects can become a mark, then you can use this to your advantage on set. If a director wants a dog to be sitting on a couch while barking, the first thing I do as a trainer is identify the couch as the dog's mark. Not all studio trainers work in *exactly* the same way—this is just my personal variation. Regardless of what object you call a mark, a studio dog knows that the mark is a place where she is supposed to stay until I ask her to do otherwise. Once a dog is on her mark, I can then ask the dog to speak, or scratch, or whatever the scene might call for. Also, in this scenario, a dog can go from one mark to another with no problem, as I would be giving her hand cues or verbal commands to direct her from one to the other.

Even though Gidget was picking up the basics at such a young age, Beans could run circles around Gidget with her behaviors, and it would be that way for the rest of their lives. It wasn't a matter of playing favorites so much as being realistic about what types of jobs these dogs would be booking. Beans had already established herself as an in-demand dog in the business, so when I worked with her at home, I would often pretend my living room was a set. I'd put my keys on the coffee table and direct her to go pick up the keys and then prop her paws up on the couch, stay there for a few seconds, then go to a mark near the fireplace, drop the keys, and wait there, before I'd have her walk over to the armchair, jump up on it, and lie down. A string of behaviors like that (rewarded and taught in stages, of course) was really fun for Beans, and good practice for when we'd get on set.

But with Gidget, I was pretty much just teaching her the basics: lying down, "on your feet" (asking a dog to get up from a sit or a lying-down position), a speak, and going to her mark. Typically the types of commercials you're going to get with a

Chihuahua or another small dog tend to be ones where the dog is on a leash or being held, maybe in a bag, and on the off chance that you do get a job with more intricate behaviors, you usually get prep time to train her.

But no matter what type of work she might land, and even though I was still a new dog trainer, I knew I didn't want Gidget to be the type of dog who got picked up and carried everywhere. She came with this bold, brave attitude of *I'm a big dog*, and I wanted her to stay that way.

When puppies are very young, there's no way to tell for sure whether they'll be good working dogs. Even if they have all the makings of an animal suited for the camera, like Gidget did at this point, things can change without a lot of warning. I once trained a pair of bulldog puppies named Frankie and Vito, who showed every sign of being stars in the making. Everything seemed to be going great as I started working with them, but when Frankie was about eighteen months old, everything just fell apart. All of a sudden he became very fearful, and he developed aggression toward people, dogs, and even kids. I'd had him all his life, and his littermate Vito had some quirks but was far more manageable. It's a classic example of how you have no idea what you'll get from a puppy when you train him for studio work. Doggy stardom, not unlike stardom for people, is truly a gamble. I was lucky to find a wonderful home for Frankie, while Vito stayed at the ranch and continues to book jobs that suit his personality.

Whether I am training a newly adopted dog or even a tiny puppy like Gidget, I'll do training sessions to socialize them in new places like pet stores to simulate showing up for work in a new environment. Obviously, a big part of this process is taking the new dog on other dogs' jobs to get her acclimated to all of the people, cameras, lights, and noises. It's important to teach her that all the activity is fun, and that good things happen each and every time she's on set.

One of the first mornings that I took Gidget to set with me was an unusual one. Typically, I'd wake up at an ungodly hour, drive for at least forty-five minutes to the ranch to pick up whatever dog I was working with for a movie or a shoot, and then drive to the set where we'd be filming. But on this day in 1994 I was working on the thriller *Seven*, starring Brad Pitt and Morgan Freeman. Brad was using one of his own dogs in a particular scene (his dogs—a Weimaraner, a hound dog, and a mutt—all had really fun names: Purty, Mr. Potter, and Saudi), so I was just there to supervise and help out if need be.

It's very unusual for an actor to use his or her own dog on a movie or TV show. What's more common is for an actor to fall in love with an animal on a job, or choose to become a dog owner after working with one. Jennifer Aniston actually got her terrier, Norman, from an animal trainer she worked with on *Friends*. When I worked on *Hancock*, Charlize Theron wanted to buy Monty, the dog we trained in that movie, but the dog himself was a valuable actor, so we just couldn't give him up! He's a sweet guy—a scrappy, street dog–looking mutt with a faux-hawk. Everybody loves Monty. He's just a cool, easygoing, afraid-of-nothing dog, and he works all the time.

Once in a while, though, an actor wants to work with his own dogs in movies. It's hard to take someone's pet (famous or not) with no formal studio training and have him work on set. Not only does it take jobs away from animal companies, but people also don't always realize how much additional work is involved for an untrained dog to be brought to set, so it usually doesn't come to fruition. Then there's the American Humane Association and U.S. Department of Agriculture (all animal companies are licensed through the USDA), who usually frown on the practice. The whole thing would also involve a ton of paperwork— and the last thing a production needs to contend with is more paperwork! Plus, actors have enough to worry about when they're filming, so adding the stress of looking after their own dog isn't usually something that enters the equation. I can think of only a few occasions where an actor used his or her own animal on film, actually: Reese Witherspoon's bulldog, Frank Sinatra, appeared with about a hundred other canine "extras" in *Legally Blonde 2*. In *Million Dollar Baby*, Hilary Swank's dog, Karoo, appears in one scene when she's driving by in a car, since it didn't require any specific action and he was hanging out with her on set anyway. These were both small scenes within a movie that didn't require any actual training.

But working with Brad's dogs on *Seven* was a lot more memorable for me. It proved to be a very exciting day, not only for Brad's dogs, but for Gidget.

On the morning of the *Seven* job, my alarm went off at six a.m. and I sprang out of bed and switched it off. I probably have the most underutilized snooze button of anyone who wakes up as early as I do. *Snooze* is just not in my vocabulary. I would much rather sleep soundly for the last twenty minutes than be interrupted every five minutes by an obnoxious alarm. I'm not one of those people who wake up slowly.

I padded through the living room in my socks to find Beans curled up in her crate, popping one eye open when I walked by her sleeping spot. She looked at me like a teenager desperate not to get out of bed.

You can't be serious.

As I put a filter in the coffeemaker, I smiled as Gidget settled her head deeper into her doggy bed in the living room and let out a little grumble. Beans had already fallen back asleep. I opened both of their crate doors, but neither one of them budged.

By the time I was swirling the sugar into my coffee, I was greeted by the pitter-pat of Gidget's paws as she tapped her way into the kitchen, still squinting in the early-morning light and lazily wagging her tail.

Okay, good morning, I'm up. What's for breakfast?

For this job, I was hired to be on set (along with an American Humane Association rep) simply to make sure everything would go according to plan, to ensure that Brad's dogs were treated well, and to help in case any problem should arise. I didn't expect to do much work at all. Not very exciting or glamorous. Well, except for the fact that I'd be working with the sexiest man alive, both officially and in my book: Brad Pitt.

I had already worked a few days on this film, and my first en-counter with Brad Pitt was far from glamorous. I had been wearing full rain gear, lying flat on my back behind an air-conditioning unit on a rooftop in downtown Los Angeles, clutching several pigeons that I would release when Brad jumped over my rain-drenched body. Lying on my back in utterly unsexy rain gear is not the way I envisioned my introduction to Brad Pitt. The dripping-wet part just completed the unsightly picture.

After breakfast, I loaded Gidget and Beans into my Ford Bronco and started the trek from Venice to Hollywood, where we were shooting. I was feeling particularly optimistic on the drive: I had an easy day ahead of me, and a new puppy to train (who, at the moment, was tucked up tightly in a ball in her crate—this dog could *sleep*).

When we pulled up to the studio I found a place to park and checked in with the assistant director. Then I went to find the catering truck to get a breakfast of raisin pancakes and a big cup of coffee. I walked back to my truck to find Gidget quite con-tent to continue sleeping. She loved that crate. It had a couple of toys and a heated disk in it, a nifty little device that you warm up in the microwave and then insert into a dog bed. Gidget was in heaven. Periodically, as I was tucking into my breakfast, she would look up at me with those liquid brown eyes that always seemed to smile, then settle right back down into her bed.

It was still early (it's pretty common to spend hours on location at a job before the work actually begins) and quite cold, so I turned the engine on, cranked up the heat, and stated reading a book on dog training. Over the years, and even today, I always have dog training books lying around—I like to see what other trainers are doing. And secretly, I think it would be quite funny to have a producer walk past the professional dog trainer they hired to be on set, and see her engrossed in *Dog Training 101*!

A couple of hours later, when the sun had cleared the top of the studio, I clipped Gidget's leash onto her collar, noticing that in just a month she'd already grown a bit—maybe even a whopping few ounces. I scooped her up and placed her safely on the pavement, and she had a little potty break before we headed inside to check things out. When you walk onto the soundstage, it takes a few seconds for your eyes to adjust from the bright sunshine to the dimly lit stage. Before you enter, you always check to make sure they aren't in the middle of filming. A big red light outside the door will flash when they are. Once the light goes off, a bell rings to signal that it's safe to go in. You may have only a couple of minutes until they're rolling again, so you'd better get in quick and get to where you need to be before film starts rolling and the sound microphones come back to life. Those mics pick up every footstep, creak of a door, or rustle of a candy wrapper, and the last thing you want is twenty people turning around to see where the noise came from that just ruined the last take!

It now appeared that they were just about ready to shoot on the *Seven* set. The hair and makeup people were doing their final touch-ups, the camera was armed with an operator and assistant, and the soft voices of the crew were fading to silence. I turned around and hurried back outside, quickly placing Gidget in her crate—the set would be shaking that day, and I thought it might be a bit much for this little girl to handle—and returned just in time to sneak in before the red light turned on. I'd use the time to work on Gidget's training in the parking lot instead, and do some work with Beans as well.

The *Seven* script called for a set that would shake periodically, because Brad's character's home was situated very close to some train tracks. The scene called for his dogs to be in the living room when the house starts to shake, so an American Humane Association representative and I were asked to observe and make sure the shaking didn't bother the dogs. I'm pretty sure they didn't even notice. They seemed just thrilled to be among so many new people and places to sniff and explore. Brad also had an assistant on set walking his three dogs and looking after them when they weren't needed to work. When someone else is taking care of your dog, it's paramount that they are "trained" as much as the dog. Otherwise it just doesn't work. Whether you've got a dog in private training with an animal trainer (which I do with some people in the L.A. area), or even if you hire a dog walker, it's absolutely necessary that they keep up with all the training principles that the owner maintains at home. If not, the dog gets mixed messages.

For the day's filming, Brad, who was playing a detective hot on the trail of a serial killer, comes home from work and lets off some steam by roughhousing with his dogs. This probably wasn't too far off from his normal routine at home, so I knew I wouldn't be needed in a training capacity so much as for professional supervision. That day, I was pretty much a glorified dog sitter. But the timing was great for Gidget, since I knew I would have a lot of downtime and plenty of opportunities to fit in some training on a set.

So I watched the scene, and when the cast and crew took a break, I went back and let Beans out for a break and a walk of her own, then wandered the property with Gidget. It was warm and sunny, just the way she liked it, and as we walked around, she tipped her nose up in the air, taking in the scents of the day.

"Time to get to work, Gidge. How's that sound?"

Gidget wagged her tail and cocked her head slightly in response.

With puppies, it's important to keep the training really fun with short sessions. It's also a good time to capitalize on their learning abilities, since very young dogs are like sponges. Everything is interesting to them and they're very eager to learn. Training a puppy is different from training an adult dog. They're new to the world, so they're going to be enamored with something novel, whereas a grown dog has already seen a lot, so something new won't necessarily cause any sort of reaction.

I had Gidget barking on command already, a behavior that was easily trained by getting her a bit excited, saying, "Speak!" in an upbeat tone, and immediately rewarding her for barking. Puppies have an amazing ease with picking up simple behaviors like these, and Gidget had learned to speak on command after just a few tries. It was already looking the same with her "mark" training.

I walked over to my truck and pulled out a small, flat piece of wood. We'd been working on this routine at home, so Gidget already had an idea about what we were doing. I placed the wood on the ground and placed her about a foot behind it. After tapping the mark with my fingers, I addressed Gidget.

"On your mark," I said in an upbeat tone while pointing to the piece of wood.

Gidget paused, and I could practically see her thinking.

Hmmm, I've done this before. . . .

She moved happily toward me, stopping just in front of the wood, giving it a quick sniff, and then looking up, standing in place.

"On your *mark*," I repeated, gesturing again. Gidget hopped on the mark and looked up at me, an expression of triumph on her little face.

After using my clicker, I calmly stepped in and reached down to feed her a treat.

Whether a trainer uses a whistle or a clicker or just says, "Good," that sound is used to let the dog know the exact moment she's done something right. After asking a dog to perform a behavior, you bridge it (click) and then pay (give the dog a treat). The bridging is the most critical part of training a behavior, because it's all about timing. The dog needs to know exactly what she did correctly in order to learn and to keep performing the desired behavior. When two trainers are working with an animal on a job together, if one misses something, the other will often say, "Bridge it!" At Studio Animal Services, we have a long-standing joke from one job where we were on set and my boss kept saying to my fellow trainer, "Bridge it, Megan, bridge it!" At the end of the day, a confused-looking cameraman came up to me and asked, "So is her name Megan? Or is it Bridget?"

Gidget and I repeated this exercise a few times, which she did perfectly with no hesitation, so I then replaced the small piece of wood with a rubber drink coaster about a half-inch thick and renamed that the mark. Making the mark smaller and smaller as you work trains the dog in two ways: First, she learns that you can call anything a mark. When I point to something and say, "Mark," Gidget knows that's where she needs to be. And ultimately, when a dog is really on her game, she can learn to go to a mark as small as a piece of tape on the ground—just like an actor does.

Working a dog on a mark also reinforces his "stay." It gives you the opportunity to provide some distance between you and the dog, and the dog gets used to staying on his mark until you release him. When you train a behavior like "stay," or "go to your bed" at home, it's always good to remember to release the dog from that behavior. I use the term *all right* with studio dogs, because it's not a word that you use all the time, like *okay*, which you might say at some point while working with your dog. When releasing a dog from a stay, you should always approach the dog and physically release him, either with a little pet on the shoulder or a gentle hand on the collar at the same time that you say, "All right." Standing twenty feet away from a dog who is learning to stay and releasing him by saying, "All right, Skipper, come on," as you clap your hands in excitement will make training a "stay" extremely hard. Your dog will always be anticipating the moment that you might release him. Of course, the dog will also anticipate waiting to be touched, but it's a different kind of energy. If you're far away and shouting, "All right!" at your dog, she's naturally going to be excited and run toward you. So instead of releasing the dog in a high-energy way, you calmly walk over, say, "All right," softly, and touch the dog on the shoulder. A calm release with a physical touch will help make the behavior stronger and keep the dog from anticipating too much. I will also walk over to the dog periodically to reward him for staying, so my walking toward him could mean many things, from a treat to a release, or that I'm just going to walk around the dog to "test" his ability to stay.

In these early training sessions, Gidget was still working with a mark that was slightly raised. It's easier for a dog to learn that way, since she can physically feel the mark and hopefully learn to land on it without looking down to search for it. Going to a mark and staying on a mark are two different behaviors. Training your dog to go to his bed, for example, is one behavior. Having him stay on his bed is another. You start with just the sending part, getting him to move away from you and get on his bed. At first, you may have to guide him on a leash to direct him. Working on the stay should be done at another time, to be clear about what you are asking your dog to do, and it will also yield better results. When your dog gets on his bed, you can bridge the behavior by saying, "Good," as soon as all four paws have made it onto the bed (always keeping your tone calm so as not to distract your dog too much); then quickly give him a treat. It's okay if he leaves after that, because you're not teaching the stay part yet. Let him understand what "go to your bed" means. Then, in a separate session, place him on the bed and teach him the "stay." When he leaves, put him back on the bed and say, "Stay," slowly increasing the time that you want him to stay there.

After about ten minutes of practice, Gidget's puppy-length attention span had hit its limit. She would still listen to me with mild interest, but she was downright fascinated by a leaf that was skipping across the parking lot. Time for a break.

I walked with Gidget to the stage to peek inside again. As we walked around the set, complete with dozens of crew members and heavy pieces of equipment being moved all over, I noticed how Gidget reacted to the whole scenario. She just took it all in, and there were no signs of stress or worry. This was exactly what I wanted to do—to develop that attitude of a big dog, with all the confidence and canine bravado that comes with it. It seemed to be working, too. She wasn't scared of much, even when I took her out to the bustling Third Street Promenade in Santa Monica on the weekends. She handled the walk along the promenade with ease. I was careful to watch her body language to make sure she wasn't getting stressed out. There is a fine line between exposing a puppy or new dog to an unfamiliar environment and to one that may be too much for her to handle. The latter could stress her out or make her fearful. At such an early stage, it's best to slowly increase your dog's exposure rather than suddenly dropping your pup in the middle of absolute chaos. I was happy to see Gidget so comfortable navigating the new situation.

I'm not scared of walking through this crowd. I've got places to go and people to meet, and hey! I'd like to meet you....

I'm so glad I did this with her early on—without that big-dog attitude, she may have never seen the success that she did. As my "big dog" and I walked around the *Seven* set, it became clear that there were no signs of things moving forward with shooting. Brad's dogs weren't even on the set yet, and the crew seemed to be taking five (or an early lunch). I led Gidget outside and sat down on the tailgate of one of the giant equipment trucks and let the leash go slack at my side. She made one full turn and settled down next to me.

Just as I was letting out a contented sigh and thinking about how lovely the day had been, I heard it. A jingle. Two jingles. Wait, was it three? I had noticed over the course of the day that when Brad's assistant took the dogs for a walk, he didn't seem to think that leashes were required. Then it hit me: Those jingles were coming from the dogs' collars. But I thought they were in Brad's trailer. . . .

They weren't. Brad Pitt's dogs were outside in the parking lot, and they were running . . . straight for Gidget! I swooped down and picked her up, holding her to my chest. The sprinting dogs wore pleasant enough expressions, like they wanted to play, not eat a snack before lunch. But even with my experience, sometimes there's no way to tell whether a big dog is looking at a little one and thinking, *Chew toy?!*

When the dogs reached us, they started jumping, and I held my breath as if I were going underwater. Startled, Gidget let out a high-pitched squeal, which made this little party a thousand times more exciting for the big dogs. The higher they leaped, the higher I stretched Gidget up over my head. I don't know whether she was frozen by fear or just trusted that I'd get her out of this mess, but she didn't squirm around much in my own mildly panicked grasp.

For what felt like hours, the dogs and I did an awkward dance. They leaped in the air and I turned my hip toward them and held Gidget against the truck. Then they'd scurry to my other side and I'd swivel my hips in the opposite direction. Where on earth was Brad's assistant? These dogs had drive. They loved our game and weren't giving up anytime soon. My heart was racing and my clothes were covered in big-dog slobber. My arms were shaking from the effort of lifting Gidget high up over my head as I felt the adrenaline pulse into my limbs.

How am I going to get out of this? I thought to myself. If I moved away from the tailgate, the dogs could easily knock me off balance, and poor Gidget would be left to fend for herself. And something told me a mauling by three big dogs—even Brad Pitt's, and even if it was good-natured—would likely undo all the "movie sets are fun!" work I'd done with her.

Man, that leashless assistant would come in really handy right about now.

Just when I was about to make a perilous break for it, someone emerged from the nearby trailer: that slim, muscled body, slightly crooked smile, and that tousled, scruffy hair. Brad Pitt was just a few yards away from me. For a split second, I almost forgot about my current and rather hazardous predicament. Then he ran toward our crazy scene—me (looking far less attractive than I would have hoped, but at least not soaking wet in head-to-toe rain gear), Gidget, and his three seriously excited dogs.

"Oh, my God, I am so sorry!" he shouted over his dogs' barks as he grabbed for their collars. At that moment, his assistant finally appeared behind us as if from nowhere. Great timing, buddy.

"Here, take these," Brad told him, the frustration breaking through his voice as he ushered his frenzied dogs toward the assistant. Then he turned to me.

"I am so, so sorry. Are you okay? Is your dog okay?"

I looked at Gidget, who seemed a little miffed over the encounter but was still very much in one piece. Then I made eye contact with Brad. My already thumping heart picked up the pace.

"Yes, I think so. I'm . . . I am all right," I stammered, cursing myself for getting lost in his blue eyes when I should have been attending to the little Chihuahua, who was now squirming to escape my grip.

I leaned down and let Gidget hop to the ground, where she began sniffing Brad's shoe and shaking out her coat.

"Are you *sure?*" Brad asked.

"Yes, it's okay, really," I told him, while silencing my suddenly teenaged brain, which was practically screaming: *Tell him you need to lie down in his trailer! This is your chance!*

"Good thing you know what you're doing with those mutts," Brad said. And with a smile, he turned on the heel Gidget had just inspected and strode back toward the soundstage. Gidget eagerly looked up at me.

What's next?

"That's enough excitement for today," I said to myself with a little shudder. We headed back to the truck, where Gidget settled in for a post-adrenaline-rush nap, and I went to the set to watch the naughty dogs film their scene.

Gidget never showed any signs of fear from the incident from that day on. That's the funny thing about "big" little dogs. They get this crazy sense of bravery from their attitude. Years later, I'd have a toy poodle named Duster, who was so small that when she was a puppy I could put her inside my boot to pose for photos. But this little dog was tough as nails. I had her at a boyfriend's house one day, and she was jumping around and playing in the yard, making those squeaking noises that bitty dogs are so known for. Little did I know that the next-door neighbor's Lab mix was watching all of this from behind his screen door, getting more and more annoyed and riled up by her antics by the minute. Before we realized what was going on, the dog busted through the screen door and went after Duster. She took off, he took off, and I thought to myself, *Well, that's it! That's the end of my dog. She's history.*

There was no calling her back, so I took off running behind Duster and the Lab mix with his owner running behind me. We must have been a real sight! So we're tearing down the street when all of a sudden a lightbulb—most likely her survival instinct—went off in Duster's little head, and she slammed on the brakes, turned around to face her would-be attacker, and just started barking in his face like a pint-size maniac! It worked too. He turned away and she chased him all the way back home.

Luckily, Gidget's up-close-and-personal encounter was with dogs who were more exuberant than vicious. She made friends with plenty of big dogs in the years to come, and was just as comfortable greeting a Great Dane as she was another Chihuahua. And she would always remember how to go to—and stay on—her mark, whether it was in a motorized boat far from shore, or on a stage in front of ten thousand people.

I didn't know it yet, but in those early days with Gidget, I was teaching the basics of the business to the most famous animal I'd ever train.

Relaxing on a rock with Duster (left) and Beans

CHAPTER 4

Discovery

Most of the animals that Sue has brought onto sets where I've worked have been better behaved than the actual actors.

—David Alan Basche, actor, *Oh, Grow Up* and *Three Sisters*

very Christmas for the past twenty years or so, I've been going to my older sister Julie's house in Vegas. And every year, before I show up, she asks, laughing, "*How* many dogs are you bringing this time?"

It's become an ongoing joke with us, because I always bring a big group of dogs with me. Beans and Gidget were mainstays, but one year I brought Rob Luketic's dog, Jackson, and other years I'd bring Studio Animal Services dogs whom I was training at the time. It's always a full house.

Luckily, my sister and her husband have the space for us. Julie has a large house and plenty of property outside of Las Vegas, plus two dogs of her own, Hailey, a Lab, and Rusty, a terrier mix she rescued from a shelter. After a day or so, her dogs acclimated to my little circus coming to town, and we would take them all out for long walks together in the morning around the neighborhood.

Julie and I also made a habit of driving out to Mount Charleston, Nevada, which is about forty-five minutes outside of Vegas. The town has a tiny ski run and a lodge house, and they get a bit of snow up there, so we would take the dogs for a romp and to soak up some of the wintry weather. One year, I rented a cabin up in the mountains with my boyfriend at the time, before going to my sister's house for the holiday. We took Beans and Gidget with us and they had a blast in the snow. I wanted to put snow booties on the dogs, but I couldn't find them small enough for Gidget. So I ended up cutting the fingers off of an old glove and sliding them on her little feet. She had an entire winter wardrobe for the trip, and she loved frolicking in the snow (though she had even more fun curling up in front of the fire). By the time we got to my sister's, the dogs were all happily exhausted.

Back in California, on many a morning as I make my drive to the ranch, a quail will sit on the side of the road, contemplating crossing it with his spouse and all twelve children piled up behind him. Then, at the very last second, they'll all make a mad dash in front of my passing car. I don't know why they do it, but it's a pretty regular occurrence. On this particular morning I was also lucky enough to spot an elusive bobcat running off the road as I approached the next turn. Sneaking up on the ranch is not really an option: The dogs can hear a car from a half mile away.

I was a good two hundred yards away from Studio Animal Services, but I could already hear the dogs' barking getting increasingly louder as I approached. The canyon roads leading up to the ranch were pretty devoid of vehicles, except for the occasional oil tanker going up to the derricks to fill up.

When I parked and opened the car door, I was greeted by the *yip-yip-howl* of Kusha, a Shiba Inu, the deep, heavy bark of Joe, a German shepherd, and the excited, yelping barks of Smith and Jones, yellow Labs whose bodies wriggled and danced in unison at the anticipation of seeing a friend come inside.

Once I walked through the gate, some of the dogs settled back into playing, or they resumed eating their breakfast, but a few continued to writhe and leap at the fence, hoping that they were the ones who got to go to work today, barking their greetings.

Someone's here!

Hey! Someone's here!

There's a truck!

I can hear someone!

This is so exciting!

Oh, it's you!

That's okay.

You will do!

I looked to see which dogs were playing in their pens, and which ones were being let out into the runs. Other dogs were finishing up the last of their meals as I walked toward the part of the kennel where we keep our rottweilers.

Typically when we get a job and the training starts at the ranch, or if we're going on set, we put a sign on the kennel gate asking the workers not to feed those particular dogs. The kennel staff comes in at six in the morning to feed and clean, which is often way before we've arrived. Anytime we prep or shoot a job, the trainers take over the responsibility of feeding those animals from the kennel workers. That way we can monitor exactly what and when they eat. The last thing we want is for the dogs to have a big breakfast before going to work—we just feed them a bit later, or in some cases, the animals will work for their food throughout the day. The kennel workers still get them out and exercise them early in the morning, so when we get there they've been out in the yard already, burning off some energy and doing their business so they're ready to load up in the van and go to set.

Karin, a trainer named Jim, and I had been prepping the rotties in 1995 for a movie called *The Fan*, starring Robert De Niro and Wesley Snipes. We had about six weeks of prep time, and we'd need all of it to get the dogs ready for their big scene. It was an ideal situation for us. Sometimes a production won't have the budget for us to prep on their dime at all. Other times, you get a last-minute call for a feature film where they've recently decided for a character to have a dog, and oh, by the way, shooting starts in two weeks.

In this particular movie, Wesley Snipes's son has a rottweiler, and there's a scene where the little boy is boogie boarding out in the ocean with his dog swimming alongside him. Meanwhile, Robert De Niro's character, who is stalking Wesley Snipes, is watching the kid and the dog play together in the water from his perch up in the hills. Then, as the waves get bigger and the kid and the dog are swimming out in the middle of the ocean, the dog panics and tries to scramble on top of the boogie board to get out of the surf, nearly drowning the kid in the process. Snipes's character is nowhere to be seen, so De Niro ends up saving the boy in one of those big, pivotal movie moments.

Exciting, right? There was just one small problem: Rottweilers aren't known to be big water dogs, so the scene was going to be pretty tricky to train. Plus, the rotties had to work with a child and a small stuntperson, so it was going to take every dog we had and every ounce of creativity to make it look seamless and real. In the end we did all sorts of things and actually got quite clever to make it work. We ended up using a black Lab to double the rottweilers (we used three of them for that scene) in wide shots. We did what's called a tail tie on our trusty Labrador, in which we gently tied the dog's tail between its legs to make it look less like a Lab and more like a rottie. While on some level it was a bit funny, it was also a little frustrating. We'd be in the middle of a scene and the tail tie would come loose and the Lab's big, bouncy tail would come popping up out of the water like a mast on a sailboat.

All the preparation and training for these water scenes took place on the beach in front of a stunning waterfront home in Malibu, so every morning the three of us would meet at the ranch to load the dogs into their crates in the van and grab a stack of about twenty towels and our wet suits. As we headed west toward the ocean each morning, passing through the groves of Santa Paula and the avocado orchards of Somis, there were two things we could count on. First, a doughnut stop in Oxnard (which resulted in Jim's daily doughnut overdose, followed by a sugar crash in the middle of our ocean training), and last, a steam shower in the beach house before we left each day. It was my own little slice of heaven. The ocean in January in California is neither warm nor calm, so that shower was my reward at the end of each day.

Over the course of all those weeks of prep work, we gave the dogs a day off here and there to just stay at the ranch and play or sleep in the sun. On one of our off days, I kept busy working with some of the other dogs on my training list, including my newest little charge, Gidget. When we arrived at the ranch on that day off from the movie prep, I set up a covered puppy pen on the porch for her. Whenever it was sunny out, this was her favorite place to be. She would play and pounce on her toys and roll around like crazy in her pen. For a total of about six minutes, anyway. Then she'd promptly lie down for a snooze in the sun. I made sure to set her up with a little doggy bed and a bowl of water until I was ready to do a session with her in the house. Even when I was off doing something else, there was always someone around, whether out in front or inside, so Gidget—or any puppy whom we put in a pen out on the porch—wouldn't be left alone for very long.

Proper socialization from the start is one of the most important qualities any dog should have. By this point in her young life, Gidget was a totally friendly little thing, open to new experiences and trusting of new people. You often have only a narrow window with a dog to establish good socialization skills, so it's really important that you embrace it. If a dog doesn't meet new people and animals in her formative months and years, she could react strongly—negatively, even—to new people and animals later in life. The dog's reaction to people or other dogs could be fearful, or

anxious, or, in some cases, aggressive. And while it's always easier to expose a puppy to new things than an adult dog, it's never
too late to work on socialization.

A big part of socialization comes down to the individual dog
and his temperament. You could find two dogs who spent the first
three years of their lives isolated in a backyard tied to a tree, and
one might end up being a great dog, while the other ends up fearful and aggressive. So while there are ground rules when it comes
to socializing a dog, there are all sorts of ways to raise a happy,
healthy dog, and the "rules" that someone may swear by for their
dog can easily be broken for another for an equally good result.

With an older dog who needs to be socialized, you would still
go through the same basic process as with a puppy, taking him to
stores and all sorts of different environments and having him meet
a variety of people. If the older dog is fearful or truly unsocialized,
an owner needs to be more cautious. A new place may be really
overwhelming, and if the dog gets overwhelmed, the socialization
lesson is not going to stick or be helpful in any way. Prospective
pet owners should note that it's a lot of work to socialize an older,
more fearful, or shy dog. But that doesn't mean it can't be done
with the right amount of patience.

As I walked around the ranch on that day off from filming
with the rotties, I checked on our bulldog Vito, swinging by
his run to make sure his swimming pool was filled. One of the
requirements with the bulldogs is to make sure they have an
easy way to cool off when they get too warm, which tends to happen to the breed when they overexert themselves. Many times
you'll walk past Vito to find him lying flat on his tummy, back
legs splayed out behind him in his plastic kiddie pool. This was
one of those days. Vito gazed happily in my direction, stubby tail
wagging back and forth.

As I worked on a few other things around the ranch, my boss
walked outside to find me and asked me to go out on a showing.

Before I left, I recruited another trainer to take Gidget inside if it got chilly. It was one of those days where sitting in the sun meant a T-shirt, but the shade called for a sweater. So by the time the sun went behind the canyons across from the training house, she'd be ready for warmer temps.

In the mid- to late 1990s, "showings" were very big in the studio animal world. They were basically just in-person animal casting sessions. Once the production company knows what they want for a project, they schedule a day to have the trainers come down and show their animals. A feature film production company had called us to say they needed a bunch of animals, including a medium-size dog. Beyond that description, they weren't really sure what type of dog they wanted, so they asked us to come by their office building in downtown L.A. with all our dogs who fit the bill. So a few other trainers and I headed out, with our best "mediums," only to find when we got there that it was an all-out cattle call. The production company had literally called every southern California animal company in the business—not an uncommon practice when it comes to showings.

I waited with the other trainers and dogs, catching up with some whom I hadn't seen in a while and meeting a few new ones as well as I patiently waited my turn. About a half hour later, when it was time for our company, I was introduced to the director and producer on the movie in an office, which, by this point, had seen dozens of dogs traipse through. So my dog, naturally, had a lot of sniffing around to do.

Wow, there have been lots of other dogs in here! I'm just gonna check things out for a minute. . . .

At any given time, each trainer has four to five dogs on his or her training list. But that leaves dozens of animals who may not have worked on a job for a couple of months, including the medium-size terrier currently sniffing around at my feet, looking very untrained.

Oh, my God, I thought nervously as I looked down at him. *Do you remember how to lie down? Were you even trained to lie down?* Needless to say, I'm not a huge fan of showings. Unless you have a dog who is rock solid, with tons of experience, the practice of showing your dogs is no picnic.

Luckily, the terrier did lie down, and we did our little show-and-tell for the director and producer, who solemnly scribbled notes from behind a desk. Fortunately, most of the time when you do a showing, the production is looking for that special dog with just the right look, so judgment may not always be passed on a dog (or a trainer) when he continues to sniff the carpet while you ask him for a "speak."

Within a few years, the practice of going to showings would dwindle and eventually disappear, and trainers started videotaping their dogs, which is an infinitely better idea for all involved. Now castings are almost always on video for commercials, and all we have to do is send the clients photos and videos of our talent. Then they can decide which animals to cast without the hassle of trainers and dogs overtaking their offices. Occasionally we still get a request to bring an animal down to audition, but it seems more common when casting a feature film or TV show, where an animal will play a larger role that might last an entire series, or be featured prominently in a movie. Commercials are usually cast and shot very quickly, so anything that speeds up the casting process and makes things easier on the clients is preferred.

When I got back to the ranch with my terrier, I returned him to his kennel and went to collect Gidget from the training house. She was showing off her chicken-eating trick with another trainer (which involves no effort or talent on her behalf, of course). As I opened the door, her big ears pricked to attention, and with a cursory glance at the other trainer, she swiveled her head around to face me.

"It's okay, Gidget," I said with a laugh. "Come here! If you can part with the chicken, that is!"

With that, a small, tan blur came scrambling across the room and skidded to a stop in front of my feet, adding in a happy little dance for emphasis. It was getting close to the end of the day, but before I left, I took her into the kitchen for a short brushup session on going to her mark, speaking, and, of course, that chicken-eating trick that she had become so good at performing as a reward.

When it comes to working animals on set, people sometimes think of them along the same lines as child stars—and all the negative connotations that come with them. As trainers, we're not there to exploit a dog or make him do something he doesn't want to do. We put so much time and energy into training our animals—years of training, really. It never ends, in fact, because we're constantly training them to do new things, so no one would ever want to jeopardize that. Many times, if something bad happens on the set, that's all it takes for a dog to think, *Well, I don't want to do* this *anymore!* And by bad, I mean anything that an animal is not comfortable with, from someone talking loudly to pulling tape off a roll or even dropping a book.

Plus, it's important to remember that an animal company doesn't take just any dog off the street and ask him to work. Can you imagine a Chihuahua who had never left her owner's living room being taken by an animal trainer and shuttled to a set to perform? Or even my dog Hank, for that matter! If a dog doesn't show the signs of being a great set animal, we find her a home where she'll be happy, and we move on. There are so many dogs out there who are driven and focused and just crave having a job to do—and also need a home. You know that feeling when you've been sick or injured and you're laid up on the couch for week? Drives you crazy, right? For most people, and most dogs (couch-potato types excluded!), stimulation, activity, and work are things that they thrive on. Dogs need to do something that burns off excess energy, whether it's a long walk in the evening, or learning new behaviors to be captured on-camera.

I see so many examples of unhappy dogs as a result of my line of work. And none of them belong to the studio animal companies. People come up to me on set all the time and ask for help with their dogs, and more times than not, I can see the story coming before they even open their mouth.

"He just chews up my yard and digs everywhere, and I don't understand it. I got a second dog so he could have a friend, and I have this huge backyard for them to run around in! But it doesn't make a lick of difference."

Well, not only does that dog want a job, I'll tell them, but he's probably going crazy locked up in a yard all day, with no mental stimulation, no structured walks, and barely any interaction with his owners. Breeding matters too. The Siberian husky, for example, is a breed that was born to work. And work for a husky happens to include running hundreds of miles, so when that dog is chewing and digging, he's really pleading with his owners: *Will someone please run with me?*

Taking into account the job that a particular dog was bred to do is a huge step in figuring out what will make him happy. Simply put, dogs need stimulation. And the dogs we train are chosen for the most part because they have a high drive, they're outgoing, and they're full of energy, so they get excited about going to work. For off-camera dogs with medium to high energy, the best thing for an owner to do is just to get out with the dog. Take a walk, a run, a bike ride, an agility class, enroll in a sheepherding course with your dog, hide his toys and make it a game to find them, or engage the dog in training sessions to teach him fun tricks. All of those things are high on a pet's list of things he wants to do. Dogs just want to be a part of what you're doing and get involved. To them, that's a job—and one that they're sure to love.

Later that week, I loaded Beans and Gidget into my truck, dropped Beans off at the ranch, and picked up one of our dachshunds, who would be working on a Limited print ad we were shooting in L.A. I was taking Gidget along on the shoot as well, to continue exposing her to new scenery and new people. Sometimes it's a good idea to bring extra dogs along to a job, in case the director wants to try another one out, or just as an insurance policy in case they change the action and you need a more experienced dog. I wasn't really anticipating that Gidget would be working at such an early age, though—she was simply brought along for the ride.

After a couple hours of work, and one photo setup with the dachshund on a leash posing with a model, I took the dog back to our base camp area and put him in his crate. Then I took Gidget out of her own crate for a little walk. Happy to have my attention after her third or fourth nap of the morning, Gidget pranced at my side as we walked around the set. She'd pause along the way to greet everyone who wanted to say hi to her, which was, as usual, quite a few people. One of those greeters turned out to be the client—a woman who worked for the Limited—and she took one look at little Gidget and gasped.

"Oh, my God, that dog is *so* cute!" she said in the high-pitched tone that Gidget tended to elicit from people. "Can we use her for one of the setups?"

"Well, it depends on what you want to use her for. She's a puppy, so she doesn't really know much yet," I replied.

"Would she sit in a bag?"

I told the client I thought we could work that out, so I walked

Gidget back to our little base camp near the set, dumped out the contents of my own bag, and placed her inside. Gidget just sat there and looked at me, ready for whatever I might ask her next. Confident that she could snag this little part, I walked her back over to the set, where the crew members were artfully arranging a tote bag being held by a model. We made a few adjustments and put some "stuffing" in the bottom of the tote to fill it out. I had a few words with the model to tell her what to do and what not to do while Gidget was in the bag, and we were ready to shoot.

In the mid- to late nineties, popping your dog in a bag wasn't a common practice by any means, though it would, of course, become very popular. The most important thing for a pet owner to remember as she's out shopping or running errands is that she's still got a dog in the bag! People seem to sort of forget that as they swing their bags back and forth, or carry the bag over their shoulder, or squished underneath their arms. It's also important to make sure the dog has enough room in the bag and that he's comfortable. Most small dogs acclimate to bag travel after a few trips in a tote.

I put Gidget inside the tote, made sure she was comfortable, told her to stay (putting my palm in front of her nose, reinforcing the vocal cue with a hand cue), fed her a treat, and then stepped back as they started snapping away. Gidget looked so cute sitting in that bag—like many Chihuahuas before her and far more after—and she was completely at ease with all eyes on her as cameras flashed and crew members shuffled about.

Ah! I can do this! Look at me; I'm sitting in a tote bag!

The shoot went really well; Gidget had officially done her first job! I was thrilled to see her succeed at this unexpected assignment. But the real surprise for me came about three months later, when I popped into a Limited store, looking for the little flyer handouts at the register that I thought would be the finished product. I had been periodically going into the store to check for the flyers, and one day, before I even walked through the doorway, a floor-to-ceiling cutout poster caught my eye. It advertised a free tote with purchase, and there was Gidget: right in the middle of the store, her head poking happily out of the gigantic tote. I don't think I'd ever been so excited to see an in-store promotion in my life! I immediately made my way to the register.

"Hi. Do you think I might be able to take that big poster with the dog in the tote off your hands when you're finished with it?"

The cashier looked at me like I had two heads.

"I train the dog in the tote, and I thought it was just going to be used for little flyers, but it's huge and . . ."

"Yeah, okay. Sure. Let me take your name and number."

She never did call me to come pick up the poster.

Gidget's first professional success was the result of the work I'd done with her at home and at the ranch—while on the set, there really wasn't a whole lot of action for me. This is the case with much of my work: The vast majority of my job happens beforehand, and then on set it's more about looking after the dogs, making sure they're safe, comfortable, and happy. But sometimes the people you work with make this harder than you'd think.

Another job early on in my career was with my company's Saint Bernard, and the day didn't go as well as I might have hoped. You get put on some funky jobs as a trainer, where you don't really know what you're expected to do, or the client isn't telling you the whole story. So you show up and it's just you and your dog, and you come to find out you've been misinformed about what you'll be doing because they didn't want to pay for prep time. The best scenario for a job is that you show up on set and you've prepped the dog for exactly what he needs to do, like with the rottweilers for their big movie scene in *The Fan.* You've spoken to the director, he or she knows what the dog can do and can't do, you shoot the scene, and everyone's happy. The worst-case scenario is that the client is not really telling you what they want the animal to do, sometimes in an effort to save money, sometimes out of just sheer ignorance. Whatever the reason, this was one of those scenarios.

I had been told that the production didn't need to hire two trainers, "because the dog just has to sit there." That was my first red flag. Rarely does a production request a dog to do nothing.

Plus, two trainers really are required for the majority of jobs. If you have a dog sitting in front of camera and the production wants her to look left and look right, you'd need one trainer on each side to call the dog for the look in that direction. Or if a dog needs to be released from one spot to travel to another and then look into a lens, you have one trainer release the dog, and another behind the camera to give the dog his next command.

And of course, when I arrived on the set, there was a *ton* of stuff for the dog to do that no one had told me about until it was time to start shooting. The job was for a low-budget children's video, and it featured a kid and a bunch of adults who were doing physical comedy—the very outlandish, over-the-top, goofy kind of comedy where the actor is playing a childish role and saying things like, "Gee, honey, come on over here!" as he slaps his thigh and swings his roller skates by the laces. There's lots of tripping, falling, and flailing, and loud, loud dialogue. Not exactly your ideal environment for a dog.

What's more, they had about ten different setups for the Saint Bernard on our one day of shooting, which they never told us about. Plus, it was about ninety-five degrees outside, and we were working with a dog that is built for more like twenty-five degrees! So there was no way all of this was going to work. Standing on set listening to what these people wanted (things that I knew I could not and would not do), I was feeling pretty annoyed but tried my best to diplomatically explain that the dog would get tired and overheated very quickly, so we'd have to rein in the amount of work for her to do. The director tried to be diplomatic as well.

"Okay, that's fine. We just need the dog to pull the kid in roller skates down the driveway for this scene. That's easy enough, right?"

Um, no, that doesn't just happen, I wanted to tell him. Sometimes people just feel they can skimp on the animal part of a production and the dog will "just do it," with no idea of how training really works. So instead of snapping, I calmly told the director that this was the type of behavior I'd need to prep, since it was totally new to the Saint Bernard. I wondered something else out loud too.

"Has the kid ever been on roller skates?"

The director piped up confidently, "Oh, yeah!"

The child spoke more softly in his response: "Well, I did the one time. . . ."

All it would take to shut down the Saint Bernard for the entire day would be for the kid on skates to fall over behind her and scare her. So we agreed to move on to another setup.

"Everyone will be in the kitchen and the mom is mixing ingredients to make cookies in a bowl. We want the dog over here and then the mom is accidentally going to drop the bowl on the floor."

Sounds fairly harmless, I thought.

"Okay," I said. "Is the bowl plastic?"

"Um, no, it's glass. We need it to shatter."

There was nothing to say but no.

"I'm sorry, but that's going to scare the dog; plus, it's dangerous."

If we knew this was the setup ahead of time, we would have taken days to prep for it, starting with the dog across the room from a bowl crashing to the ground to see how he reacted. We also would have checked with the prop department to see what we could use instead of a glass bowl. As the dog's comfort level increased, we'd drop the bowl from a greater height and move the dog closer and closer to the action until we were confident that she felt fine with the scenario and we could duplicate it safely on set. We'd never just show up at a job and allow someone to smash a glass object two feet away from our dog.

This wasn't looking good.

By this point, the production crew was getting rather irritated with me. They even called my boss, stage-whispering through the conversation.

"She's telling me I can't do this, but it's in my script—I need to! That's why we hired you!"

My boss just replied calmly, "Sue's in charge, so if she's saying the dog can't do it, the dog can't do it. She's not going to do something to jeopardize the dog's safety."

This client really thought he could get us to go down there and then pull the wool over our eyes about what the action was and have us do it. So I explained again that if something happened and the dog got scared, she was not going to work, and not only for this job. A dog can get spooked and never work again. And this was not a particularly brave animal to begin with. The production crew looked at me like I was insane.

"Come on, that dog's never going to remember!"

Right.

Needless to say, on that day, the show did not go on.

I got home that night and collapsed in a heap on my bed. Annoying as the circumstances were, I smiled, thinking back on our big Saint Bernard that day, eagerly looking up at me, ready to get to work, blissfully unaware of how crazy and potentially scary that job could have been. Even on my worst day, I couldn't imagine working at any other career.

From the time I was a kid, I was absolutely sure I didn't want to be in an office. It was a class that I took back in England that confirmed this important fact for me. After much debate, my mom had insisted that I take typewriting and shorthand in addition to my photography class. I loved that one, and spent hours in the darkroom, developing prints. I was dreading the other two classes, but I didn't realize just how much I would despise them until I showed up to the first day.

The afternoon of the first typewriting class, I sat down with thirty other students with those big, clumsy typewriters poised in front of us on tiny desks. For the next half hour, I sat listening as the instructor droned on about the importance of typing at a high rate of words per minute, and practicing my own typing: *Cat Rat Hat Sat . . . Cat Rat Hat Sat . . .* on and on and on until I was sure my eyes were crossing.

I felt like I was going deaf from the constant clacking of the keys and the disgruntled sighs from kids throughout the room. It was like a symphony from hell.

I can't do this, I thought. *I'm going insane. I simply cannot stay in this room!* With shaky hands, I pushed my chair back from the desk and hurried to the front of the classroom, having no idea how I'd get out of this, but feeling more determined than anything to do so.

"I just realized . . ." I said to the teacher, without any idea of how I'd finish my sentence. But I knew I couldn't type another *cat-rat-hat-sat* sentence if my life depended on it.

"My sister!" I blurted, as the instructor looked at me quizzically. I tried to compose myself.

"I'm sorry. I meant to say, I forgot that my sister is . . . coming in from the States! And we have to go pick her up from the airport."

And with that world-class lame excuse, I turned away from the teacher, walked out, and never went back. I never wanted to sit in a room and type at a desk again—I would go crazy, plain and simple. Today, I do realize that working in an office is not quite as horrific as my tandem typewriting class, but still, get me outside and on the move as often as possible! Even though I had no clear idea as a teenager of what I wanted to do with my life, I did already know that it had to be bigger than anything I could find in my tiny village.

As kids in my high school classes started figuring out what they wanted to do with their lives—there were future doctors, vets, lawyers, and pilots all around me—I was floundering. But I knew that whatever direction I took, having fun needed to be a big part of the equation. At seventeen, I found a job that fit that bill, and I became a live-in nanny for an English family with a huge, beautiful home in a picturesque village called Bray, nestled on the River Thames. One day, when the three kids were in school, I met a wonderful woman named Noelle who had a couple of horses. She had two boys who had gone off to college and there was no one to ride her horses, so she invited me to go riding with her. We would take the horses out during the day to Windsor Great Park, which, for centuries, was the private hunting ground for Windsor Castle. Her house was part of the estate, so she'd been given a key to access all the gates leading into the park.

Riding on horseback through the park was nothing short of breathtaking. The scenery alone looked like something out of a BBC series. My neighbor had a beautiful brick-and-flint lodge house that was hundreds of years old, right on the border of the park. We would ride to the top of the Long Walk, which led all the way to Windsor Castle. Nearly three miles long, it runs up a hill toward the back of the castle, and it's surrounded by huge old oak trees that have been there forever. Then, at the top of the hill, there's a statue of King George III on horseback that denotes the end of the walk. You can see the vast woods and the polo grounds, and we could even ride through parts of the estate where Princess Anne trained for the cross-country portion of her three-day event trials. There we were: a seventeen-year-old English girl and her well-to-do older neighbor, cantering along past these massive jumps that princesses sailed over atop fancy, world-class athletic mounts. The whole thing was just surreal. *Kings and queens* had ridden where we were riding. It was simply amazing.

My nanny job afforded me my first trip to the States as well, since I'd go on vacation with the family to their house in Fort Lauderdale. There was no looking back after that. After all, I was in search of that perfect job that would provide the fun I was looking for. Whenever I got a job over the years that I didn't find enjoyable, I would leave it and do something else after lasting only a day or two. Not exactly my parents' dream! When I moved to Florida from the U.K. hoping to train dolphins, I took a bit of a detour first.

While I was a nanny, I had met a guy named Chuck on the beach in Fort Lauderdale, who worked at a hotel across from the family's house. I took the kids to the beach during the day, and Chuck worked on the beach, renting lounge chairs and sail-boats to beachgoers. We dated that summer and, like any good summer romance, I didn't want it to end.

When Chuck and I said our good-byes, he told me he wanted me to come back. I loved the idea so, back in England, I quit my nanny job and packed up my bags for my big move to America. But Chuck had only meant he wanted me to come visit! We would joke for years to come that when he picked me up at the airport, he was shocked to see all of my luggage and thought, *Damn, she's got a lot of stuff for a two-week visit!* Several years later, we were still together.

Eventually, Chuck and I got married and I would help him out by working at the hotel, selling suntan lotion and renting out sailboats on the beach. In short, a dream summer job! Not long after though, I wanted to get back on track with my dolphin-training plans, and I applied for an entry-level position at Ocean World. During my time at Ocean World, I found out that some of the trainers I worked with had attended a two-year exotic animal training and management program at a school in California. What was more, they had friends in their graduation class who had gone on to do studio work, training animals for movies and television.

I was intrigued.

"They do *what?*" I'd ask my fellow trainers. "Really? Work *on set* with animals?"

I'd never entertained such an idea, much less known someone who did that kind of work, or even understood it to be a real job. You see animals on TV and in the movies all the time, but it never occurred to me that there must be a trainer working with that animal on set too. I quizzed my fellow trainers nonstop. Ever since my sister had taken me to the BBC set, I had it tucked away in my mind that I'd love to work on set one day. So when I put the two together, sets and animal training, I was completely sold. I gave my notice at Ocean World and made the cross-country trek, just like that.

I got an apartment in Manhattan Beach with three other women from a roommate-finder service (I'm still friends with two of them today), and I set up an interview with Birds and Animals, a studio animal company that does the big animal movies like *101 Dalmatians* and *Hotel for Dogs*. I was hoping my marine-mammal training background would be enough to get my foot in the door. They weren't hiring until the spring, though, so in the meantime, I needed a job. My next gig was a bit of a departure from animal training (depending on whom you ask!). For my first three years in California, before I first made the call to Studio Animal Services, I worked at Chippendales. Yes, *that* Chippendales. I was going after the fun factor after all!

My road to actually landing that job was just as much fun as doing it. My sister Julie, who lives in Las Vegas, used to be a dancer, and her husband, Ken, did lighting for many of the shows along the Strip. One weekend I left California behind to go see her and brought my friend Lori along as well. We wanted to see a show, but didn't have much money, so we flipped through a leaflet of Vegas entertainment to look for the cheapest option. The Chippendales male revue show fit the bill, so we set off for the Strip.

Though it was the cheapest option, we still didn't have quite enough money to scrape together for a pair of tickets. So Lori set up at the roulette table, and before long we had the additional funds we needed for two tickets to the early-evening show. When we arrived at the theater, we joined a very long line of ticket holders, all waiting for first-come, first-served seating.

"We can't sit in the *back*," Lori lamented.

Then I noticed a guy leaving the theater with a bunch of microphone packs. He must work for the production, I thought, and I decided to drop a name to see if it might help. So I asked if he knew my brother-in-law.

"Sure, I know Ken," the guy told me.

"Is there any way you can help us bypass this line so we don't have to sit in the back?"

The guy was happy to usher us to the VIP section, so we were among the first people to get in. And it was *well* worth it. Lori and I loved the show, and when we got back home to California, we decided to organize a girls' night out to the Chippendales club in L.A. I wasn't working at the time, so when Lori called to make a reservation, she jokingly asked the person on the other end of the phone if they had any job openings.

Despite my standing next to her and mouthing, *Nooo!*, Lori pressed on, and actually found out that they were looking for someone to work on the weekends answering phones and helping out with some filing and organizing in their offices in Santa Monica. I interviewed for the job and got it.

I was a jack-of-all-trades and a master of none at Chippendales. For the first few months, I took reservations and did filing on the weekends. That led to assisting with some casting and working at the club a couple of nights. Then, as the company got busier, I took a full-time job assisting the owner. I also continued my work with casting and ended up doing nationwide searches for guys who would eventually be photographed for our yearly calendars. Some would go on the road throughout Europe, working on one of the many stage productions that were more Broadway-style shows than Hollywood male revues.

But after years of working with all those lovely men, I needed to focus and get back on track with my animal training. So one day, while sitting at my desk in Santa Monica, I picked up "The 411," an industry handbook for different companies in the entertainment business, and worked my way down the list of animal companies. I called them all. Most were not hiring and others did not answer, but then, finally, I got through to Studio Animal Services. I went for an interview and they took me on as a volunteer—the entry-level job for all trainers—and I never looked back. Within my first month or so, I was lucky enough to get on set assisting other trainers on numerous shoots and making the most of every opportunity to learn the job. Some trainers started out at Studio Animal Services with no experience—just a love for animals and a healthy amount of common sense—while others had been through an exotic-animal training program. I quickly learned that no matter what a person's background may have been, it was all about making the most of the opportunities to assist, and learning as I went along.

But even for an established animal trainer, the job has plenty of *un*glamorous moments. The evening after the catastrophic Saint Bernard shoot I'd worked on, I went to bed early because I had a peculiar job to do late at night. One of our rats at work had babies—we train rats periodically, along with the ducks and squirrels, goats, and other unexpected animal actors—but the mama rat wasn't taking care of them, so I took a baby rat home to feed and care for it. I had been getting up every three or four hours throughout the night to syringe-feed the little guy for several days.

And oddly enough, Gidget fell into the routine as well. It turned out she loved this little rat! So that night, when I woke up around midnight to feed it, as usual, Gidget peered out from her crate and I opened the door to let her out. She followed me into the living room, squinting as I turned on the light, and sat next to me as I fed the tiny rodent. Then, when I was finished, she washed the rat, licking the extra formula off of its face, cleaning it up.

Gidget and the rat had become fast friends. It was the sweetest, weirdest thing—she was so excited to see this little thing and clean it up. As the rat got older, I continued to let her interact with it, sometimes placing the rat on Gidget's back and letting her walk around with it (both animals happily thinking this was quite normal!). But that night was clearly an opportunity for her to nurture her new friend. I smiled at her as I walked back to bed.

"You are the cutest, funniest little dog."

Gidget looked up at me and wagged her tail dutifully.

See you in a few hours.

My Taco Bell neon sign—a Christmas gift from the company

CHAPTER 5

Taco Bell Comes Calling

What most people don't realize is, the trainer and the animal have a very professional relationship on set. The trainer has to command the respect of their animal, and that respect goes both ways. Sue was also very protective. There was only one Gidget, so we had to be careful around her! She was like a superstar.

—Buzzy Cancilla, producer

"Guess what Gidget does now!"

My triumphant early-morning greeting caused a stir to ripple through the quiet office. Deb looked up at me with a barely detectable eye roll.

"What?"

"Gidget can fold socks!"

As quickly as my coworkers looked at me, they turned away, albeit smiling. Deb turned back to her paperwork, nodding her head.

"Okay, that's a little ridiculous."

But actually, it wasn't. At my new apartment in Venice, Gidget had somehow figured out a way to fold all of my roommate Don's socks. Ever since she was a little puppy, she loved to pick up pretty much anything off the floor. And socks appeared to be her specialty. Especially those that belonged to Don.

If she were dealing with the shorter, athletic type of socks, she'd just grab them in her mouth and be on her merry way. But with the longer varieties, like tube socks, Gidget figured out that if she picked them up and ran with them, she'd get tripped up as she took off. So with the longer ones, she perfected this little move where she'd yank her head up in the air over and over, like she was furiously nodding in agreement with something. And in doing so, she'd get more and more of the sock balled up in her mouth, folding-slash-rolling it up in the process.

Okay, so maybe I'm using the term *fold* loosely. But it was a pretty hysterical habit. I went about my business in the training house and gathered up everything I needed for the day's shoot.

Gidget had just booked her first official job after being selected last-minute to appear in the Limited print ad: a commercial shoot for the fast-food restaurant Hardee's. I was excited that she'd booked her first real gig, but the process was pretty uneventful, and she landed it like our dogs land any job. The production company called, asking for a medium-size dog and a small one, and we sent them a photo of Gidget and they selected her. I drove her out to the studio with a lot of confidence in the little dog. She was able to pick up all the behaviors I was teaching her really quickly. Nothing had been a struggle, and it became very clear that this little Chihuahua was a worker. She was always happy to have a job, and whenever she had one, you could see a shift in her body language and personality. As with many talented studio dogs, you could clearly tell when she was ready to work. With some dogs, you're constantly fighting for their attention. They see other things going on around them, all of which they find much more interesting than what you're asking them to do, so you have to work that much harder to keep their focus while on a job. This was far from the case with Gidget.

When we got to work at the Hardee's shoot, Gidget was her usual, professional self. This job wasn't very difficult, but she still pulled it off seamlessly. As I guided her through the setup, Gidget was totally focused on me, eager to do whatever I asked of her next. It was pretty simple: The script called for her to sit in a kitchen watching someone eat a breakfast sandwich. We had another dog, a spaniel mix named Spudder, working on the ad as well, and my fellow trainer and I had a fairly easy day with these two. Oftentimes, an animal isn't the main "story line" of a commercial, and that was the case here. I think Gidget's screen time ended up being just a few seconds. So it goes in our industry sometimes. Not every role is a star-making turn.

The next morning when we got to the ranch, I worked on some of Gidget's behaviors with her out on the road in front of the property. The key to training a young dog is to keep the sessions brief and enjoyable. They don't have to be *as* short as when you're working with a puppy, but as soon as training gets long and tedious, a dog isn't going to be all that excited to learn. There's no set amount of time for sessions, but you want to keep them short, sweet, and fun. It depends on each individual dog too—some like to work longer than others. It's just important for *you* to quit before *they* quit so that the training is always a positive experience. And training a dog with toys as a reward is also a good idea, since at some point—especially with small dogs— they're going to get full from all the treats and your bag of tricks will be empty! And while there is a contingent of people out there who don't believe in using food to motivate a dog, the simple fact remains that a dog treat shortens the learning curve. Again, each dog is different, so some dogs will prefer toys to treats or vice versa. Beans, for example, would work all day for a tennis ball.

If you're training a recall outdoors—getting a dog to come when he's called, off leash—the process is going to move along a lot faster if that dog knows there's a treat in it for him when he gets to you. Randomly reinforcing the dog with a treat, maybe fifty percent of the times he comes back, will make the behavior even stronger. Random reinforcement works much better than rewarding the dog every single time—it keeps her on her toes so she wants to continue to please. Then, once the behavior is firmly established, you can slowly phase out the treats.

It's the same way with pets—you don't want to reward them with a treat every time. Sometimes at home or at the dog park, you may not have a treat handy, so the behavior is just getting reinforced with affection, or by throwing the dog's favorite ball a few more times.

It's pretty much a necessity in the studio world to use treats—without them, we'd be hard-pressed to have our animals ready on time for each and every job. Say we get a call on Monday morning with a request to do a Target commercial on Friday where the dog needs to walk over to a couch, pick up an object, and carry it to an actor. Then, over the next day or so, we'll send them photos of our dogs and they'll pick the one they want. Then the clock starts ticking and we have until Friday to perfect the behavior with the dog. Doing that without treats would be next to impossible. But for a pet owner, using treats as rewards is a personal choice. Still, even with my pets, I've always used treats to initially train a behavior before moving away from food.

It's a bit like going to a casino and gambling. If you got your money back every time you bet a quarter in the slot machine, that might sound like the best trip to Vegas ever at first, but it would get kind of boring if you won every single time. (Lucrative, sure, but exciting? Not so much.) There's a distinct excitement in not knowing. And it's the same with random reinforcement with a dog.

Toys, of course, are the other key training method after treats. And to get a dog excited about a toy, you have to encourage his play drive or prey drive, depending on the breed. Most people think that all puppies naturally have a play drive, but it depends a lot on the breed. Jack Russells, for example, will be very excited about a toy with a squeaker in it, or maybe a tennis ball. You need that trick in your back pocket (literally) for when the dog gets full and won't be motivated by food anymore. It comes in quite handy when you've got a less than perky pup on set and more shooting ahead of you.

Yeah, I don't really care if you have steak; I'm not hungry. . . . *Wait, what? You've got my tennis ball!?*

Pull that favorite toy out of your pocket and suddenly the dog has a new lease on life. So it's a matter of figuring out what type of toy excites the individual dog, and then working on that drive so you can benefit from it down the road.

Back at the ranch during our training session, Gidget and I moved into the training house, where we focused on "hide your eyes," a behavior where the dog lifts a paw and puts it over her face. This is usually an easy move to teach a young dog or a puppy. All you do is lightly place a Post-it or a piece of tape on the dog's head so it hangs annoyingly over the eyebrow, which makes the dog want to swat at it. As soon as they do, you bridge the behavior with a click or another sound. Then you gently remove the Post-it if the dog didn't knock it off with a swipe of his paw (also part of the reward) and then pay the dog with a treat. Animal trainers often joke that it's called "paying" because the dog is working for the treats the way people work for a paycheck.

As easy as it was to train Gidget to hide her eyes, it was about a thousand times harder when I tried to train my dog Beans. Whereas puppies will add a new trick to their repertoire in a matter of hours (if that!), it's a whole other story with a seasoned, studio-trained adult dog. After two weeks of attempting to train it with Beans, I pretty much gave up. Like other older dogs, especially studio dogs, she was very desensitized to strange things, since we'd done so much with her over the years. Other trainers and I had put clothing on her as well as headpieces, like little crowns on her for TV commercials, and we often had her hold stuff in her mouth that would end up touching her face. Often-times, studio dogs and pets (to an extent, anyway) have seen and experienced so much that they won't be enthralled with something new the way a young dog would be. When I put that Post-it on Beans's head, she just sat there.

Oh. Okay, Mom wants me to sit here with a Post-it on my head. I'll just sit still then.

She couldn't have cared less. I had to work overtime to convince her that she *should* care about that Post-it. Instead, Beans assumed it was part of a behavior I was teaching her and agreeably went along with it (such a good dog, right?). Six months later, when Beans and I were sitting in the kitchen, out of the blue I told her, "Hide your eyes," and she did it! It's easy to drive yourself crazy as a trainer when you're trying to get a behavior, but if you walk away from it and try again weeks—or even months—later, sometimes the dog will decide to offer it up.

While Gidget and I were working on her behaviors, a call came through at the office from another animal company casting for a Taco Bell commercial. Just like the day I found Gidget, that call for Taco Bell was nothing out of the ordinary, nor did it show any potential for doggy superstardom. It was just another job. Taco Bell was shooting a commercial and they were looking for two Chihuahuas, one male and one female, to star in it. So the office sent in a picture of Gidget and the production cast her, along with a male Chihuahua named Dinky from another animal company.

Gidget was due at the shoot that Monday morning, but I was already booked on another job, so a trainer named Jeanine took Gidget to shoot the Taco Bell commercial. This is a pretty common practice among trainers, since our jobs tend to involve travel. There's just no way to guarantee that a trainer will be available for a particular animal's job, especially for a one-off like this one.

Even though Gidget had done well in her work for the Limited and Hardee's, this was her biggest job to date; plus, there were multiple behaviors required. Even when all bodes well, you never really know how an animal is going to work under that kind of pressure. She'd be on set longer, the crowd would be bigger, and she would have to perform. Dogs may not know the meaning of the word *pressure*, but they can certainly feel it.

When Gidget was originally cast, the plan was for her to play the shaky little "girlfriend" dog of the main dog they'd be shooting. But a few days before the dogs were due on set, the director decided to switch things up, as directors sometimes do. So Dinky, the male dog, would actually play the girlfriend role, while Gidget would play the male dog, the lead role. We didn't know it then, but that last-moment swap was huge. The girlfriend part in the ads spanned only a few commercials, and without the switch, Gidget would never have become the Taco Bell dog, never walked the red carpet, appeared in movies, met celebrities, or been the subject of a book.

The evening after the shoot, Jeanine called me with a glowing review.

"She was so good. She did everything I asked and was happy as could be!"

I was thrilled that Gidget's first big job was a positive experience, and helped her settle in at home. After a quick round of greetings with the other dogs, she made a beeline for her bed. She'd put in a full day at work after all!

Within a month or so, Gidget's Taco Bell commercial began airing, and something funny started to happen. I was on a shoot in downtown Los Angeles with another dog, and Gidget had come along for the ride. I hadn't seen her commercial yet myself. On breaks, as I walked her around the set, I noticed several crew members pointing at her. Not sure why the little dog was being gossiped about, I continued to walk around base camp and do a little training with her while we were at it. While I was still bringing Beans along on shoots and to the ranch with me, for this particular job I left her behind. Downtown L.A. is full of funky parking areas and interesting characters, so I didn't want to leave her in a locked car for long stretches of the day.

As the shoot progressed, so did the stares. Gidget wasn't even working, but everyone seemed particularly taken with her. Soon, one of the camera operators tapped me on the shoulder.

"Excuse me, but is that the dog from the Taco Bell commercial?"

I told him she was, and a flurry of compliments came our way. And I swear, Gidget seemed to eat them all up, dancing around at my feet as people came over to talk.

"I saw that commercial! It was so funny!"

"That dog is adorable."

"It made me hungry for tacos!"

For people who work in the studio industry, a cute animal commercial isn't exactly an earth-shattering piece of work. There are plenty of appealing ads out there, so it takes something pretty special for people to buzz about one the way they were about Taco Bell.

In the days that followed, we encountered more and more fans of the commercial. As exciting and flattering as it was, I still didn't imagine a big future with Gidget and the fast-food industry.

A few weeks later, the next call came in.

Taco Bell wanted to do not just one more commercial, but an entire series of them down in Miami in the winter of 1997. As luck would have it, I was otherwise engaged again, working on the movie *Enemy of the State* in Baltimore, so another trainer would take Gidget down to Florida while I worked up north on the movie.

A couple other animal trainers and I were working on *Enemy of the State* for an integral piece of the plot—even though it was only a quick blip on-screen. When a person gets murdered, an unlikely piece of evidence surfaces thanks to, randomly enough, a scientist studying the migration behaviors of Canadian geese. The scientist in the movie has a video camera disguised in the bushes around a lake to track the geese, so he inadvertently catches the crime on film. Where do the animal trainers come in? Well, contrary to what moviegoers may assume, you can't just take a bunch of wild geese and throw them on the ground in a group and hope they stay there. So we spent a few weeks training the geese to stay in one particular area.

I also worked with a cat on the movie who belonged to Gene Hackman's character. I often get asked when I'm working with a cat, "Do you starve him so that he'll work on set?" It's a frustrating misconception about what we do as animal trainers. The truth of the matter is, studio cats are healthier than most cats sitting at home on the couch.

Chrissie, one of the trainers at Studio Animal Services, once did a promotional tour with a bunch of cats from our ranch for a cat-food company. People would approach her at the pet shows where the cats were working and say, "Your cats look *so* thin." But the vet who was working there would step in and explain.

"Actually, the cats you see working here today aren't thin at all—they're at an ideal weight. About eighty percent of people's cats at home are actually overweight. We weigh out the studio cats' food every day so that they maintain a normal size."

The *Enemy of the State* cat appeared in quite a few scenes, including the one where Gene realizes he's been located by a government agency, so he grabs all of his belongings from his home, cat included, and flees to a safer location. Gene was a really nice guy, and always made my job easier with his pleasant tone and willingness to cooperate with whatever we needed for the animal's sake.

There was one scene that was fairly tricky to shoot. The cat, an orange-and-white tabby named Aladdin (who was hired along with a slew of teammates who doubled as him for other scenes), was supposed to be sitting on a chair while the camera is on a dolly track behind him, shooting over his shoulder as Gene exits the room. So there was no way for me to stand in front of the cat, since I'd be right there in frame like an unplanned cameo in the movie. The cat didn't need to do any particular action in the scene—the director, Tony Scott, just asked that he sit there and look off into the distance in the direction of Gene and the front door. When it came time to shoot, the usual activity started up: The camera on the dolly had to move, which meant there were a few people involved with that process. In total, there were about ten people working behind the cat and the camera, including me, which could prove very distracting. It's like when you're in a very quiet room and the slightest noise will draw your attention. It was very tempting for the cat to turn around and check things out behind him instead of looking straight ahead. Luckily, Deb (our best cat trainer at the ranch) had initially trained him, and by now he was a seasoned performer, able to take direction from me even while I was standing behind him. Everything was going well until Aladdin went to stand up just as the director called, "Action!" So I quickly made the sound we use for a cat that means "stay," and without turning to look at me, Aladdin promptly lay down facing the doorway that Gene Hackman was standing in. I silently thanked Deb for laying the groundwork with our hero cat, the main animal we use for a role. (We always name our cat teams in themes, and this team had a Las Vegas theme, with the names Aladdin, for the hotel, Vegas, and Reno.)

Next, we filmed a scene in an abandoned warehouse—which would get blown up in the middle of the movie—and the special-effects team was actually packing it with explosives as we filmed. A little unnerving, let me tell you! It wasn't until the actual blowup day that they would rig up the detonators, of course, but it was still hard not to think about it as we heard the special-effects guys working on the explosives on the other floors in the building. A couple of days later I went down on my day off to watch them blow up the warehouse. They had five cameras on the ground, plus one in a helicopter to capture it all. And they shut down about four freeways—not so much for safety reasons, but because I'm sure it would prove a little distracting to nearby drivers.

During our time in Baltimore, while staying at a residential hotel, we had arranged for an extra room in which to keep two of the cats. I had one cat in my room, and my boss had the dogs we used in the movie in his room. This happens quite often when we have a lot of cats on a shoot—invariably, some of the them get their own room to themselves, without a trainer staying with them (in this case, a king-size room with a loft and minikitchen!). On one of our days off, another trainer and I were coming back from lunch, just strolling leisurely along the pathway that went around the hotel. And there, lying fully stretched out in our path, was an orange-and-white cat. We stopped. We stared. And while both of us were struck by the coincidence that a cat who looked just like ours was rolling around in the sun ten feet from our hotel room doors, we carried on, stepping over the cat and heading for our respective rooms. It wasn't until I was sliding the key card in my door that I stopped, gave it some thought, and walked back around the corner. I looked at the cat again. *Hmmm, maybe I should check the cat room just to make sure*, I thought to myself.

Upon arrival at the hotel, we'd had a very thorough conversation with the manager and staff, including the housekeeping department, so everyone was aware that this room had two cats in it with no humans. So under no circumstances should housekeeping or other staff members enter the room without our consent. That way, we could ensure that neither cat would sneak out when the door was opened. I put the key in the cat room door and stepped inside. I immediately spotted one of the cats from the team, Reno, but no Aladdin. I checked the bathroom, under the bed, in the closet, behind the curtains. Still no Aladdin. I opened the front door, peeked out at the sunbathing cat, and looked back at Reno, who was purring quietly on the bed, giving nothing away. The cat lounging outside *was* Aladdin! My first reaction was to get a little irritated, to say the least, as I jumped to the conclusion that housekeeping had opened the door, allowing our main hero cat to escape.

Lucky for us, he had decided to stay close by and do a bit of sunbathing, rather than traipse through the city. I reached down to pet him and he rolled over on his back. I scooped him up and promptly returned him to his hotel room. I left the room, closed the door, and, while standing in the breezeway contemplating whether I should lodge a formal complaint with the hotel manager, I noticed some movement out of the corner of my eye. As I turned to face the door, I witnessed the makings of the great escape. The door handle from the cat room was twitching up and down. I folded my arms and waited, determined to see how this would play out, while marveling at the ingenuity of these two resourceful cats. Reno, I'd come to find out, would hang on the door handle, so that his weight would allow the door (a heavy fire door, no less) to open a crack, and Aladdin would nudge it open and squeeze out before the door shut behind him. Only this time, when the door opened a crack, I was standing there to greet Aladdin, who happily rolled over when he saw me, still quite pleased with himself. I laughed to myself as I realized that their master plan fell short: They never figured out a way for Reno to get out after Aladdin! From that day on, we shut the door with a newspaper wedged in the doorway so that it would stick. No more kitty field trips on this movie!

Another small animal actor we trained for *Enemy of the State* was a Pomeranian named Dracula who played Will Smith's character's family pet. Studio Animal Services has always had Pomeranians, and for some reason they all have vampire-themed names (no, they don't bite). After Dracula, we had a Pomeranian named Lestat, who played Mr. Muggles on the TV show *Heroes*. In *Enemy of the State*, Will's character's home is vandalized, and the intruder even spray-paints the dog green. As busy as I was training the animals on that film, I also had time to sit back and watch the Will Smith phenomenon at its peak. There were massive crowds of girls outside of wherever we were shooting for the entire two months we were there. They seemed to follow him wherever he went. And they always did the same thing, screeching in high-pitched voices.

"Will! Will! *Wiiiiiiiill!*"

Believe me, it got old.

I also had some personal business to attend to while I was in Baltimore that winter. For a while, I'd been thinking about getting a toy poodle. I had seen one in a magazine, and it was so cute that it just got me thinking about what dog I would get next, and I figured that a poodle might be a good choice to join Gidget, Beans, and me at home in California. A red poodle, to be exact! So on days off from shooting I looked up some breeders and found one who would be able to show me puppies. I went to look at them without any definite plan to keep one, though I should have known how things would end. Really, when are you ever going to leave a litter of adorable puppies—the exact type you're looking for—and *not* take one home with you? I certainly couldn't.

I brought the new toy poodle puppy, whom I named Duster, back to my room at the hotel and quickly discovered that this dog was insanely smart. I had no intention of training her for studio work; I just wanted another pet, but it was lots of fun to discover just how bright she was. Since it was cold out, I decided to paper-train Duster instead of taking her outside for housebreaking. She didn't have a single accident, happily doing her business on the paper from day one before retiring to her crate.

If a pet owner is going to paper-train a dog, the most important thing to remember is that once you introduce that option in your home, it's difficult to take it back. Once a dog is paper-trained, you run the risk of the dog going to the bathroom elsewhere in the house, unless you are very careful to designate the dog's particular potty spot. Otherwise, the wee-wee pad you've got in the corner may not look all that different from your area rug! If an apartment dweller paper-trains a dog and then moves to a house, that dog is not automatically going to understand the new concept of going outside to go potty. So if you want to paper-train, be prepared to use that method for the rest of the dog's life. It is possible to retrain a dog's bathroom procedure and "undo" the paper-training in exchange for potty time outside, but most people simply don't have the time for this, and that's when they run into problems.

While I was in Baltimore, another trainer named Megan took Gidget down to Miami for the next series of Taco Bell commercials. As much as I would have liked to take her myself, this is just the nature of our business. Oftentimes, a dog who lives with (or is trained by) one trainer will go on jobs with another, depending on everyone's schedule. Megan had known Gidget since I got her, and they spent a few weeks together before going down to Miami, getting to know each other and prepping for the new ads. Over the course of those six commercials, Gidget had to wear clothing—not her favorite part of studio work—stand on a fire escape, ride a skateboard, and even run alongside a moving bus.

Before I left for the movie job, I dropped Gidget off at Megan's with one very special accessory. Like any small dog, Gidget would get full pretty quickly while working, so you could pay her with treats for only so long. Once she got full, holding a piece of chicken out on a bait stick would no longer elicit that happy, eager response. So when you needed an intense look from a dog for the camera but she's got that Sunday-after-lunch-just-want-to-lie-on-the-couch expression instead, there's got to be something extra-special on hand to perk her up.

For Gidget, that toy was Mrs. Hedgehog. I didn't allow her to have the little stuffed hedgehog all the time, for two reasons: first, because she wouldn't be quite as motivated by her everyday toy as a special one, and second, because my other dog, Beans, loved to decapitate those toys, ripping them apart to get to the squeaker. So I sent Megan to Miami with Mrs. Hedgehog and specific instructions not to give it to Gidget until she needed a little motivation on set. Gidget was just crazy for this toy (it's very popular—still available to buy online today!). She had lots of toys, but she loved Mrs. Hedgehog the most. I think she just liked the way it felt, the way she could grab the whole thing in her mouth and squish the squeaker inside. She would toss it in the air and throw it down on the ground and pounce on it with reckless abandon. And since she really saw it only when we were traveling or working, we got the same adorable reaction from her each time.

Oh, my God, it's Mrs. Hedgehog! Let me have it! Please, can I have it? I need it now, now, now!

Whenever it looked like she was fading a bit, I could just hold up her Mrs. Hedgehog near the camera or at waist level and she'd get refocused and excited.

And Mrs. Hedgehog would come in handy in Miami—Gidget had her work cut out for her down there. For the bus commercial, she had to not only run alongside the bus on a real street, but also glance up at the bus periodically, since the commercial had her "talking" to a passenger on board. So for a couple weeks at the ranch, the trainers prepped her with one trainer in a car and one calling her from point A to point B. They started out having the car drive very slowly and making sure that Gidget never stepped off the curb, which was just three feet away from the moving vehicle (for obvious reasons!). And they paid her with treats for looking at the vehicle while running in a straight line next to it. Pretty impressive for a Chihuahua! It was becoming quite clear that Gidget was incredibly brave, and didn't act her size under any circumstances.

Gidget performed with all the chutzpah we'd come to expect of her. A training assistant rode on the bus as Megan called her on the curb on a real street in Miami. Our prep time had served her well, and the entire crew worked hard to make sure Gidget was safe every step of the way. With each take, she seemed more and more sure of herself.

Over the course of the six spots, Gidget happily rode atop a skateboard, ran through doggy doors, and did a lot of work on the crowded streets of Miami. For one spot, she crested a hill with a crowd of two hundred extras behind her waving flags and chanting. Even when moving buses weren't involved, her safety and comfort were paramount. Megan learned to watch for a twitch of the ear that signaled that Gidget might be uncomfortable with something. The little dog loved the work and never ran away from anything—it was more like watching her mind work and being able to read the signals if she didn't trust something or someone. And she had no trouble at all with holding a small piece of wood called a bite stick in her mouth. This was a tool to keep her mouth propped open at just the right position to get a light reference in her mouth. That way, the postproduction people could animate her mouth with her famous tag line, "*Yo quiero* Taco Bell," and it would look realistic—as though Gidget were actually speaking. That technology would later change, but at first it required Gidget to hold that bite stick.

The only real trouble that came out of those shoots was in the morning or evening, when the air was chilly. Directors often call for a "wet-down" on streets and sidewalks, because it makes them look better on film. But for a Chihuahua who detested the cold, wet-downs were no walk in the park. Gidget's role in the Taco Bell ads called for a very particular look: ears pricked, eyes wide, and head high—an overall look of pride and confidence. But the minute she got chilly, that look would be lost (dogs can't help appearing a bit pathetic when they're cold), so the first of many space heaters was brought onto the set for Gidget.

By the time filming wrapped in Baltimore, I'd had ten-week-old Duster for only a short time, and we had a big flight home ahead of us. It was more than four hours of flying time before our plane change in Denver. So the morning of the flight, anticipating a nightmarish trip, I woke up at five a.m. to start playing with her. Duster ate up the attention, and anytime she went to sit down, I'd encourage her to stand up and keep playing with me—wearing her out in the process—in anticipation of our flight. I made sure her little paws stayed in motion until we were on that plane and she was sleepily tucked inside her carry-on bag.

During the four hours en route to Denver, I didn't hear a peep from Duster the whole time. My play-till-you're-pooped plan had worked! But when it was time for the plane change, I knew she would have to go to the bathroom, and I couldn't leave the airport to take her outside. So, on a hope and a prayer, I carried the tiny poodle into the handicapped stall in the ladies' room and laid down a bunch of paper towels on the floor. I lifted Duster out of her carrier, and before I could figure out my next move, she walked over to the pile of towels, peed and pooped, and traipsed right back into her carrier!

I get it. I have to go to the bathroom here.

It was amazing. Here was a ten-week-old puppy who had never seen a paper towel or a public bathroom—let alone an airplane— and not one bit of it fazed her. I marveled at my great find as I leaned back in my seat on the final leg of our journey home. As the airplane climbed higher and higher into the sky, my excitement to introduce Duster to my dogs grew, and to see them myself for the first time in months. I missed Gidget and Beans while I was away, but since I was working on a movie with other animals, I was distracted and kept busy with them and with Duster. It would be harder if I were a traveling salesperson and suddenly had no contact with any dogs. But now that I was headed back home, I realized just how thrilled I would be to reunite with my pack.

On the set of Gran Torino *with Clint Eastwood*

CHAPTER 6

Call Times and Downtimes

I've worked with a lot of animals on film: dogs, cats, horses, orangutans. It's always been a lot of fun and a bit of challenge. I enjoy it very much, especially when you have good animal handlers who know when to come in and when to step back. My trick is always to try to become as friendly as I can with the animal on a movie. On *Gran Torino*, I tried to get our dog Holly comfortable being around me. Sue gave me treats to put in my pocket so Holly got used to taking them from me. That way she wasn't only looking for the trainer to come reward her. A lot of times, trainers forget that there are other elements of the movie going on, but Sue never forgot that. In the old days with the orangutans, I'd do the same thing. I'd come to work and put a bunch of dates in my pocket and then I'd sit and eat a date, looking off in the distance like I wasn't paying attention. And then out of my peripheral vision I'd watch the orangutan looking at me, wondering, "When do I get some?" And finally I'd go, "Oh, you want one too?" So I'd give them one and then they thought I was okay. I think animals that work in film like to have a job. You can see that they're trying to please the trainer. But they also seem to enjoy certain rewards, nice conditions, and a lot of people paying attention to them. Like any actor!

—Clint Eastwood, director and star of *Gran Torino*

When I got home to California, I immediately went through the meet-and-greet process with Duster, Gidget, and Beans. It went quite easily (too easily, I'd later discover). With a weekend off of work, I settled in at my apartment for a lovely two days of doing as little as possible while I recovered from the jet lag and the cold—I wasn't used to East Coast winters after being spoiled by the "cold" months in California.

That night, I ordered a pizza and plopped down on the couch to watch copious amounts of bad TV. Gidget, who'd been snoozing, of course, got up slowly, stretching each little leg as she stood and yawned and trotted over in my direction. I invited her to join me, and, after a moment's consideration, she hopped up onto the couch and settled into her favorite pillow. I'd been leaning on it, so it had that convenient little depression, perfectly Chihuahua-sized, that she could curl up in for the next nap of the evening.

Those first few days at home with the dogs were quite peaceful. As the years went by, however, it became evident that Duster was going to be the type of dog who required your attention twenty-four hours a day, seven days a week. And with two laid-back, surfer-girl type dogs already living with me, it was bound to be problematic. In no time at all, Duster decided she wanted to be in my lap whenever I sat down, and trailed me anytime I walked the five feet from the couch to the kitchen. I've never had a dog like that. Gidget and Beans were always quite relaxed when it came to my whereabouts. They were more than happy to laze around on the deck, interested in my location only when they were hungry or on the move from one sunny locale to the next. Over the first couple of years of living together, when I showed affection to the other dogs, Duster started to become jealous. She wouldn't bark or act out the way most dogs would, though. That would be child's play to Duster. Instead, she plotted against the other dogs, almost like Beans did early on with Gidget.

Sure, that may sound dramatic, but it's one hundred percent true. And it was really quite funny to think that a dog could come up with this stuff. She was like a little person stuck inside a poodle outfit! Blows my mind to this day.

Duster's first scheme went as follows: At the end of a meal, she would save one kibble of dog food while the others gobbled up every morsel. As her roommates dispersed, getting up for a drink of water or to walk around the house, she would take that one kibble and walk it over to one of the big dog beds in a high-traffic area of the living room where everyone would pass by, and she'd place it on the edge of the bed. Then, like a tiny, curly-haired cougar, she'd crouch behind the bed and wait patiently for another dog to walk by.

All right, bring it on. Who wants it?

And she would just wait, patient as could be, for another dog to come upon the lone kibble, and then go in for the kill.

Oh, look! There's a piece of kibble on that dog bed!

The moment one of them went for it, Duster would pop up from behind the doggy bed and sound the classic poodle alarm, that high-pitched *Rah! Rahrahrahrah! Rah! Rah!* And then she'd throw herself at the other dog, attacking its nose. Who knew a toy poodle could be capable of planning such a carefully timed attack? I'd correct her, of course, but pretty soon she'd wait until I was out of sight, and she started incorporating the routine into nearly every mealtime, cementing herself as the villain of the house with each kibble placement.

Eventually, I had to end the mealtime attacks by putting Duster in her crate as soon as she finished, leaving her to look longingly at the single uneaten kibble left in her bowl. But that just made her even more creative.

Pretty soon, at other times of the day—probably more often than I knew—if there was a toy that Duster wanted, but Gidget or Beans was playing with it, she would get herself all worked up and frustrated about her misfortune.

I. Want. That. Toy!

She'd yap her little head off, but they'd just look at her with disdain.

You silly little dog. Bark all you want, but you're not getting this toy.

The joke, it turned out, was on them. Whenever they'd deny her the plaything she desired, Duster broke out her secret weapon: the living room window. This was the window that every dog owner has in their home—the window that all the dogs peer out of and bark at when they hear someone pulling up to the apartment.

So when the toy was not relinquished, Duster would relent, taking just a few steps away before popping up her little head and scampering to the window as if she heard someone approaching, and start barking. Then the other dogs would follow suit, running to the window and barking like crazy to alert me to visitors.

Someone's here! Hey! Someone's here!

And the minute the other dogs did that, Duster would jump away from the window and run back to grab the toy that the other dogs had forgotten while barking at the invisible visitor. And so it went in our house for a couple of years. Duster was always jealous of the other dogs and kept coming up with sneaky ways to pick fights with them. Eventually, I knew I'd need to find another home for her. Luckily, I had a perfect new owner in mind. An acquaintance of mine was a big traveler, always jetting off to another part of the world, and she was looking for a small dog to take with her. I said she could try out Duster for a week or two to see how things went, and she fell in love with the little poodle right away. I never saw Duster again! I was sad to let her go, but this little girl really needed a person who wanted to be close to her as much as she wanted to be close to them. A classic "only dog," she did best without any canine roommates. And that was just never going to work in my household. Beyond the full-time dogs—who would continue to multiply as the years went by—I would often bring home dogs from work for a night before they had a job, and I couldn't run the risk of an unfriendly interaction between a working dog and Duster.

Periodically, I would get reports on how Duster was doing after she left my house, and it was always reassuring to know I'd found her the perfect owner. Calls and e-mail would come through like, "Duster's in Belgium!" Or, "Duster's on a yacht in the Pacific Ocean." Duster became more of a world traveler than most people I know, even making a trip to the Berlin Wall. To this day, she goes everywhere with her owner and just laps up the attention (and lap time) she gets all day long.

After my minibreak following *Enemy of the State*, I got back to work at the ranch, where it seemed like we were booking more jobs than ever. The Taco Bell ads were taking off, but we had plenty of other jobs as well. It was fun to be busy, but my call times (the time that the crew, animal trainers included, is expected to be on set) seemed to be getting earlier and earlier. On some mornings, I wouldn't even bother to bring Gidget along with me, since she seemed so peaceful and content snoozing away as I headed out to my truck before the sun came up.

It was the spring of 1998, and I'd moved from my Santa Monica apartment into a new house in Lake Hughes, California. It was the first house I'd ever bought (with a doggy door, no less, so the dogs could come and go freely), and I was quite pleased with it. Lake Hughes is about an hour north of Los Angeles, situated high up in the mountains, thirty miles away from the hectic bustle of the city. It had a gorgeous view of the lake, which appeared as still as glass on a calm day. The house was surrounded by a thick cover of pine trees that looked particularly picturesque in the winter, when they'd be covered in soft mountain snow.

But my commute wasn't easy. A winding mountain road with hairpin turns can be unnerving—especially after eighteen-hour days, of which I was putting in plenty these days. The commercials just kept rolling in, and I was bringing plenty of dogs into the house the night before a big job. Meanwhile, Beans was becoming quite a star in her own right.

Ever since I got her from the shelter and began training her, Beans had booked tons of jobs and made a real name for herself in our industry. She was one of the busiest dogs at our company for most of her life. I think it was just fate or dumb luck that I picked her the way I did (first dog I saw at the first animal shelter I visited!) and she turned into such a star. She never did a feature film, but she'd often have two or three commercials airing at the same time—quite a big deal in the studio-animal industry. Beans was just so incredibly smart. She would learn a new behavior in a single training session, whereas it might take another dog several sessions to pick it up. For a while, it seemed like no matter what job we heard about, my boss could hardly resist putting her up for it. "Let's send Beans's picture in for that" became a common mantra around the office. She was my trial-and-error dog when it came to training, but ever since I'd started my job in California, she ended up being the dog everybody talked about and trainers hoped to take on a job, because she always did what she was asked and made a trainer's job easy.

Beans's first big job was for Miller Genuine Draft in 1994, and the commercial featured a guy sitting at a bar with a tattoo of a dog on his arm. He's trying to get a bartender's attention but no one is noticing him, so the tattooed dog on his arm—played by Beans—comes to life. She started out standing on the bar; then she had to run down the length of it, reach down into a cooler, and grab a beer bottle in her mouth. Finally, she had to run it back to the guy before jumping back into his arm (in postproduction, of course). That's a lot of behaviors for a dog to do all at once, but for Beans, it was a piece of cake. Then she booked a Visa commercial where she walks past a guard at Buckingham Palace and has to lift her leg as though she is doing her business right there on his leg. And she even booked a small part in *The Fan*, the Robert De Niro movie that featured our rottweilers. A lot of times when trainers bring extra dogs to the set of Tony Scott's movies, he'll find a way to put those dogs in the film too, since he's a huge animal lover. That's what happened when I brought Beans to the set. He took one look at her and that was it.

"Let's put her in this scene!"

And we did, even if it wasn't the most logical scene in movie history. Robert De Niro's character is walking to an office building to meet someone, and then all of a sudden, there's Beans, trotting alongside him! I chalk it up to some sort of artistic directing decision that was over my head.

After a slew of commercials and her little role in *The Fan*, Beans even landed a guest-starring role on *Baywatch*. My little cattle dog costarred with two of the biggest beach bunnies on the planet at the time, Pamela Anderson and Yasmine Bleeth, during the show's eighth season. Their characters found Beans down on the beach after her owner had drowned, and they decided to keep her and train her to be a lifeguard (a logical decision on this TV beach). They even did a whole slow-motion montage with Beans and Yasmine running down the beach with their little red life preservers. As easy as it may be to poke fun at the plot-lines, the production on that show was like a well-oiled machine (emphasis on the oil). Those people know how to make a TV show on a budget.

Normally, as you move on a shoot from one set to another, you take your animal and put her into her crate and you've got a nice break, maybe a half hour, while the crew moves the lights and cameras and sets everything up for the next shot. But on *Baywatch*, I would literally walk off set, lead Beans to her crate, open the door, and when she had one paw inside, they'd be calling me for the next setup.

"Okay, we're ready! Let's put the dog in."

This happened time and time again. At one point, I had to tell the first assistant director that Beans had been working all day and needed a break before we kept filming. Studio dogs understand their downtime and enjoy it quite a bit. When they go into that crate after a lot of work, they know they'd better take advantage of their downtime and sleep. The dog doesn't peer out from her crate, wondering what's going on and wishing she could come out and make new friends. The crate is like an actor's dressing room: After a few hours and many takes, she's going to want a little rest time, and the crate becomes the dog's home away from home.

Of course, there are always people who aren't very dog savvy who insist upon calling a dog crate a "cage" and make subtle but judgmental comments about it. Today, of course, dog crates are totally acceptable, but back in the midnineties, people weren't so familiar with them. They were starting to become more commonplace as people used them for training and housebreaking. But back then, people who weren't housebreaking a puppy would walk past and give you this look like, *Aw, look at that poor dog!*

I was once on a job in Tennessee with two dogs shooting a commercial, and people just went crazy about the crates. Granted, there aren't a whole lot of commercials being filmed in Tennessee, so people weren't used to seeing studio dogs in the first place, but it was a little strange just how fascinated they were. People would walk past them and go on and on about how sad it was that we were putting our dogs in cages. I tried to explain that we weren't going to let the dogs run willy-nilly around a set and expose them to possible harm or injury; nor was the crate a "cage" to begin with. But no one was buying it. "A dog in a crate? That's the darnedest thing!" I heard it time and time again. That is, until I introduced them to Chewy.

Chewy was a Heinz 57 mutt: all sorts of breeds put together in one shaggy, golden, fifty-pound body. And he absolutely loved his crate. Actually, he was obsessed with it. Plenty of pets are like this too, in the same way people might feel about their beds. So, after I'd heard one dog-in-a-cage remark too many, I just couldn't take it anymore.

"Hey, you guys . . . do you want to see how much this dog loves his 'cage'? Here, let me show you."

And with that, a slightly stunned crowd of crew members and onlookers followed me over to Chewy, who was sitting patiently on his most recent mark even though we were on a break from filming. I knew the door to the dressing room where we kept the crates was open, so I led Chewy over to where he'd have a straight shot. I gave him a pat and he looked up at me, ready for action. I gestured in the direction of the crate room.

"All right, go on!"

And with that, Chewy took off running from the set, tearing across the soundstage, through the door, and down the hallway. The crowd of people chattered among themselves, asking one another where Chewy could have possibly gone.

Once I heard the telltale clatter of the crate door, I led the crowd back to the room with the crates and there was Chewy, lying down in his crate with the door wide-open, happy as could be, with his paws tucked neatly under his chin.

"See how much he loves it? The crate, not a cage, is a little sanctuary for a dog. They know they can go in there and rest, which they love to do. You love to go to bed after a day at work, right? It's a good thing. See?"

I think they saw.

Back at home, my dogs were heading for their own crates for the night. I'd averaged those killer eighteen-hour days over the last few weeks, and I couldn't wait to enjoy some much-needed downtime at home. And some quality time with my bed! It seemed my dogs felt the same way.

Of course, not all of the jobs I work keep me quite so busy. Several years later, I worked on a movie that was probably the most easygoing, pleasant job I'd ever worked on. And it was thanks, in large part, to the prep I did for it before I even got there. Not to mention one very good dog.

Holly was a yellow Lab that I had trained from the time she was a puppy. She was a little wild and crazy in her younger days, as most Labradors are, but as she got older she had calmed down a bit. Holly lived at Studio Animal Services and was part of the pack that Karin took out on her mountain-bike rides.

It was the summer of 2008 and Hollywood was on the verge of a major actors' strike. Clint Eastwood's production company had contacted Studio Animal Services to provide a dog for his next movie. Normally my boss, Paul, would go on the Clint Eastwood jobs, as he had been doing since around 1983 on *Sudden Impact*. This time, though, Paul was going to be on vacation, so I was lucky enough to go to Detroit that summer and work Holly on the film *Gran Torino*.

I had worked with Clint once before in 2007, on the thriller *Changeling*. On that movie, he was directing and I was charged with tossing chickens (gently, of course!) in front of the camera during a scene shot at a remote location in the Mojave Desert.

"You are an excellent chicken tosser," he'd told me. Sometimes I can hardly believe this is my job.

For *Gran Torino*, Holly was hired to play Clint's easygoing companion, Daisy, so for a full month before filming, I worked with Holly on a behavior called "go with." I knew that the script called for Clint's dog to spend a lot of time with him on his porch, so I needed to teach her to stay with him and relax, no matter what else was going on around them. Her focus needed to be on Clint, not me.

Typically, when a dog is working on set, once he's completed an action or behavior, he might glance at the trainer for the next cue. It's always a fine line to get the dog to do these behaviors without it looking like a trainer is standing off-camera telling him what to do. Still, it's quite endearing to see how much they want to do the next action and look forward to what you'll direct them to do next. This movie was different, since there really wasn't much for Holly to do except to hang out with Clint.

Before I left for Michigan I worked daily with Holly on "go with." Training this behavior on a seasoned dog means she will eventually relax into that behavior and hang with that actor whether he's walking through a house, jogging on a beach, or walking up some steps to a front porch and sitting in a chair. A dog that does this well might go and lie down next to the feet of the actor after he has sat down, reinforcing with the audience that this dog does, in fact, belong to this character. So I worked Holly with anyone who would help me, and conditioned her to do lengthy "go withs." I wanted her to settle in with that person and not always be looking at me for direction or a treat. The goal was to get her to look at the other person instead, and simply act like his dog. In lieu of a treat she would sometimes just get a scratch behind the ear or a "good girl."

After a month's worth of training at the ranch and on set while I was doing other jobs, it was time to leave for Detroit. Everyone was cautioning me that filming could be shut down at any moment, since the actors' strike was coming. And when it did, we'd have only a couple of weeks to wrap the movie.

Luckily, I was on set with a man who's known for his speed. Clint is famous in the industry for knocking scenes out in one take. Very few rehearsals, no second takes. He says his lines on the first take and it's a perfect delivery almost every time. So even if Hollywood did shut down as a result of a strike, two weeks seemed like a totally reasonable amount of time in which to finish up our movie. After all, Clint has been known to shoot an entire feature film in about thirty days!

The first day we got on set—a rough residential neighborhood in Detroit—Holly checked out everything and everyone, getting used to her surroundings. But as it turned out, I'd have to get used to mine.

When it came time for Holly's first scene with Clint, I walked her up onto the porch and placed her on a "down-stay" next to him. I made eye contact with Clint, who smiled at me politely.

"Cute dog," he said in his signature gravelly tone.

"Stay," I told Holly, as I backed away from the two of them sitting on the top step of the porch. I walked to a position off-camera where I could see her and she could see me. I held my hand up in a "stay" signal and tried not to stare at her too intently. As a trainer working an animal next to an actor, it is always your job to work without drawing attention to yourself or distracting the actor. Of course, there are times when the animal has to do some outrageous stunt that requires lots of verbal cues and hand signals. In those cases, you may have to "jump in" on the actor's lines, meaning you can speak in between the actors' scripted dialogue. This was not going to be that kind of movie.

Before the cameras started rolling, Clint reached down and

patted Holly's head. He immediately looked taken with the sweet Lab and made some kissy noises in her direction.

Holly took this as a cue to jump up and lick his face. (Who wouldn't?)

"Down," I said gently, walking toward her.

But Clint raised a hand and nodded in my direction.

"That's okay," he said. "She can sit, stand, lie down, whatever. She's just playing a dog, after all," he added, and smiled at Holly. This was certainly a softer side of Clint Eastwood than most people would expect to see. Holly relaxed too, and looked as happy to be working with Clint as he was with her.

As we continued to work that day, I would place Holly with Clint, hand him a couple of treats to put in his pocket, and tell her, "Go with," and simply walk away. Sometimes I hid behind a tree; other times I turned away from her, so she wouldn't be tempted to look at me for cues. Holly quickly acclimated to her task. She was hanging out with Clint Eastwood, and nothing more. (Not a bad gig, right?) My work with her in the weeks before filming had really paid off, and she happily hung out by his side day after day and didn't have a whole lot of action behaviors to perform. After all, Clint's character was an older, crotchety guy who enjoyed the company of his quiet, older dog.

As the weeks progressed, I got very comfortable with the fact that all I needed to do throughout my time on the movie was to place Holly by Clint's side, whether she was sitting, lying down, or standing, and then promptly walk away. It was then Holly's job to remember that she needed to stay with Clint no matter what, even if he got up from his porch seat and walked down the steps and across the lawn. I could be sure that the prepping I had done with an extended "go with" had paid off, and I ended up having one of my easiest and most memorable jobs in Detroit that wonderful summer.

The strike never ended up happening, and Clint, true to form, finished filming in just about six weeks. On the last day that we were scheduled to work before heading back to L.A., I was saying my good-byes to the crew and I stopped to talk with Clint as he was on his way to lunch. He mentioned how much he liked the friendly Lab and wanted to take her home with him, but his allergies would make it unbearable. I assured him that she was returning to California and going to live with a family in Calabasas—with Deb's sister, actually—so she would be living a nice semiretirement as a pet. Then he continued.

"I want to thank you. I've been doing this for a long time. I've worked with a lot of animals and trainers over the years, and you did an excellent job."

I thanked him, feeling slightly embarrassed at first. What had I done on this job, anyway? Run away during filming and left him to fend for himself with the dog? But in truth, that was exactly what I needed to do. Whereas some trainers might feel the need to control the situation with the dog on the set, I was able to go with the flow. This was how Clint worked, and I'd done my preparation with Holly, so everyone was happy. Animal trainer life lesson? Sometimes less is more.

Gidget posing in front of the Hollywood sign

CHAPTER 7

Stardom

One of my favorite memories of Gidget was when we were in Arizona filming a Taco Bell commercial. Just as Gidget did not like extreme cold, she also couldn't work in extreme heat. So, as her trainer at that shoot, I got to benefit from her needs on set. Normally, I am lucky to get a pop-up tent and a fan on set. But seeing as it was ninety-five degrees at eight a.m., we had to come up with an alternate plan. Production gave us an air-conditioned motor home, so I got to hang out in there with the star of the commercial! We had snacks, a couch, and movies to watch all day during our breaks. Thanks for that, Gidget!

—Deborah Dellosso, animal trainer

You could say that a celebrity can really tell she's made it in Hollywood when people start coming up to her and saying she looks just like herself.

It's usually around the time of an actress's big breakout role that the phenomenon begins. She'll be out shopping, or maybe she'll be at the airport heading out of town, and someone will walk up to her—one part shy, one part slightly crazed superfan—and gently broach the subject.

"Um, hi, I'm sorry to bother you, but I just had to tell you, you look just *exactly* like So-and-so!"

Now, in the early days of fame, the budding starlets of the world would probably giggle, maybe even blush, and tell the stranger that she is, in fact, So-and-so. The fan would then squeal and scramble to find a pen and something for her to sign, excitedly asking about her costars, life in Hollywood, and "Where did you get those cool sunglasses?" This might go on again and again, until one day, the conversation starts taking a different turn.

"Oh, my gosh, hi, I don't mean to interrupt you, but does anyone ever tell you that you look just like So-and-so?"

"Oh, yeah, I get that all the time. I'm not, though. Sorry!"

After about six Taco Bell commercials with the other trainers, Gidget—now a bona fide celebrity herself—experienced that very phenomenon. Not directly, of course: People would be coming up to *me*, asking if the Chihuahua I was walking was the Taco Bell dog. It happened on airplanes all the time. Chihuahuas were having a moment in the late nineties; between Paris Hilton carrying one around and Gidget appearing on TV every day, they were becoming more and more popular. It was a similar phenomenon to Dalmatians gaining popularity after *101 Dalmatians* and cocker spaniels having their moment after *Lady and the Tramp*. Chihuahuas were "it," and Gidget was *the* Chihuahua.

When I first started traveling with Gidget, I'd open her carrier once we were seated and she'd pop her little head out. (People would also comment on how good she was and ask me if I drugged her to keep her behaving. Um, nope, just a trained dog who's used to being in a bag, thanks!) Then, after Gidget would take a peek outside her bag, the people sitting near us would look at her curiously for a minute or two. Then one would pipe up.

"You know, she looks just like the Taco Bell dog."

"Oh, it is the Taco Bell dog."

And then the twenty questions would start. Followed by another twenty by that person's seatmate. And all I'd want to do was go to sleep! So we got wise to the phenomenon real quick. Gidget would stay in her bag for most, if not all, of the flight—she was as happy to snooze there as anywhere—and if I heard her moving around or something, I'd unzip the bag to check on her. Then, if someone saw her and started asking questions, I'd shut it down.

"You have a dog in there? I didn't even notice! Hey, that dog looks like the dog that's always on TV."

"Hmmm, yeah, she does, doesn't she? She's not, though."

I had Gidget's on-air persona working in my favor too, since the actor who provided her voice is a man. So, naturally, people thought the Taco Bell dog was a boy. But my use of the proper pronoun to describe her tended to get me off the hook.

By now, Gidget was filming a new commercial nearly every month, and since it had become a full-blown campaign, it was decided that I would be the one to prep her for and train her on all of the commercials from then on out. When I missed the first commercials, we had no idea they would take off the way they did, so other trainers were able to take the jobs. But now Gidget and I were a team, and we had just been booked to film three commercials in New York City. We got the storyboards for three separate ads pegged to the *Godzilla* movie, in which Taco Bell would be a product placement. So Gidget had been hired to do three commercials called "Drive-through," "Trap," and "Screamers." "Screamers" was just a short commercial for a kids' meal in which they show a clip from the movie. Then they cut to Gidget, who's letting out this big scream, and her mouth is filled with huge teeth like Godzilla—added in postproduction, of course. The other commercials, one in particular, were much more interesting to film.

For "Drive-through," Godzilla would go through a Taco Bell drive-through and Gidget would be riding on his tail, so after he places his order, she's carried up to the speaker to place an order as well. We planned to shoot it on a green screen, but we needed Gidget to be able to sit on something that would go left, right, up, and down with some fluidity to it, like a big tail. The best solution, we figured, was to use a dolly, which is the platform that a camera sits on when filming certain shots in a movie. Oftentimes, the camera operator will be sitting on it as well, on a stool attached to the base. So we contacted Chapman, a company in L.A. that makes dollies, and we asked if we could come prep at their facility, and if they'd rig up a special arm and a platform that Gidget would sit on.

They agreed, and we set up the disk-shaped platform for Gidget. Next, we got her comfortable with the disk being her mark and we had her sit there as it moved all around. She couldn't have cared less, and she happily sat as the platform reached higher and higher up into the air. Because of her training, Gidget knew that when I asked her to stay on a mark, she should not move off of it, even if it reached well up into the air. I completely trusted that she would do just that. So after our prep time in L.A., we had a meeting with the producer and the director, in which they explained the other ad, "Trap."

"Trap" would become one of the more iconic Taco Bell ads, in which Gidget is trying to catch Godzilla, and when she finally spots him, she quips, "I think I need a bigger box." There wasn't much action required of Gidget in filming, but they wanted her to be sitting in an alleyway in Manhattan at night, in the winter. I explained that it would be difficult for her to do this if she was cold. We talked about incorporating a warm disk like the kind I used at home, where you heated it up, hot-water-bottle style, in the microwave and tucked it in a dog bed. Perhaps we could use it underneath a fake manhole cover, I suggested, so Gidget would be warm and happy while sitting on her mark.

At this point in the campaign, to get her to say, "*Yo quiero* Taco Bell," we did what's called mouth manipulation. As Gidget looked into the camera, I'd stand behind her and open her mouth. They needed a light reference inside of her mouth in whatever type of light we were shooting. She was so good and easygoing about this. I would move my fingers around her jaw and face, since that gave the postproduction crew plenty to work with when they animated her mouth. That way, they could see what her face really looked like as her mouth moved when she was "speaking" to make the effect as realistic as possible. Plus, it was like a minimassage for Gidget, who would close her eyes sleepily as I moved her mouth. As the computer-generated work evolved, I didn't need to move her mouth around so much. I would just pop it open for their light reference inside her mouth.

It really is amazing what they can do in postproduction. Back in the day, you always had to completely clear the frame after setting an animal. I once shot a Maytag commercial with the classic Maytag basset hound when I experienced this change for the first time. We were shooting in a field and they needed a very wide shot, so I'd have to work really far away from the dog, who, like your typical basset hound, would prefer to sleep on the couch than do the string of behaviors I'd asked of him. Not a whole lot of work ethic! So I would have to stand about thirty feet away from the dog, trying to get the same kind of response that I would if I were three feet away. I was totally sweating it. They called us in when they were ready for the dog, and I showed him to his mark.

"That's good; now just take a step back so you're out of the light and you can stay there," the director told me. "We can remove you in post."

I was slightly amazed, not to mention thrilled.

What do you mean, you can "remove me in post"? I silently wondered. But I did as I was told, reveling in this unexpected bonus.

While I'm sure this technology was available for many years before this particular commercial was shot, it just wasn't the norm to hear those magic words on a commercial set. It makes our jobs so much easier overall.

When we arrived in New York City to shoot the Godzilla Taco Bell commercials, a Lincoln Town Car was waiting for us at the airport to shuttle us to the hotel. The first thing I would always do in a hotel room for Gidget would be to set up her little dog bed. If it was cold, I'd put the heat on, and seek out the sunniest spot to plop down her bed. Sometimes it would be on a windowsill, other times on an armchair where the sun filtered into the room. In this room, a love seat was situated right near the window, and despite the chilly air outside, the sunlight and the nearby heater made for a toasty spot for Gidget. And while many dogs would sniff every inch of an unfamiliar hotel room, Gidget was quite pleased with my hotel room routine for her, and once I had her bed set up, that was it. She'd jump in and be happy as a clam, no exploring necessary.

Okay, thanks. I'm good to go!

The first spot we were going to film was the "Trap" commercial, and our call time wasn't until one a.m. So Gidget and I tucked in for a nap that evening around ten, and when the wake-up call came through at twelve thirty, neither of us was too thrilled.

I wrapped Gidget up in her little sweater, which was never an easy task. I always put one on her if we were going to be in the cold for a while, since Chihuahuas get chilly so easily. She tolerated the sweaters for the most part, because she knew on some level that they kept her warm. But she would never help you when you tried to get one on her. In the dim light in the hotel room, I had to reach through each tiny leg hole and pull all four of her legs out one by one, with no assistance from the little sweater hater.

You are putting this on *me. So I'm going to make you put it on me and I'm not going to help you in any way.*

Once we were both sufficiently bundled, we headed down to the hotel lobby. I could see plenty of people coming in for the night—and even more still out on the town. Guess it really is the city that never sleeps.

The same Town Car that had dropped us off earlier in the day was back, idling outside for us, and Gidget, suddenly energized by the cold, picked up a bouncy trot when she saw it and eagerly hopped inside. Once we arrived on set, I walked Gidget through a crowd of production people. I heard a few murmurs about how cute she was, and someone asked if he could have a picture taken with the Taco Bell dog. Sure thing, I told him, just wait until after we wrap.

It's really important to keep any sort of doggy meet-and-greets to a minimum before shooting begins. That goes for Gidget and the vast majority of other studio dogs, because all that social interaction can wear them out and you'll have a less enthusiastic and peppy dog on your hands when it comes time to shoot. Every now and again I'll have a dog who breaks this rule and I want him to meet everybody. This might be the case with new dogs who are unfamiliar with being on set and need a fun introduction to the environment, so they get to meet everyone. Sometimes if you show up on set and all your dog has to do is walk on a leash (which is not very taxing), then the crew can say hi to the dog if they want. It all depends on the individual animal and what he has to do that day. It's similar with a pet—especially if you want to burn off his excess energy. If you have a dog with lots of energy, taking him on a structured walk through a bustling neighborhood will burn off more energy than an hour playing ball at the dog park. Making a dog use his brain will tire him out and burn off that excess energy far faster than plain physical exercise will.

Years later, I'd do a commercial with a dog named Monty (who'd go on to film *Hancock* with Will Smith and Charlize Theron). Monty had a lot of action to perform over the course of the day—and he was surrounded by onlookers who wanted to pet him and play with him before he started working. It can take a lot out of a dog when twenty or thirty people are coming over to greet him. It's like being on a business trip and having to socialize with twenty or thirty people before you get to your meeting—it can be really draining. It's even more so for a dog, because they're usually so excited to meet every new person. As a trainer, I just want to keep the dog calm and relaxed when he's not shooting. In this case, Monty had to interact with an actor on-camera, so we wanted to save all that excitement for the actor. I was having a hard time keeping the people from production away from the dog, and I had to keep explaining the situation to them.

"You can pet him, no problem, just as soon as we wrap. I'm trying to conserve his energy for the shoot."

But that wasn't good enough for one guy, who kept coming over to Monty, whom we had on a "down-stay" while we were waiting to shoot. He would either pet Monty or stand a few feet away and stare at him, cooing baby talk (which still engages the dog and gets him excited). I asked nicely if he could wait until the dog was finished working. His response was far less polite. He was clearly a little irritated and didn't quite believe me.

"Is it *really* such a big problem to pet the dog?"

Here we go again.

"Actually, yes, it is," I began. "What happens when the dog suddenly decides he doesn't want to interact with the actor anymore because he's bored with him and remembers he had more fun with *you*? And then runs to you during the scene? Are you going to be the one who explains yourself to all these people trying to get their shot?"

Yes, sometimes I have to train people too.

The problem gets about a thousand times worse when you're on a job with puppies. Obviously, everyone wants to pet puppies. So I'll tell production ahead of time that nobody should pet them and we don't even want people in the vicinity of their puppy pen until shooting is done for the day. We even put signs up and place the puppy pen in a decidedly low-traffic area.

But of course, on one job, the clients came over and gazed over the side of the puppy pen, ignoring the sign entirely. One of the clients jumped to explain herself when I came over.

"Oh, I know that we can't *pet* them, but we just wanted to look at them."

Okay, great, but I just had six sleeping puppies who saw someone new coming over, so they're now jumping up at the sides of the pen, desperate to meet you and using up their energy with every leap.

Hi! Who are you? What are you doing? It's so good to meet you!
"I'm sorry, but that's just as bad as petting them. They're eight weeks old and we're trying to save their energy. Can you please wait over there? I promise you can pet them after we finish for the day. We just want you to have the best, most excited puppies possible for your commercial."

So I was prepared on Gidget's Manhattan job to keep her fans at bay until we were finished.

I made my way through the crowd convened in the alleyway, which fortunately didn't include too many onlookers (Wall Street isn't exactly a late-night hot spot in the city). Then I led Gidget to the trailer that served as our dressing room to get her situated and warm inside.

After making sure that Gidget was relaxed and comfortable, I left the trailer to scout out the set. When the crew gets ready to set up a shot, I always go to the set before they finalize the lights and scenery to make sure I have a spot to stand or kneel. I need to work my animal without being in anyone's way and to make sure my spot isn't in front of a great big light, which would cast my great big shadow onto the set! There is nothing worse or more embarrassing than arriving on set and finding that you have absolutely no place to stand in order to do your work. All it takes is ten minutes beforehand to let the shooting crew know where you will be positioned to avoid problems later.

Once I'd found my spot on the "Trap" set, I checked for the props we needed in that setup. To start, I'd need Gidget's hero collar. A hero prop is one that might be scrutinized closely in a scene—something that appears in every shot, like Gidget's collar, so it would need to look the same across numerous commercials. Sometimes there will be two, three, or more of these items as an added security measure in case one gets lost or damaged. I also needed to make sure the rope she would be holding in her mouth was the same type of rope we'd been prepping with all week. That may sound insignificant, but a slight change in the size or texture of a prop can throw off a dog like a Chihuahua, since they aren't naturally retrieving dogs. As I spoke to the first assistant director about the shot, I realized there was no special manhole cover to keep Gidget warm where she had to sit. We were in an alley near Wall Street at two a.m., and it was about thirty degrees with snow flurries. To make matters even more complicated, the crew had done a wet-down on the pavement. So now not only was her mark cold; it was also wet. I couldn't help but laugh to myself. This was going to be interesting. When the weather was this chilly, I'd still take Gidget out for walks in her little sweater or jacket, but it was never a prolonged event. In this weather, she would basically just sleep until you woke her up to take her outside for a potty break, and she'd quickly do her thing in order to get back inside. Lengthy visits to the great outdoors just weren't her thing in the winter.

So while a sleepy Gidget stayed warm in the trailer, I had the crew set up heaters on one area of the chilly sidewalk. That way, the spot where Gidget would be sitting could stay warm and dry. I then brought her out, directed her to her mark, and asked her to hold the rope in her mouth that was attached to the box meant to catch Godzilla. Gidget knew what's called a "trained retrieve," meaning if I asked her to hold something—anything—in her mouth, she would do it, even if she wasn't particularly thrilled to do so. Now, if I told her to hold on to her stuffed toy, Mrs. Hedgehog, and get on her mark on a soundstage, she'd be bouncing around like an Easter bunny. But sitting in a cold alleyway at two o'clock in the morning holding a piece of rope? Not so thrilled.

So Gidget sat there with her ears pinned back, looking downright miserable as I danced around trying to get her to join in my exuberance.

"Gidget! Good girl! Gidget! Hold it! Hold it!"

Are you frickin' kidding me?

I felt so bad for her and tried to figure out another way to make the situation more comfortable. This was another instance when my job was less about being a trainer and more about protecting my dog. In this case, it was my job to protect her from the elements. Then the director, Rocky, with whom we'd worked on a few commercials—albeit in far warmer weather—chimed in.

"Why does she look like that, Sue? She doesn't look very happy."

I took a quick inventory of Rocky's wares: sheepskin boots, down jacket, wool hat, gloves, a blanket wrapped around him, and a few jet-engine heaters positioned around his chair.

"Rocky, do you see what you're wearing? And all of your heaters? And you're *still* cold? Well, look at where she's sitting. And what she's wearing. It's below freezing and she's sitting on cold concrete, naked. What about that do you think would make a Chihuahua happy?"

Rocky let out a little self-deprecating laugh, realizing the irony of it all. We put Gidget back inside the warm trailer for a bit while we rethought our strategy and repositioned some more heaters around her mark.

I asked the first assistant director if he would ask all the extra people hanging around the set to leave. We needed as little distraction as possible tonight.

"Everyone who is not directly involved with this shot," he announced on the megaphone, "please clear out."

Just like any good diva, Gidget had her people—me—to do her bidding! So with a now smaller crowd around us, I worked on getting Gidget to give us that happy Taco Bell–dog look, with her ears up as she held the rope. It was a challenging shot to get, but we did it, and we shot the remainder of the ad on an indoor stage. The next day, we filmed the "Drive-through" and the "Screamers" ads, which ended up being a total breeze.

It was during this series of ads that Rocky began an unusual practice with Gidget. Before we started shooting, he would always pick her up so they could share a little moment before he called, "Action." And then he did the oddest thing: While holding Gidget in front of him, he'd speak quietly to her—and blow directly into her nose! I think he believed that this added to her performance on set and influenced how she worked. She just sort of tolerated these moments with Rocky, though I would see a peculiar look on her face from time to time.

Okay, what is he doing? Mom? Seriously, what is he doing?

But who knows? Maybe he was onto something! We did get a great bunch of commercials out of those days in New York. Although I do wonder if the nose blowing had anything to do with Gidget's naughty phase that would surface years later, when she'd bite at people's noses. Maybe it was her little form of payback for Rocky's unconventional directing method.

It was while we were in Manhattan that Gidget also developed two of her funniest habits. By this point, we'd spent a lot of time in hotels, and Gidget developed a behavior that the other trainers and I jokingly called "mad dog."

Gidget's absolute favorite thing to do in a hotel was to run at top speed down a hallway. If there was a really long, carpeted hallway on our floor, I'd put her on the floor and take off her leash. Then I'd do a little play jump in her direction to get her excited, and she'd bow her little head down at me in response. Then, before you could blink your eye, she would take off and run as fast as her legs would carry her down the hallway. She'd do this over and over, running laps around the hall. The dog would just *fly*. You see this kind of thing all the time in dog parks. One dog will take off running, hunkered down with his back legs seemingly churning faster than the front, jackrabbit-like, as he tears around in a circle. It's a small moment of delighted madness. Hence, mad dog! It became a never-fail habit anytime we were in a hotel, and it always cracked me up to think about people in their hotel rooms, wondering what that crazy pitter-pat sound coming from the hallway could possibly be.

With all the commuting from airports to hotels, hotels to sets, sets to hotels, and hotels back to airports, the production company would send limos—Lincoln Town Cars, usually—with private drivers to shuttle us around. So Gidget became quite accustomed to this mode of transportation. In Manhattan, there are usually a slew of limos sitting outside of the bigger hotels. And when a doorman would open the passenger door of one of them, Gidget would start pulling to get over there.

Ah, yes, there's my ride. Come on, Mom, let's go!

It was really very cute.

In fact, she got so used to walking out of lobbies and hopping into limos that she seemed to eschew other modes of travel. Every now and again we'd have a little downtime to go sightseeing while on location, and the last day of shooting in Manhattan was one of those times. So another trainer and I headed out of the hotel with Gidget at my side. We walked over to the doorman hailing cabs, and there was Gidget—trying her best to haul me in the other direction toward an open limo door. My fellow trainer and I doubled over laughing.

"Um, Gidget, we're taking a *cab*, not the limo!"

But Gidget thought every Town Car was hers and she needed to get in it. It's a funny behavior to have attached to your dog: friendly, outgoing, gets on well with other dogs, loves the sun . . . and prefers limos.

One of our later trips to New York was to shoot a Taco Bell commercial in Times Square, and once again, we had an early-morning call time. Luckily for Gidget, it was July, so this time I was wearing a T-shirt at one a.m., and she had no need for heaters. Our set that early morning was smack-dab in the middle of Times Square. The city closed down all the streets leading into the busy crossroads and the production positioned their own movie taxicabs to give the illusion of one huge traffic jam, with Gidget sitting right in the middle of it. A rep from the film office nearby told me that this was the first time that Times Square had been completely shut down for a shoot. I have to admit, it made us all feel very lucky to be shooting in this spot, like a bunch of VIPs—with an even more important Chihuahua.

With Gidget warm and comfortable, all she had to do was sit in the center of all the taxicabs as a giant camera crane swooped in overhead. Taco Bell got their shot and we headed back to the hotel in a matter of just two hours. Not a bad night, and a vast improvement over wet pavement and snow flurries!

Since that day, I have seen and heard about numerous scenes in commercials and movies where Times Square is featured and obviously had to be shut down for the production. So I'm not sure I believe that piece of trivia the rep had shared with us (maybe he tells everyone that to make them feel special?), but it made for a fun evening.

After our trio of Manhattan commercials pegged to *Godzilla*, Gidget and I returned to California. I still took her to work most days, leaving her to sleep and socialize in the office if I was training or on set with another dog. But nothing compared to the fun and stimulation of an actual set, so I'd still make a point of bringing her and Beans on other dogs' jobs when I could.

Working at the ranch one day, I found myself employing an old technique from Ocean World while working with Brandy, the pit bull on my training list. When you're training dolphins, you obviously can't put a leash on them or even reach out and touch them when you're teaching new behaviors, which poses a unique challenge. But you have their brains on your side—dolphins are so incredibly smart. At Ocean World, we used whistles to bridge behavior, not unlike the clickers we tend to use with dogs, to indicate to the animal the exact moment that they've done something right and that a reward will follow shortly. If you're training a dolphin to jump out of the water and through a hoop, you can't exactly reward him the second he performs the part of the behavior that you're shaping—that may be the height of the jump or going through the hoop. So when he does that part of the behavior, that's when you bridge it with a whistle so he knows what part he did right. Then the reward follows as soon as he returns to you at the side of the pool.

It's very similar to when you're doing off-leash training with a dog. If I'm teaching Brandy to do a "down-stay" thirty feet away from me, obviously I can't make any corrections or give her rewards with thirty feet between us. So I have to build that trust with her and feel confident that she understands what I'm doing and what I'm asking at five feet before I move ten, twenty, and finally thirty feet away. It takes a lot of patience, but the payoff comes when the dog does just what you're asking and knows a reward is to follow shortly.

Another staple of dolphin training that translates to dogs is called target training. I learned how to do this with our dolphins, seals, and sea lions at Ocean World. Just like a dog learns its mark, we teach these animals to identify a target, usually a tennis ball at the end of a long stick. And through trial and error, you get the dolphin to jump out of the water to touch the tennis ball with his nose, and each time he does this, he gets a reward. It's pretty basic stuff. Soon you can move that tennis ball all over, even while you stand up on a ladder, and the dolphin knows to leap out of the water and touch it. Obviously, when you're doing a show for an audience, you're not holding the target stick out there. Instead, you are showing off the final result of adding a hand signal to the behavior and removing the target stick to produce the finished behavior—a jump in a certain part of the pool. Constant reinforcement is used to get the initial behavior (touching the ball with the nose), and then intermittent reinforcement is used to shape the behavior and maintain it.

So after working with Brandy, I brought her back to her run and took out Kusha, one of our Shiba Inus, the Japanese dogs that look like miniature Akitas. He'd been hired to do a commercial in which he needed to jump up in the air from a standing position. So to shape the behavior, I used a homemade target stick—a tennis ball stuck on the end of a broomstick. Just like the dolphins, he quickly figured out that every time he touched the tennis ball he'd get a treat. So we started out with the ball at his eye level, and I gradually raised it up until I could get him to do a dramatic, pro basketball–worthy vertical leap into the air. It's pretty endearing watching a dog figure something like this out. The first time I held the target stick at my eye level—I'm five-eleven, so this was quite a leap for a little dog—Kusha looked at me, then at the tennis ball, as though he were carefully calculating his next move.

Hmmm, now how do I get up there? Well, maybe if I just throw myself at it. . . .

So when we had perfected his amazing vertical jump, I worked on transitioning him from responding to the target stick to responding to a hand signal or a voice cue. I had used the word *jump* when I had asked Kusha to leap in the air and touch the target, so the transition was an easy one when I removed the stick.

Another trainer at the company had also been a marine-mammal trainer, so the techniques weren't entirely foreign to our other colleagues. After giving Brandy a break in her run, I brought her back out to work her in target training as well. We'd been working on it for a couple weeks, and I could tell she remembered what she'd learned. With Brandy, I had used my fist as a target. So we stood in the shade on the porch, and I told Brandy, "Target," and she jumped up and touched my hand with her nose. I paid her a treat just as Karin walked by, smiling.

"Ah," she said with a knowing grin. "That's right. I forgot. Another marine-mammal trainer!"

A few days later, I booked another out-of-town job, so I decided to leave Gidget at my fellow trainer Megan's house. Megan lives in one of those southern California neighborhoods where all the houses have a similar look. It had been a year or so since I last visited Megan at home, and in a brief phone conversation the night before, she told me, "I should be there by three o'clock, but if I'm not, just go on in."

I pulled into her driveway and did a little bit of a double take. *Wow, Megan's done a lot of landscaping*, I thought to myself. Admiring the work as I headed to the front door, I knocked and waited. Then I peered through the kitchen window but heard nothing. I picked up Gidget's crate and her dog food, and she followed me with all the confidence of a small child relying on a grown-up to take care of her and know what's best.

We went through the side gate to the backyard, and I was thoroughly impressed with Megan's garden makeover. The yard, which goes up a steep hill behind the house, was now beautifully landscaped, with a pool, a cabana, and plush lounge chairs.

Mildly annoyed that I hadn't received any invites to pool parties at Megan's newly improved home, I placed Gidget's crate inside the garage door, along with her food, and looked around.

"Cool, she finally put in a doggy door," I thought aloud. So instead of checking the side door to see if it was open, I just held the doggy door open and Gidget hopped through. I watched as she went over to the couch and lay down.

"Be a good girl!"

She looked at me with wide eyes, put her head down, and kicked out her legs. Obviously, this was a dog who was very adaptable! How many dogs can you shove through a strange doggy door and have them curl up on the couch and go to sleep?

As I was driving away, I called Megan on her cell phone to let her know I had dropped off Gidget at her house.

"Huh, that's weird," Megan replied. "I didn't hear you in the back when—"

Before she had a chance to finish, I interrupted.

"And by the way, Meg, you never told me you and Tom were doing a big garden makeover. Your place looks amazing!"

Megan sounded baffled.

"*What?*"

Then she paused, as if scanning her living room for any sign of the little Chihuahua, and perhaps glancing outside to see what makeover I was talking about.

"Wait, are you home?" I asked.

"Sue, Gidget's not here. When did you come over?"

Then it dawned on me. The houses all looked alike. . . . Megan hadn't done any landscaping.

"Oh, my God, Megan! I shoved her through the doggy door of someone else's house!"

"Why . . . would you do that?"

Megan's voice teemed with laughter that only escalated my own panic.

"Megan! I'm turning around!"

We quickly figured out that I had been to a neighbor's house— luckily the neighbor was a friend of Megan's as well—and I'd let Gidget through *her* doggy door.

"No, Sue, don't do that; you'll be late for your job. Let me go and find her."

Ten tense minutes later I got a call from Megan that Gidget was safely at her house. Fortunately Gidget didn't seem to be rattled whatsoever by the accidental break-in. Apparently, there was a slightly miffed cat who lived there, but luckily that was it.

I still think back in horror at my mistake, but I also wonder what the homeowner would have done when she got home to find the Taco Bell dog lounging on her couch!

★ ★ ★

Within a month of being back home from our adventures in New York City filming that round of Taco Bell ads, I really started to notice just how much attention the campaign was getting. You could hardly turn on your TV without seeing one of the Taco Bell ads, and the products began popping up everywhere—plush Taco Bell dogs, toys in kids' meals. . . . Gidget likenesses were *all* over the place. If she were a human star, she would have had quite the inflated ego! Plus, an interesting new Gidget phenomenon had developed. I'd become quite good at keeping people from freaking out when they saw her—I was pretty darn believable when I said she wasn't the Taco Bell dog, I suppose. But among acquaintances, people on sets, and some fans, everyone started to think that they had a dog who looked just like Gidget. And it was funny timing too. Since Gidget's campaign had become so huge, we needed to find a backup for her, but I was having trouble finding a similar-looking Chihuahua. And the strange thing was that most of the time, the dogs people would show me looked nothing like Gidget!

We always try to have a backup dog when we shoot, and generally that dog will look just like the hero dog (the main dog we're using on-camera), so we can switch them out while shooting. Perhaps one dog is sweet and lovable with an actor—in that case, we would use that dog for all the interaction shots, hopefully getting some nice, natural behavior between them. Maybe the look-alike dog is better suited for action scenes, so we'd use that one for the scene where the dog is called to run full-speed down the driveway and up the stairs to the porch and put his paws on the door to open it. It's much better to have more than one dog for action shots when you have a lot to shoot, because it not only provides you with more options (maybe dog A barks differently than dog B and the director likes one bark better for a particular shot), but it also provides each dog with valuable downtime so they can get some rest in while at work.

Now, I'm not speaking from a professional-animal-trainer perspective here when it comes to these non-look-alike look-alikes. These dogs didn't share Gidget's coloring, and sometimes they weren't even Chihuahuas. One day I was walking Gidget to the set and a fan came up beside me. Gidget fans all tended to act in a similar fashion: They'd give me a cursory glance, but then their eyes lit up and locked on the dog. I could have an entire conversation with them and they wouldn't look at me once. They were so taken with Gidget that they'd just stare at her the entire time.

So this particular fan, after making a fuss over Gidget (who always ate up this type of attention—she was a gracious star, to be sure), pulled her wallet out of her bag.

"I have a dog," said the woman, "who looks *just* like her!"

I smiled politely as she shuffled through her wallet for a moment, and then proudly produced a well-worn photo of her pet. The dog might have been Gidget's size, and had some pretty expressive ears, but that's where the comparisons ended. This dog was black and white. Seriously. Not even close to the fawn color of Gidget's coat, and this woman's dog was not even a Chihuahua.

Looking back, I think it's kind of sweet that so many people with dogs who looked nothing like Gidget would proudly show off their little doppelgängers. It must be what it's like when someone thinks her child looks just like some famous actor.

After several such fan interactions, I was shooting a commercial in L.A. one day when a crew member I'd worked with before started chatting about Gidget.

"My girlfriend has a Chihuahua who looks kind of like Gidget and she just had puppies," he said.

Sure, I thought to myself. *Everyone has a dog who looks like Gidget. This one's probably a Dalmatian or something.*

But I was wrong. He showed me a photo of the dog, and she

did actually look a bit like our little star. She was a fawn-colored Chihuahua and her features were similar to Gidget's. I asked how old the puppies were and if any were still available. He called his girlfriend from the set and we made an appointment for me to see them.

The next day, I stopped by her home to check out the puppies. She had three left, and one was this teeny, tiny little thing with a look and color just like Gidget's. In fact, he looked a lot like she did as a puppy. Some people think that Chihuahuas all look the same, but they actually come in all shapes and sizes. Since the puppy's mom looked similar to Gidget too, I put a call in to my boss, then scooped up the tiny puppy and off we went.

Back at home, I introduced my dogs to the new addition, whom we named Moondoggie, Moonie for short, after the TV Gidget's boyfriend. I made the introductions one by one outside, as I always did with new dogs, taking special interest in how Gidget would react to a new friend who was closer to her size than her other roommates.

She thought he was fun for about thirty seconds. As Moonie scampered around Gidget, urging her to play with him, she looked at me with a combination of boredom and disgust.

Okay, this was cute. Now get him away from me, please.

But Moonie couldn't be moved so easily. He tried to sidle up next to her from the left, then from the right, but Gidget kept repositioning herself on her little pillow, trying to ignore his attempts at affection. When that didn't work, she jumped up to play with him, batting her paws in his direction and bowing her head down at his feet. Then, before I knew it, she jumped on top of him and pinned him down in a move reminiscent of how Beans used to wrestle with her. Suddenly, Gidget didn't look quite so annoyed anymore.

Aha! Something smaller than me that I can boss around!

Within a few months, Moonie went to live with another

trainer. With all the traveling I'd been doing with Gidget and for other jobs, I didn't have the time to devote to a new puppy. And my next trip was going to be a fun one: We were heading back to New York for the premiere of *Godzilla* at Madison Square Garden.

This trip had all of the fun of the last Manhattan journey, with almost none of the stress, since Gidget was the star attending the premiere. The movie people wanted Gidget to walk down the red carpet, and Taco Bell had given me and another trainer a clothing budget, since we'd be photographed on the red carpet, so we got to go on a little shopping spree in New York City for the premiere. My job may not usually be as glamorous as people might think, but on that day it was!

Gidget arrived on the red carpet with a small entourage: myself, the other trainer, the creative directors of the ad agency, and a handful of executives from Taco Bell. The movie people had really wanted Gidget to walk down the red carpet, but with the crush of reporters and photographers on the other side of the velvet rope, no one would have noticed a tiny Chihuahua. So I was urged to pick her up to make the most of the photo ops. Bleachers were set up for the fans to get a glimpse of the movie talent, and when they caught sight of Gidget, the crowd exploded in cheers for the Taco Bell dog.

As always, Gidget was unfazed by the mayhem and just rested calmly in my arms as a publicist shuttled us down the red carpet for interviews and photos. I looked over my shoulder to see which stars were making their way down the carpet with us and nearly did a double take when I saw who was following us.

Muhammad Ali.

The champ.

I was stunned. I thought about yelling back to the fans, "People, Muhammad Ali is right behind us. This? Is a Chihuahua!"

But I thought better of it and dutifully completed my interviews while people oohed and ahhed over Gidget. It's not that I didn't love and appreciate what a celebrity she had become, but Muhammad Ali? Come on! If there was ever a star who would overshadow a dog, I would think Muhammad Ali would be it.

The rest of our red-carpet journey was a blur. It was really just a mad dash of sound bites and camera flashes and, "Sue, this is *USA Today*," and, "Sue, this is *Entertainment Tonight*," and, "One last question for Sue and Gidget, please." Crazy. I know we started at the beginning of the carpet and then somehow we got to the end, but by the time we finished, I didn't remember much of anything!

We dropped Gidget off at the hotel so she wouldn't be stuck on my lap for the movie, which I knew would be too loud for her, and returned to Madison Square Garden. (She was used to spending time in hotel rooms alone—I would leave her in her crate, in which she had her bed and a toy or two—and we always told the staff not to enter.) For about ten minutes the other trainers and I got a feel for what it would be like to be celebrities, getting shuffled in and out of back entrances and limos with walkie-talkie-armed assistants taking us here, there, and everywhere. The next morning we flew back to L.A., and Gidget was as well behaved as ever in her dog carrier. Little did I know that she was about to embark on a new phase of Chihuahua behavior.

Modeling sweaters with Moonie

CHAPTER 8

The Naughty Movie Star

Gidget was a queen. She had opinions about everything and was more than capable of letting us know what she wanted and needed. When it came to early-morning call times, she hated leaving her warm covers before she was ready. Most dogs will rise with their humans no matter the time. Not Gidget! She would have to be pried from her sleep with much fanfare and encouragement. Similarly, she knew whom she wanted to greet and allow to adore her. Many times she would refuse visitors for no apparent reason, turning away from their attempts to touch and fawn over her. She knew when she didn't care for someone, and that was enough of a reason! Despite her size, she carried herself like royalty. Prancing, nose held high, she entered into each situation with grace. Gidget was hardworking and never quit, even when conditions on set were less than pleasing to her. She had a lot of try in her. What a great queen she was throughout her life.

—Megan Valinote, animal trainer

As Moonie grew out of his puppy stage, it became readily apparent that he'd never be a proper backup for Gidget. As a small puppy, he bore the closest resemblance I'd seen, as both of them were really tiny and had similar puppy features. Still, it was becoming clear how unique-looking Gidget really was. I'd been chatting with breeders about the trouble I was having finding her a look-alike, and they all agreed on one thing: Gidget was larger than the average Chihuahua. At eleven or twelve pounds (depending on the day, like any woman), she was so big for her breed that many people would ask me if she was mixed with something else. She wasn't, but since Chihuahuas come in so many shapes and sizes (most being smaller than her), I realized that my dream of a backup just wasn't going to come true. Moonie would only reach about six pounds fully grown, and he was the closest match I'd found, so it was time to throw in the towel.

Even though Gidget didn't have a dog to double her in more complicated setups, she did have a lighting stand-in named Taco, who was owned by another animal company and would sit on her mark while the crew set up the lights instead of having

Gidget spend all that time just sitting. We put him in for smaller sequences to give Gidget a break, but over the course of all the commercials, he appeared very sparingly. In total, we would do around forty Taco Bell commercials, including test-market spots and regional ads. At least half of the commercials were nationally televised.

The morning of our latest Taco Bell ad, "Serenade," I was taken, as I often am, by just how amazing the crew was with Gidget. It wasn't a particularly complicated commercial. A woman is listening as a man sings a romantic song, presumably to her, but she quickly realizes it's actually the Taco Bell Chihuahua singing to a man nearby because he's got a Mexican pizza. Gidget didn't have a whole lot more to do on this shoot than stand on her mark. Still, our assistant director, Lee, ran an incredibly tight ship. He was as strict as could be when our little star was involved.

"I don't want to see one person move," he'd bark over the megaphone. "If you're going to talk, leave the stage now. Gidget's coming to set."

I can't think of a single human star who's given that type of treatment (okay, well, maybe a few . . .), but when you're working with animals, it's incredibly helpful, because it allows you to feel confident when you get on set. You want to be able to trust that no one is going to do something stupid, like move a giant light while Gidget's nearby (one fell behind her a couple of commercials earlier and it scared the daylights out of her), or drop an apple box and startle the poor thing.

Lee announced that they were ready for Gidget, and I let her out of the dressing room. It was amazing to watch this little dog find the camera on her own. She had an uncanny ability to seek out the camera in any situation, and without any help from me. I made a point never to lift her up onto a set. Instead, I let her use her nose and find her way around on her own, because it was more fun and engaging for her that way. As she trotted through the set, her little head swiveled from side to side, as if she were greeting her crew.

Hey, everyone, how's it going? Ready to get to work today? Hey, Andre, how ya been?

Whenever I picked Gidget up and placed her somewhere, there was a subtle but noticeable change that came over the little dog. Instead of her proud, happy attitude, it was like she got deflated a bit, and lost her edge. No matter how small they are, and whether they're in front of the camera or not, dogs need to just be dogs and do things under their own power. Otherwise, you get a different attitude from them—even a naughty one, as I'd soon find out.

Sniffing away and wagging her tail as she made her way through the crew and the equipment, Gidget headed straight for the camera. This kind of behavior is pretty unusual, even for a seasoned studio dog, but since Gidget's role called for her to look directly into the lens, she had developed a great relationship with the camera. She always sought it out with a determined look on her face and seemed so proud of herself when she found it. And then she'd just sit there still as a statue and gaze, almost lovingly, into the lens. It cracked up the crew for most of the campaign. And she did it every single time. I could be halfway across the stage, but when I released her, she'd be off, just like that.

While there was certainly something funny about it, whenever Gidget found the camera, people would also come up to me and say that watching her do it was the most amazing thing they'd seen on a job. And it *was* amazing. I'd never seen anything like it before—that's for sure! There just aren't many jobs like the Taco Bell campaign. If you watch any of the big dog movies, the animal is usually playing or running, or interacting with the actors. They're doing dog stuff, basically, not just sitting back and looking and talking into a camera. But Gidget's job for most of the commercials was to have a quiet dialogue with the camera lens. After a while she just knew her job—so well, in fact, that half the time I didn't even have my bait stick (a long forklike device that holds the dog's treat) over the lens. Even big-time directors of photography would be amazed at how this little four-legged actor always knew exactly what to do.

As for Taco, instead of getting him off the set by this point, as his trainer usually did right before shooting, she had kept him in front of the camera on Gidget's mark. She was working him a little bit to keep the job from getting boring for him, since he didn't usually see much action. Neither she nor Taco seemed to notice one very determined Chihuahua making a beeline for that very mark. When Gidget made it to the top of the stairs and, lo and behold, Taco was still there, she didn't slow down. She ran right up to him, dropped her shoulder like a tiny football player, and—I'm quite serious—body-slammed him out of her way! Taco scrambled to his paws to face her and the two sniffed at each other for a moment before Gidget plopped down in front of the camera.

Sorry, buddy. You're on my mark, and you should be long *gone by now!*

And with that, she gazed into the lens.

The crew let out a collective gasp. No one could believe the audacity of this little dog! It was like she had her job in mind and nothing could stop her.

I'm here, this is my mark, and I have to look into the camera. . . . What is this dog doing in my way?

The funniest part was that Gidget held no ill will toward Taco. They were friends and were always happy to play together in a dressing room before shooting began. We couldn't let them play together too much for fear of wearing them out before they got in front of the camera, but they were definitely buddies. Just not when it came to the limelight, apparently!

Shortly after Gidget's diva day on the Taco Bell set, we got a call at the ranch from someone looking for a Chihuahua to star in a feature film. Gidget was too busy, not to mention under contract to work only for Taco Bell. It's not that common for an animal to be under contract with a company. The only other example we've had at Studio Animal Services was a team of cats who were under contract to work only for one computer company (though they were free to film ads for other products). These types of contracts really spring up only when something truly takes off, like the Taco Bell campaign.

So since Gidget was otherwise engaged, we put Moonie up for the role in the movie. He landed it. He was still living with another trainer, but when he booked the movie—a romantic comedy called *Legally Blonde* starring Reese Witherspoon, about a sorority girl who goes to Harvard Law School—Karin and Paul decided I'd train him on the film and he'd come home to live with me.

Despite Gidget's mixed reaction when she first met Moonie, once the new Chihuahua got older, she seemed far more content to have a buddy nearly her own size. When I first brought Moonie home to prep for *Legally Blonde*, the two of them had the cutest little interaction, jumping around and bowing as they greeted each other. This became a standard greeting pretty much anytime they saw each other after being apart for a while. Unfortunately for Moonie, another standard behavior was developing as well.

After their first week back together as roommates, for some odd reason, Gidget began washing Moonie's face and ears on a regular basis. He would just sit there and tolerate it, but it was kind of a bizarre behavior. She would slowly and carefully lick Moonie's entire face, even his eyeballs, and he'd sit there with this slightly confused expression on his face.

Is it over yet? Okay, it's not. Do we really have to do this? When is this going to end, anyway?

Moonie sort of enjoyed the washing ritual, but when Gidget seemed to become truly obsessed with the practice, he would just stand up, turn around, and lie down in the opposite direction. Those days, Gidget was sleeping in my room, on a dog bed placed on an armchair. Instead of my figuring out another bed for Moonie, it was easier just to put them both in Gidget's bed at night. Moonie was too small to jump on the chair, so when I lifted him up to Gidget's bed, she wasn't so sure it was the best idea.

I love him, but . . . really? He's gonna share my bed?

Moonie wasn't entirely sold either, giving me a sideways glance and a flick of his ears that I knew meant he was feeling unsure.

Um, just so you know, I'm not all that comfortable with this arrangement.

But then, after what appeared to be a wordless conversation between the two Chihuahuas, they wiggled into position in the single dog bed, looking pretty darn content, with Gidget conceding her space to her buddy.

Okay, lie down. Get comfortable.

Before I knew it, our *Legally Blonde* prep time was over and we were due on set for the first day of filming. Moonie, who played a dog called Bruiser, had his first scene with Reese that day, and the pressure was on. I'd been working with him for some time, of course, but the first impression between a dog and an actor is paramount. There was going to be a lot of interaction between Bruiser and Reese's character in their scenes together, so it was important that Moonie relate directly to Reese, rather than focus on me. When the cameras are rolling, a dog needs to be looking at any number of things: another character or an object, or just gazing off in a certain direction. But if the dog's eyes are fixed on me, we have a problem.

This was Moonie's first real test. And while he showed no signs of stage fright, I was anxious enough for both of us. So instead of the typical freeze-dried chicken or liver treats that we often use to reward an animal on a shoot, I brought in the big guns that day: hot bait.

Hot bait is a term we use for a true delicacy in the dog world—real meat. In this case, I had chicken—moist hunks of chicken—and I had an intimidating place I wanted to put them: Reese's hot little hand.

Sometimes actors are amenable to this proposition; other times they're far from it. And while Reese had been very nice and friendly on set thus far, I didn't know what to expect when I asked her to hold meat in her hand while filming a scene. Was she a vegetarian? A vegan? Even if she wasn't, she was still a big star.

The next time the director called for a break, I took a deep breath and approached her.

"Reese, can we chat about the dog for a few minutes?"

"Sure!" she replied in her charming Southern drawl, so it came out sounding more like, "*Shore*."

I explained the best techniques for rewarding a dog, and told her that for Moonie to work well with her from the start, he needed to focus on her, not me. And in our line of work, there's no better way to get a dog to focus than with food.

"Great," she said agreeably. "I'd be happy to hold a treat for him."

"There's just one thing," I began. "The treats are, um, well, they're chicken. As in, actual pieces of meat. If you wouldn't mind too terribly holding that, I mean—"

"Sue," Reese interrupted me, squatting down to scratch Moonie under his chin. "If I have to slather my legs in chicken grease to make this work, I will. I'll do anything for this little guy!"

I was stunned. She couldn't have been nicer or more agreeable. Moonie must have felt me relax, because he put his paws up on Reese and gave her a big kiss.

After some final prep on our part, it was time for Moonie to make his debut. The director called, "Action!" and Moondoggie and Reese became fast friends. The first scene we worked was the one where Reese's character, Elle, arrives at Harvard, toting Bruiser in her arms. There's a great still shot of this moment in which you can actually see her clenched palm (with the chicken inside!) as she's looking up at a grand Harvard building. The meat was in there for quite a while too, because I asked her not to reward Moonie until the end of the scene. But she couldn't have cared less.

As for Moondoggie, he became quite enamored with his costar, and especially enjoyed all the scenes where he got to sit inside her purse. As a result of all the "bag training" I did with him for the movie, to this day, you can signal him to jump into any handbag. Sometimes he'll even do it without your asking. Polite of him, right?

The second scene we shot with Moonie and Reese was the one where he has to go pick up the envelope that someone slides under the door and bring it over to Reese. Moonie had to learn to retrieve a flat object, which, when it's placed on the floor, is pretty difficult for a dog to scoop up. So we had to bend it in the middle in order for him to slide his little chin underneath it and bring it over. After some trial and error we had that part down, but then came a more difficult proposition: He had to keep holding the envelope while Reese picked him up and put him on her lap. That's a lot of complicated behaviors for a rather simple-looking scene.

Most dogs, especially little ones, turn to mush and deflate when you pick them up—they tend to lose their work attitude, which is why I never lifted Gidget onto sets. So when Reese would lift Moonie after his retrieve, he'd drop the envelope. One of the hardest parts for him over the course of the whole movie was hanging on to that envelope as Reese lifted him into her lap. Once we got that behavior down, if she so much as tapped the envelope on her arm or leg as she lifted him, it was just an excuse for him to drop it. So I had to instruct Reese to turn Moonie away from her body as she scooped him up so the envelope wouldn't bump into her.

There are so many actors who wouldn't give me the time of day for such a request, and would just pick up the dog any old way. But not Reese. She was so good about working with me to figure out the best way to pick up Moonie without giving him the excuse to drop the envelope. She just *got it*, and always wanted to do whatever would help Moonie succeed.

The night after Moonie's big letter-carrying scene, we drove home in my truck, both of us feeling rather content. Whereas Gidget would have been fast asleep five minutes into the drive, Moonie was on high alert, standing in his crate in the backseat, watching the action of downtown Los Angeles whiz by as I drove home.

An hour later, when I pulled up to the house, Gidget's little head popped up in the window. I could only imagine how much carefree lounging she and the other dogs had done at home and in the backyard all day—until Moondoggie arrived, anyway. Moonie was excited to be home too, and dashed around in little circles in his crate. I put the truck into park and watched as Gidget bobbed her head up and down in the window, eagerly awaiting her friend's arrival.

I opened Moonie's crate and picked him up. The moment I placed him on the ground, he knew that was his cue to race to the front door. Gidget's head disappeared from the window and I imagined her flying across the hardwood floor to get to the door to meet her buddy. By the time I had put my key in the lock, Moonie was already warming up the happy dance he did every time he saw Gidget.

As soon as I opened the front door, they were all over each other, play-wrestling to the floor, and then jumping up to chase each other and running around in circles.

"Hey, guys," I said, and they snapped to attention, looking at me with matching tails wagging a mile a minute.

"How about some dinner?"

They looked at each other in a moment of apparent consultation. *Yeah, that sounds good; let's go!*

And we all made our way into the kitchen to eat.

As the filming of *Legally Blonde* progressed, Reese fell more and more in love with Moonie. Before we would shoot a scene she would give him a little hug and a kiss and he would lick her face in return. She would always refer to his breath as smelling like roasted fish garbage. I think she actually said that on Leno. He definitely did have interesting breath. So the two of them would always have their little moment exchanging kisses before the director signaled the start of a scene. Reese would do anything for him and thought he was the greatest.

Once in a while I'd also bring Gidget to the *Legally Blonde* set to get her out of the house. One day on set, a producer asked to have his picture taken with Gidget, so I put her on one of the director's chairs and he posed next to her. Just then, Reese happened to walk by.

"Who is *this*?" she asked, walking over to us.

"This is Gidget; she's the Taco Bell dog," I replied.

"No!"

"Yes!"

"Shut up that is not the Taco Bell dog. Are you sure?"

I laughed and assured Reese that I was positive that this was indeed Gidget. She gasped and turned toward her trailer.

"Oh, my God, I have to go get my camera!" she said, nearly breaking into a jog. "I can't wait to tell my mom I met the Taco Bell dog!"

That's the wonderful thing about dogs—they're the great equalizer, rendering both everyday people and A-list stars giddy in their wake.

Another fun element of filming *Legally Blonde* was the extensive wardrobe. For Moonie, that is. Luckily, he was very amenable to the proposition.

Some dogs just don't care about wardrobe. I'd later get a very smart bulldog named Serious to train, and he booked a job where he had to sit on the back of a motorcycle (stationary, of course) wearing Doggles, a.k.a. doggie goggles. He'd never worn them before, but he just sat there like it was something he does every day! For most dogs, wearing glasses or anything else over their eyes is pretty much the most annoying request you can make, since all they want to do is swat it away. But not Serious! It really just depends on the dog. Everybody's seen those Christmas pet photos where you've got dogs with antlers on their heads or giant bows around their necks. Some animals tolerate that stuff and others don't. Like Gidget, whom I'd often find at home on a winter day with one leg sticking out through the neck hole of a sweater, looking at me with a mixture of frustration and relief that I'd come home.

I was trying to get it off!

So you can imagine how much fun we had with the series of Taco Bell commercials where Gidget had to wear her little Che Guevara hat. With dogs who don't love wardrobe, we use two trainers: One pays the dog or distracts her, while the other puts on the item of clothing, or the dreaded hat. Then you bridge the behavior as usual and the next reward is taking off the wardrobe. Gidget knew that, at some point, the hat would come off, so she would tolerate it pretty well.

If I can sit here and be good with this stupid little hat on, eventually she'll take it off of me. . . .

We also helped ease her frustration by bringing in our secret weapon: Mrs. Hedgehog. We could have Gidget in head-to-tail accessories and she'd forget all about them if Mrs. Hedgehog showed up. Anytime I tossed that little toy in her direction between takes, she would race to pick it up, the tips of her ears flapping around as she ran. Then she'd tackle it and toss it up in the air, only to wrestle it back down to the ground again.

The really tricky thing with Gidget and wardrobe was that the client always wanted that Taco Bell dog look: very alert, with eyes wide-open and ears perky. But when you're training a dog who doesn't like wearing things, the personality just deflates and the dog kind of shrinks a little in appearance. So then you have to work a little harder when you're shooting to get the dog to be happy. You put the hat on, or the headphones (Gidget's least favorite accessory of all the Taco Bell commercials), and her body language would just sink.

I don't wanna *wear this.*

So to compensate, I would be twice as peppy (and consequently, twice as annoying to everyone around me) to get her back to that look that they loved. It's the most draining thing to shoot when an animal has to wear something or he's contained somehow. He's starting from a five when you want him at a ten, so every little thing needs to be exaggerated.

"Gidget!" I'd squeal in a tone so high-pitched I'd even annoy myself. "Look here! What a good girl! What a *good girl!*"

It was exhausting.

Watching Moonie deal with wardrobe on *Legally Blonde* was nothing short of hysterical. He was the complete opposite of Gidget—he *loved* to wear clothes. Whereas Gidget would wait for you to reach in and pull each of her legs through the sweater holes, begrudgingly allowing the practice but not helping in the slightest, Moonie always wanted to help.

To put a sweater on him, we'd stand him up on his hind legs, slip the sweater over his head, and then, on his own, he would punch his front feet through the armholes without waiting for assistance. He knew exactly what we were doing and he loved it.

We're putting on a sweater!

Not only was it a riot, but it also made me happy to know he enjoyed his wardrobe, since there was so much of it on that movie. At times, he had to wear some pretty elaborate outfits, like the Jackie O. getup, complete with a pillbox hat and skort. All of Moonie's wardrobe for *Legally Blonde* and *Legally Blonde 2* was designed and made by Fifi & Romeo, an L.A. boutique specializing in dog clothes and accessories (And as much as people joke about dogs looking embarrassed, myself included, it's just not an emotion that they're capable of. Thank goodness; otherwise Moonie would have been humiliated by all the cross-dressing he was forced to do on the big screen!) He had something crazy like twenty-three wardrobe changes in the second movie, but he couldn't have cared less.

Right around the time that I learned just how easygoing Moonie could be, it became clear that we were entering a new phase with Gidget—the naughty phase. Due to her increasing popularity and our circumstances navigating through crowds and traveling, I was breaking my own cardinal rule and picking her up and carrying her a lot more often.

When we went to New York for *Godzilla*, people started to get really brazen with Gidget. I'd be checking in at the airport or the hotel and people would come right over to her, squat down, and put their faces next to hers to pet her. Which happens to be my number one pet peeve.

I'm always happy to have people pet my dog, provided she's well socialized, but it's so important to ask first. I just don't understand why people don't get this. Especially when it comes to kids. I can't tell you how many times I've had children come up to my dogs and pet them without asking—and without their parents correcting them. So essentially, the child is learning that it's okay to go up and pet any strange dog, exposing both themselves and the animal to possible injury or harm.

So whenever a child comes up to me on a set or when I'm out and about and asks, "Can I pet your dog?" I always take the time to positively reinforce them. That tends to elicit a really cute and proud response from the kid—plus, I know they'll probably ask again the next time they want to pet someone's dog.

"Sure, you can pet the dog," I'll tell the child, "and thank you so much for asking; that was very nice of you. Not many people

ask, and it makes such a difference when they do, so thank you."
(I guess I'm training the children of southern California, too!)

Adults are just as bad. I've been on the road or waiting in a line, and while my back is turned, someone will just come over and scoop Gidget up without so much as a casual glance in my direction! It still shocks me when people act this way. People don't walk over to babies and pick them up (and babies don't have sharp teeth and bite when threatened!). I just don't understand it.

In any case, due to the behavior of such fans, and the sheer size of the crowds we had to navigate in our line of work, I was forced to start carrying Gidget more than I ever had. And it took its toll. As soon as I picked her up, the Chihuahua started to come out—the typical snippy, yappy behavior that is stereotypical of the breed. The minute you take a dog and put her in your arms or your lap, you're elevating the dog's status and changing her attitude and behavior. And despite all her great training and easygoing personality, I could still feel that shift in Gidget.

Ha, look at this! A human is holding me. I am now more powerful!

All the small dog breeds, from Chihuahuas to Yorkies and Maltese, just sink into your hip and go, *This is kind of cool. I don't have to do much of anything, or worry about getting stepped on. But if somebody comes into my space, I'll protect myself—and you.*

When an owner has got their little dog in their lap, as soon as that dog starts yapping and biting at people, they tend to say, "It's okaaaaaay," and pet the dog. But all that does is positively reinforce that dog's bad behavior.

The first time that Gidget was truly naughty came at a rather unfortunate time.

She'd been hired by another animal company to play a Chihuahua (go figure) in a movie called *Crazy in Alabama*, directed by Antonio Banderas. She was one of three Chihuahuas in the scene, so it wasn't like they wanted the Taco Bell dog for the movie. She was just playing your average, everyday little dog.

Of course, this dog was anything but average, so on the day that we met Antonio, he knew just who she was and was eager to meet her.

"Hey, I heard this was the Taco Bell dog," he said to me when we were on set. "My kids love her!" He was picking her up between takes (yes, he'd asked), and at one point, he lifted her to his face and cooed to her in the standard baby talk that Chihuahuas tend to get from people. Then, without warning, Gidget pulled back a bit as if saying, *I don't like this* . . . and bit him on the nose. Antonio Banderas! I was mortified.

"Oh, my God, I am *so* sorry!" I told him in a state of shock. I'd never seen her do anything like that before, and I couldn't believe my luck that the first time would be with a director on set.

Luckily, Antonio thought it was funny. He actually laughed and joked about how ridiculous it would be to tell his kids that he'd been bitten by the Taco Bell dog.

And thus began a new phase for me—the careful phase. Every day from then on, I'd watch Gidget's body language and behavior closely to make sure she was comfortable with new people. I'd also try to keep her out of other people's arms. Thinking back on it, I wonder if this was her idea of revenge for all those times that the Taco Bell director blew in her nose! Either that or she just got fed up with so many strangers petting her. My carrying her around, thus elevating her sense of power, certainly didn't help.

For their roles in *Crazy in Alabama*, Gidget and the two other Chihuahuas had to jump around on a bed where Melanie Griffith's character had stowed a human head inside a hatbox. So we would put Mrs. Hedgehog or pieces of chicken inside it so she'd get excited and try to get into the box to uncover the source of the smell (luckily, the prop department left the actual smell part of it up to us, so the scent was just chicken). This was a more natural behavior for Gidget than for Moonie, who simply didn't have that particular type of drive. He would just be like, *Oh, a hatbox? There's chicken inside it? That's nice. I'll just sit here and wait for you to take it out.*

Luckily, after the biting incident, Gidget was well behaved on set, but I was still extra-vigilant on our next trip—back to New York for a trade show with Taco Bell. They'd asked for Gidget to be there in a booth for photo ops with fans. We had her sitting in a director's chair and asked people to pose next to her so that we wouldn't run into any snapping problems.

Of course, some people would bring their faces in close to hers and squeal over how cute she was.

You're insane, lady, Gidget's body language would say, but I kept a close watch on her and we got through the trade show without any "love bites," as people like to call them when a little dog is involved. (To which I always want to say, "You wouldn't call it that if a pit bull bit you!")

We also had another, far bigger commitment for Taco Bell in 1999 in Nashville. The parent company had Taco Bell, KFC, and Pizza Hut all together for a huge presentation in a massive stadium. Gidget was the big surprise guest. They actually had her and me stay in a different hotel from the rest of the convention so it wouldn't get out that she was there. As soon as a couple people noticed that the Taco Bell dog was in town, word would spread like wildfire and the surprise would be ruined. It was like traveling with a huge rock star! We had daily covert operations for her to take walks outside.

But the action they wanted Gidget to do onstage was even trickier than keeping her presence a secret. The plan was to have Gidget come out onstage from one side, and R2-D2 (the real one!) would come out on the other, since Taco Bell had filmed a series of commercials for the new *Star Wars* movie. I explained to the organizers that I couldn't tell them what she would do without rehearsing next to a moving, talking robot. Not to mention how she'd cope with the thunderous applause that was sure to accompany her surprise appearance.

I knew that Gidget could go to a mark without seeing me, but with all the commotion and the strange robot moving toward her, I feared she might go, *Ohhh, what's going on? I can't see my mark; I'd better just stay here in the curtains.* We decided to give her a slightly raised mark so she'd have a clear and defined target to focus on, and so we made the mark a small box with a padded top.

To make matters even more complicated, there was a huge orchestra pit in front of the stage, so the closest I could be to Gidget was in the front row of the audience, wearing all black to blend in, hopeful that she'd be able to spot me. The idea was that if she saw me, I'd get her attention and send her to her mark, and her ears would perk up and she'd look happy after she saw me. *Oh, there's Mom. And hey, there's my mark!*

And on top of all that, they were filming the event with three cameras—and one of them would swing down on a huge arm and follow Gidget as she traveled across the stage.

So we rehearsed in pieces, starting with Gidget simply running out onstage to the sounds of recorded applause playing over the PA system, increasing the volume as we went. I had an extra-long bait stick, so I would pay her over the orchestra pit when she landed on her mark. Next, we added the camera, and she seemed to be fine with that too. Fortunately she knew cameras, because otherwise we probably never would have gotten her to calmly walk across the stage with one in her face (whereas most dogs would be like, *What the hell is this thing swooping down from out of the sky?*). In any case, it's so important to introduce elements of a complicated scene one at a time so the dog feels successful with each behavior and doesn't get overwhelmed.

Next, we worked on Gidget's cue. Since I couldn't exactly stand in the audience and shout, "Gidget! Go to your mark," my fellow trainer Ginger would start with her behind the curtain. Next, she'd whisper, "Go on; go to your mark," in Gidget's ear. Then, being the happy-go-lucky little dog that she was, Gidget would eagerly run out to the mark. Of course, the Taco Bell people wanted her to just walk out, but we started out with her running so that the work was fun and she wouldn't get bored. Then, when she felt good about running out to her mark, we slowed it down with the command "go easy," which, to studio dogs, means "slow down." So, as a joke, I told Ginger to just *whisper*, "Go easy," in Gidget's ear when it was showtime to keep her calm and slow. I had no idea that it would actually work. We wrapped up our rehearsal after a few hours and I went to bed that night hoping that the little dog could pull it off.

When we arrived the next morning at the arena, we were shuttled to a dressing room that Elton John had used the night before for his concert. How's that for star treatment? They didn't have time to clean it out from the night before, so the room was still decorated with several bouquets of flowers. Gidget was truly in good company. Colin Powell was the guest speaker right before Gidget's appearance, so I listened to his speech backstage while she sat at my feet. I'd recently learned that the production people wanted Gidget to exit the stage on this long ramp, which we hadn't prepped. We also weren't able to rehearse the part where R2-D2 would be "speaking" to Gidget and she'd respond in the prerecorded voice of the actor who did her voice in the commercials. I said a quick, silent prayer that she'd pull all this off.

Before I knew it, it was go time. I stood in my all-black ensemble in the audience and watched Ginger whisper, "Go easy," in Gidget's ear. Then, like a consummate professional, the little Chihuahua calmly walked out onstage with a giant camera looming right in front of her face. She just bebopped along like this was an everyday event for her. The audience went nuts. The stadium, which was easily packed with ten thousand people, positively erupted. Gidget reached her mark and sat down. As the cheers died down, they started the tape with R2-D2's voice. I crossed my fingers.

As she'd practiced, Gidget sat there facing forward. Then, as the voice emanated from R2-D2, she turned her head slightly to look at him, which was actually perfect, because it looked like they were having a conversation. The brave little dog had a look in her eye that only I could decipher as she checked out her robot costar.

Ummm, I don't know what you are, but you weren't here yesterday when we rehearsed this. . . . What the heck, I'll go along with it.

When it was all over and it was time for Gidget to exit, I got her attention and signaled her toward the runway and walked in that direction myself. And without a moment's hesitation, Gidget turned and trotted offstage without a care in the world. I was truly amazed. It wasn't a big commercial, a movie, or a red carpet, but at that corporate convention in Nashville, I felt prouder of my little charge than I'd ever been. This was no small feat, and an incredibly daunting task for a Chihuahua! But not this one. Yet again, Gidget impressed me with what a star she really was. Not to mention what a good dog.

Shooting a Taco Bell ad on Lake Powell

CHAPTER 9

Fears and Triumphs

Working with dogs on set is as hard as you make it. "The movie" is of little significance to Gidget or any member of the animal world. Talented as she is, Gidget was simply looking for some positive attention and her next snack.

—Charlie Herman-Wurmfeld, director, *Legally Blonde* 2

Living in a beautiful community atop a massive hill forty-five miles north of Los Angeles had its perks as well as its downsides. To get home, I took the winding Lake Hughes Road up the hill on a long scenic trek. Lake Hughes Road is basically twenty-five miles of nothing, in a metropolitan sense, anyway. At most, you'll see a half dozen other cars during the entire drive. Canyons and creeks cover the landscape, and every now and again a deer or fox will dash through a hedgerow as you drive by. After it rains, waterfalls pop up in the rock formations. The rock walls, many of which jut straight up in the air, can also foster dangerous mud slides and rock slides. Drivers are warned of this possibility by several disconcerting SLIDE AREA signs along the road.

On top of the hill sits a very small community without so much as a major grocery store—residents make sure to hit one of the big chains in Valencia, thirty miles away, before going home for the weekend. But for small things, like milk, bread, and conversation, there's always Papa's Country Store, a quaint, weather-worn shop that merits little explanation beyond its name.

My dogs did just fine when I made the move to Lake Hughes, since they're exposed to new places all the time. So their attitude in the new house was pretty much, *Hey, this is nice!* They thought it was the coolest thing to explore their new surroundings. And cool surroundings they were: About halfway down Lake Hughes Road, I soon discovered a little ravine that leads down to a tiny, seasonal river. It dries up in the summer, but it's a lovely, peaceful spot during the rest of the year, and the dogs love it, hunting lizards (or anything else that moves) and snapping tree branches and sticks to carry around as they trailblaze their way through the water. Of course, I always have my camera at the ready in these moments. I love catching my dogs in action, and have plenty of photo albums to prove it.

For most socialized dogs, moving should not be looked at as a source of stress (it's stressful for humans, sure, but generally not for well-adjusted dogs). If your dog is used to going to many different places with you, even vacations (that you take with or without your dog) shouldn't be stressful. Of course, a dog who never leaves the house is going to be stressed by changes like these. The more socialized a dog is, and the more new environments he's exposed to, the less stress he'll face overall. Plus, it's funny the way a dog's memory works—you could be gone for ten days or ten minutes and get the same reaction upon your return. There have been times when I've gotten out to my truck and realized that I forgot my cell phone, and when I got back to the house, the dogs were like, *Oh, my God, you're home! We missed you!* So there's no need to stress about a move any more than a quick outing, really.

It was while living in Lake Hughes that I also acquired a new pet.

One afternoon at work, I set out on a casting search in Temecula, a town just outside San Diego, so I was scouring breed rescues to look for just the right dog. I needed a golden retriever, so I went to one breeder whom we'd used to acquire the dogs for

Gidget as a puppy.

The new addition, sprinting on the beach at top speed.

Beans playing her favorite game
with Gidget before they became
friends: Pin Down the Puppy!

A young Gidget, working on her poses.

Feeling the holiday spirit and posing for my annual Christmas card.

Trying to figure out what to make of my sister's tortoise.

Gidget with Jeanine Barry, the trainer who worked her on the first Taco Bell commercial.

Gidget, Daisy and Duster waiting for a training session
at the ranch.

Going for a ride with Megan Valinote,
Gidget's trainer for the Miami Taco Bell
commercials.

Taking a snooze with Mrs. Hedgehog at a New York hotel.

Three happy dogs: Holly (from *Gran Torino*), Beans and Smith at a dog park north of Detroit in 2008.

Sue Chipperton

Exploring the private jet we took to New York to open the stock exchange in 2000.

Gidget checks out the view from her seat on a private jet.

Sue Chipperton

Like many travelers, slightly annoyed at the airport check-in.

Working Gidget on a dolly for the Taco Bell commercial where she rides on Godzilla's tail.

Gidget and Moonie posing for my annual Christmas card.

Moonie snuggling up to Beans at home.

Unfazed by her rather creepy costar, Gidget knocked 'em dead on this Taco Bell commercial, in which we had a special A/C unit fed into the vehicle just for her!

Gidget in her boat on a Taco Bell commercial, stopping by to say hi to the guys, including Johnny Knoxville (left).

Paying Gidget with a piece of chicken on the end of a bait stick during her boat shoot.

Hank getting in on the fun on our favorite stretch of the beach, just north of Malibu, with Beans and Tula playing in the background.

Jackson, Tula, Hank and Beans on a twilight hike in southern California.

Hank, Tula, Gidget and Beans at Lake Elizabeth in 1999.

Shelley Leidner

Sue Chipperton

Best buddies Hank and Tula sharing a dog bed at home.

On the set of *Titanic*, we dressed in wardrobe to blend in (this is me!) and released a couple of dogs to mill around the dock during the boarding scene.

Sprig in 2010, contemplating a dip in the doggie pool at home.

Sue Chipperton

Serious hard at work with his first celebrity, Toby Keith, on an industrial ad for the country star's concert tour.

the TV show *Providence*. When I arrived to look at dogs that afternoon, I noticed that the breeder also did Weimaraner rescue. As I walked around her sprawling property, I noticed one dog run with a Weimaraner in it. Just like Gidget had captured my attention several years back, this dog grabbed my gaze and wouldn't let it go.

He was a blue Weimaraner, which I'd never seen before. The breed is usually the brown or silvery gray color that you see in William Wegman's photos. But this dog was a very dark bluish gray color with bright yellow eyes.

"Oh, my God," I said to the breeder. "That is the handsomest dog I've ever seen!"

Apparently he'd been adopted out twice, unsuccessfully. Now he was going to his third prospective home, this time with a family in Las Vegas that weekend. But I knew that when it came to breed rescue, dogs got sent back all the time. Most rescues have it in their contract that if an owner cannot keep the dog, they can return it. The reasons Hank was sent back, I'd later surmise, were that he could be a bit aloof, he wasn't exactly a cuddle bug, and his defense mechanism was to run. Not exactly selling points for many dog owners!

"Okay, well, if for some reason you get him back, please let me know," I told her, crossing my fingers that for whatever reason, this gorgeous guy would find his way back.

One month later, the beautiful blue Weimaraner returned. I got a call from the breeder that he was mine if I was still interested. I drove out and picked him up that same day and decided to call him Hank.

And just like that, Hank became a member of my crew. He loved the beach as much as Beans and Gidget, so the three of them would have a ball tearing across the sand together. But Hank was also a bit of a quirky guy. He definitely had a flight mode when he got spooked. I found out that another animal company owned a ranch up in Lake Hughes where they kept their surplus horses who weren't working all the time, and the company let me ride them for fun. The hills, canyons, and fire roads in the area are so extensive that you could spend ten years riding through them and never see the same spot twice. Beans loved to come with me—I could control her off leash no matter what was going on—and eventually I thought it would be great if I could take Hank. I knew he wasn't as adaptable as Beans, but I figured I'd give it a shot.

It was a complete and utter disaster. He was totally skittish around the horse, constantly giving me this wary look of, *What the hell is that big thing you're sitting on?!* Then, on one of the fire roads, he twisted his leg and started limping. So I was a good mile away from the ranch where the horse lived and I had a dog who was limping, so I dismounted to check him out. Now I had a horse who was freaked-out because I was freaked-out, and there wasn't a tree in sight to tie up the reins, so I held them in one hand while reaching out to Hank, who wouldn't come anywhere near me because I was holding the horse! That was Hank for you. And his quirks extended beyond just strange horses— he wasn't all that intrigued by strange people, either. Whenever I had company at the house and he was expected to greet them, he· would only begrudgingly comply.

Look. I. Am. Wagging. My. Tail. Back. And. Forth.

Slow and deliberate, every time. Hank's got these big, mournful eyes, but he's totally sweet and affectionate, just in his own way. One of his cutest qualities comes out when I return home and he greets me, whether I was gone for five minutes or two hours, by putting his big, solemn face right up next to mine, wagging his stubby tail with all the exuberance he's got.

Hank has always loved his hikes (provided there are no horses involved), and in later years he came in quite handy while I trained our Jack Russell puppies, Sprig and Decoy. As Beans got older and could no longer hike long distances, I subbed in Hank as my cotrainer and little helper. Oftentimes with puppies who have had some training, teaching them a recall is difficult because they don't like to leave you. But having another dog who can draw them out and get them going gives you the opportunity to then call them back. And Hank turned into a great dog for that, acting as my sidekick to get the dogs to travel away from me.

As it turned out, all the cute things about my new dog—the way he'd wag his stubby tail, and his big ears flopping around as he greeted me at the door—were pretty much reserved for me alone. There was just no way he'd make it in studio work, because the sweet, endearing personality I saw at home did not show up on set whatsoever. Hank just wasn't a real social kind of guy. He was so hopeless in front of a camera, in fact (to say that no personality came through would be an understatement), that it became a standing joke at work. We'd get a call for a Weimaraner and we'd be like, "Well, we can't send Hank because, well . . . because he's just pathetic!" But the truth was, we wouldn't think of sending him out on a job because he wouldn't enjoy it, and that's really the bottom line.

Hank is hardly the only dog who didn't take to studio work. I've had plenty of cases where it's pretty obvious that an animal isn't going to work out. Maybe he's scared of anything going on above him, in which case the sound boom that inevitably appears during most scenes will be just too much for him to cope with. Or maybe meeting new people becomes a real process and the dog has to be around someone new for a long time before he can interact with and trust them. What we need in a studio dog is one who can show up on set, walk out of his crate, and get handed off to an actor for rehearsal. There are so many dogs in shelters who are willing and happy to work that it's just not worth the time and energy you'd spend trying to get a shy dog to adapt. Besides, it's supposed to be fun! And since we never send an animal who doesn't work for us back to a shelter, that dog will find a good home, and we'll also be rescuing another from a shelter at the same time.

I once got a beautiful rottweiler named Bella who I thought would be perfect for studio work. The problem ended up being that rottweilers and German shepherds are typically cast as "mean" dogs—like the barking, snarling, agitated one behind a fence at a junkyard, or the dog who does a "hit" (a trained attack)—but Bella could never be one of them. She was just a big softie with no drive for that kind of work. But as it happens with so many of our adoption stories, the perfect home for Bella was just around the corner. A trainer from another animal company was out at Studio Animal Services for a couple of days prepping a job and she saw Bella in the exercise yard and asked about her. It turned out that the trainer's in-laws were looking for a sweet, lovable rottweiler. Luckily for all, I happened to have a sweet, lovable rottweiler whom I was looking to place! Today, Bella lives out on a huge ranch outside of San Francisco with that trainer's in-laws, another dog, and a big, hundred-acre backyard.

About two years after we wrapped on *Legally Blonde*, we got a call about the sequel. Much to our surprise, the production company wanted us to come out and *audition* Moonie for the role of Bruiser in *Legally Blonde 2*. As far as we were concerned, Moonie was one of the stars of the first movie, and we were incredibly surprised that they'd even consider using another dog to play Bruiser. How could they recast the *Legally Blonde* Chihuahua? So it goes in Hollywood, but luckily, Moondoggie landed the role. Again.

As Moonie got to work on his second feature film, I noticed that the biggest difference between him and Gidget was that Moonie tended to be a little more cautious when he was working. He was great with his behaviors and did a lot of things well, but if you were to look at them like two actors, Gidget was the seasoned veteran, whereas Moonie was the young whippersnapper who would ask, *Am I doing it right? Is this how you sit on a mark?* He was a little more exuberant, and you had to calm him down a bit. You'd have him stand on a mark and he'd want to bark or spin around in a circle. So I often needed to plead with him: "All you have to do is stand there. Okay? Nothing more." When I was working with him on the envelope retrieve in the first movie, he would even mistake it for his mark and run over to land proudly on top of it!

For one scene in the first film, our director, Robert Luketic, told us he wanted Bruiser to snarl. Snarling is not in Moonie's nature at all, so I put a lot of time into trying to elicit a snarl. We'd get him very excited about a bone and then sneak in to steal it from him in the hope that he'd show some sort of displeasure. Then we could try to elevate that into a snarl or a little growl. But Moonie was such a sweet, good-natured little soul he would just be like, *Okay! You can have that bone!* So we had to go back to Robert and tell him we were sorry but we wouldn't be able to get Moonie to snarl. Robert was very confused. He hadn't meant to ask for any sort of angry snarl out of Moonie; he just wanted us to be able to elicit any old sound from him, as though Moonie were having a "conversation" with an actor. So it all worked out just fine, but we learned an interesting lesson: To an animal trainer, a snarl is a snarl—a very particular sound and look. But to the average person, that word doesn't necessarily carry such a particular meaning. Lesson learned! And sweet Moonie never became the snarling type.

Moonie was also a little bit more cautious on the second movie than the first. On a feature film it's a lot harder to rein everybody in and control the environment than on a commercial shoot where you're doing a campaign and the dog is the star. On a movie, there are a lot more crew people and equipment. Some people have tunnel vision, thinking only about what they have to accomplish. You have hair and makeup people stepping in for final touches on the actor, so you make sure to place the dog on his mark after they are finished. But then someone rushes in for an adjustment and whips out a can of hair spray, feverishly spraying down an actress's hair while the dog sits in a sticky mist. Or perhaps a flag needs a piece of tape, so someone steps in and loudly rips a piece of tape from the roll right by the dog, making him jump. So a trainer has to constantly be on the lookout. Then there are amazing crew members who may have dogs themselves, or have worked on a big animal feature, and they really get it. They'll come over to tell you, "Hey, I just want to let you know I'm going to move that light." I could kiss any crew member who says something like that.

It's amazing how the littlest change can derail a dog. Ever since the day that the light fell behind Gidget, which was a complete accident and no one's fault, she always thought there was going to be somebody standing behind her getting ready to drop something. Moonie had a similar experience on *Legally Blonde 2*. He was a warier personality to begin with, always looking around the set checking things out, wondering, *What's that person doing over there? What's she doing down that way?*

When a dog (whether a studio dog or a pet) jumps in fear at something, the last thing you want to do is coddle him. If the dog knows any sort of behaviors or tricks, this is a great time to ask him to sit or speak, because it distracts him from the fear and gives him something else to focus on. If a garbage truck drives by you and your dog on a walk, for example, and it makes a scary noise and the dog spooks, you should not acknowledge that fear. Instead, immediately divert the dog to something else, like a trick, to change his mind about what just happened. People coddle frightened dogs all the time and it's the worst thing you can do. It's like when a kid falls down on a playground—her reaction to the fall can depend a whole lot on *your* reaction. If a parent goes, "Whoa! You went flying for a minute there, huh? That was cool! Let's go play on this slide instead," then the child is a lot less likely to cry than if the adult says, "Oh, no! Honey! Are you okay?" The same goes for a dog who already has a fear in place. If she's skittish in a certain situation, try to keep her focus on you instead of what scares her. It's all about distraction and redirection.

When we shot the scene with Moonie and the actor who played the doorman in Elle's building, one of the second assistant cameramen kept slating the clapper board (the piece of equipment they use right before the director calls "action!") in an extremely—and unnecessarily—loud manner, and it kept scaring the heck out of Moonie. And despite my begging and pleading (and the AC's repeated assurance that he wouldn't do it again), the clapper board continued slamming and Moonie became more and more nervous. A few days later, we shot a scene where he's sitting in Reese's lap, and she gets really excited to hear some good news, so she rapidly claps her hands together. And poor Moonie just couldn't handle it. With a wild, "I can't take this!" look in his eye, he actually jumped out of her lap to get away from the clapping. As luck would have it, that was the day a bunch of movie execs were on set. It took a lot of work and distraction to convince him to get back in Reese's lap when he knew the clapping was coming.

And it didn't end there. In the laboratory scene where they're testing makeup on Bruiser's mom—played by Gidget!—Moonie has to run along down a long, empty corridor. We shot the scene in a big glass office building with concrete floors, so when the camera guy slated loudly for the umpteenth time, it was not only a loud sound, but it reverberated through the whole building. Poor Moonie had become a jittery mess with his ears pinned back, anticipating trouble, practically shaking when he saw the camera. Not good. This was the last straw.

"*Okay*," I announced, my voice brimming with frustration and emotion. "He has to take a break!"

I whisked Moonie off the set and went downstairs to the room where we kept the crates. The producer came down to ask me what was wrong, and I explained that, no matter how many times I asked, the assistant cameraman refused to slate quietly, and that anytime he so much as appeared on set, Moonie was beside himself.

A couple hours later, when we returned to work on the lab scene, a producer (a.k.a. my hero) made an announcement to the camera department loudly enough for the entire crew to hear.

"I do not want to hear the slate one more time on this movie! There is no need for it and I do not want it to happen again. *Not one more time.*"

I never heard the slate again for the rest of the movie.

Still, thanks to that assistant cameraman, Moonie has an issue to this day with any slapping, smacking, or clapping sound. Studio dogs are probably among the bravest animals out there, but they're still dogs, and fears can take their toll.

With the longer-term phobias, there are a few ways to help a dog overcome a fear. One of my dogs used to be terrified of my then-boyfriend's motorcycle, so I'd prepare her dinner out on the driveway while he started up the bike from a distance. This dog loved her food, so it was a fitting solution. The next day, he moved the bike to the driveway and started it up while the dog was eating, and pretty soon, she would be eating from the bowl placed underneath the parked motorcycle. Of course, if a dog isn't food driven, he'll just think, *I don't care; that thing is scary; I don't need to eat.* So then you can think about distracting him with a favorite toy, but not a belly rub or any other sort of affection, because that just tells him that feeling scared is an acceptable reaction.

As Moonie continued to work on the *Legally Blonde* films, jumping into a handbag became pretty much his favorite thing to do in the world. I remember Fifi & Romeo designing the pink "Kelly" bag for Moonie, in which they substituted one panel of the handbag with mesh, so that Moonie could see me through it as I gave him directions. This way, when I asked him to lie down, I could pay him with a bait stick through a little open compartment in the mesh while he was still lying down. Otherwise, I'd have to walk over to him and reach inside the bag, which would make him pop up, which might confuse him about what he was getting paid for. It made the behavior that much stronger.

Once Moonie had his bag behaviors down, he was so darn cute to watch working through his repertoire. There's a scene in the sequel where he and Reese are in a courtroom and Bruiser is in the bag, unbeknownst to the audience. Then, like a little gopher, he pops up and puts his paws up on top of the bag, as though he was perking up in response to the characters' dialogue. He learned that when I asked him to get into a bag, he was supposed to lie down and stay there until I asked him to pop up. And he learned to get up when I signaled him with a hand cue or the term "all right!" paired with a high-pitched tone. Each time, Moonie would pop with the speed and exuberance of a jack-in-the-box, and the quickness of one those little Whac-A-Mole guys you see on the boardwalk at the beach. And the behavior translated to pretty much any bag. No matter what the shape or size, if a bag is placed on the floor, he'll still try to jump inside it and pop up on command!

For *Legally Blonde 2*, like the first movie, I had Moonie for a good four or five months, and he was a joy to have at my house. He got along well with the other dogs. He and Gidget were always happy to just sleep out on the deck in the sunshine. And when we worked on prep for the movie, he was such a good little guy, always willing to try to put his heart into giving new things a shot.

It was a busy time for me, between Moonie's features and Gidget's ongoing Taco Bell campaign. Our latest commercial was called "Theme Song," and it was a *Shaft*-themed spot in which she had to trot along, set to seventies music, of course, and glance over to the camera so they could do a freeze-frame of her head. Pretty soon after that, we worked on a commercial where Gidget rides in a taxi looking out the window. We had another trainer, Andrea, holding her in the cab while I was posted on the side of the road. Gidget had her head out the window and I called to her to get her to look in my direction. Now, this was a dog who understood her limitations and those of her surroundings. She was always good about not leaping off of high places because of her size, but on the taxi commercial she did the strangest thing.

As the cab drove by and I called, "Gidget, look!" this brave little dog threw her paws up on the window and tried to jump out of the moving taxi! Luckily, Gidget was wearing a harness tied to the seat and Andrea was right there, so she didn't really stand a chance. Still, it was such a funny, endearing moment of Gidget just trying to do her job the best she could. I called her, so without giving it a second thought, she responded with, *I'm coming!*

The biggest, most obvious example of how brave Gidget had become came when we were on location in Lake Powell, Arizona. It was one of the most fun Taco Bell commercials we did throughout the entire three-year campaign. The story line went like this: Three guys are sitting in a rowboat, eating chalupas, when out of nowhere, the Taco Bell dog appears right next to them on the water in her own motorized boat. The scenario may sound odd today, but remember, this was the little dog who tried to capture Godzilla in her ad campaign!

To prepare Gidget for this shoot, like any shoot, I tried to mimic the actions as closely as possible in rehearsals to get her comfortable with what she'd be doing. There was just one problem: How do you mimic a motorized boat ride in the middle of a lake, when you don't have a boat *or* a lake to prep with?

The best we could do was practice in my boss Paul's swimming pool just outside of L.A. Much to my amazement, I was able to find a Gidget-size raft that would float under her weight when we sent it out into the water. It wasn't quite the middle of a 186-mile-long lake, but it would have to do.

A week before we were due on set in Arizona, I loaded the dog and the raft into my truck and drove to Paul's house. I really had no idea how Gidget would react to the scenario, so I just broke it down to the basics. As on all the other jobs we'd done, she had a mark. In this case, like many others, it was a small cushion, and I placed it inside the raft. I introduced Gidget to her mark, and then set it inside the raft, which I'd placed in the water at the edge of the pool.

"Go to your mark," I told her, and she happily obliged, hopping inside.

Then I carefully pushed it out to the middle of the pool. Gidget looked cool as a cucumber, and even when the raft took a turn away from me, she just looked around a bit and then locked her eyes with mine. Well, that was easy!

Next, just to be sure she had it down, I grabbed Paul's pool skimmer and gently poked at Gidget's raft to simulate the movement she'd experience in the motorized one on the lake, since it was only February and too cold for me to get in the water with her. As I sent the raft in different directions, Gidget just shifted her weight on the cushion to keep her balance, and kept her eyes calmly on me. Even Paul looked impressed.

"Well, let's hope she's this good when it's the real thing!" I said with a laugh.

A week later, we arrived on the shore of Lake Powell. It's a huge, beautiful body of water filled with massive red rocks that form caves and coves, and in the warmer months, it's one of the biggest houseboat party destinations in the country. That winter, of course, it was relatively empty, and I marveled at the scenery before we boarded the speedboat that would take us to our location: a houseboat posted out in the middle of the lake.

When we got to our spot—over an hour away from shore—the prop master first tested out our little vehicle, sans Gidget, who was curled up in her crate fast asleep, with no idea just how far we were from land. I had a blanket wrapped around her to keep her warm, since her comfort in the cool temperatures was always our biggest concern. She had proven herself time and time again, so by this shoot, it didn't even really occur to me what I'd do if she danced around in the boat, or worse, tried to jump out. I trusted her that much.

After testing the boat on its own, we placed Gidget's mark (a small cushion like the one we practiced with, plus a heating pad inside of it) in the boat and I instructed her to go to her mark. Gidget was happy to oblige.

She leaned back on her hind legs and leaped inside the boat. This one was bigger than the raft we'd practiced with, but Gidget knew that her mark was a safe zone where she could stay and feel secure, no matter where it happened to be located.

I rewarded her with a piece of chicken and she looked up at me eagerly.

So, where are we going in this thing?

Turned out, she was going pretty far. To get the shot done just right, the prop guy operated the remote control and sent Gidget's boat out a solid hundred feet out from where I sat on the houseboat with the crew. At first, everyone seemed to hold their breath as Gidget motored out on her own. But I had every confidence in my little dog.

As the boat traveled farther and farther away, Gidget just sat calmly and kept her eyes on me. As the filming with the actors began, she would even have to do what's called a "work away," where her back is to the camera—and to me—and she'd need to look in another direction. So when she arrived at the boat with the actors, I asked one of them to help me by rewarding her with a treat. (One of those actors, it turned out, was Johnny Knoxville, who would later go on to *Jackass* fame.)

The script called for Gidget to be looking at the three guys for most of the shoot. When she first came upon them, I knew she'd do that naturally, since she'd be curious about these people in a boat next to her. And she did just that, keeping her eyes on the men as her boat traveled toward them.

Hey, what are you dudes up to?

Then I asked one of the actors to feed her the treat from his boat, so that in subsequent takes she'd still stay focused on him. It worked like a charm.

And so went our day, with a happy, agreeable dog doing what she did best. Of course, we did have one bit of excitement. The last shot would take place much closer to the shore, so we drove the houseboat back out there—this time with a wide-awake Gidget taking in all the sights. And while it was the off-season and relatively empty, we noticed that we still had an audience: a lone coyote.

He was a good distance away from where we were shooting (not to mention on land, not water), but his presence was a bit unsettling nonetheless.

"Can coyotes swim?" we asked one another with nervous laughter.

I'm still not sure if they can, but luckily this one did not. He simply wore a curious and slightly puzzled expression as he watched us work—keeping an extra-watchful eye on Gidget.

That looks like lunch. . . . Why is it zipping around on a boat?

By day's end, Gidget had three new fans in the actors she'd worked with. They asked for a quick photo with her before we wrapped, and Gidget was happy to pose with them, her tail wagging furiously as she worked her charm on the men.

Back on land, Gidget stood beside me as I prepared to load her into the truck.

"Bye, Gidget!" called one of the actors. "Great work today!"

She glanced in his direction, gave a cursory tail wag, and sat down at my feet, clearly ready for her favorite activity after working.

Is it naptime?

As often as Gidget had amazed me with her work ethic and drive, this was a new high. She had just spent the day in her own boat out on a huge lake. You'd think a dog would be at least a little concerned. But not this one.

Still, like Moonie and like all dogs, Gidget did have her moments where something scared her. In addition to the light falling behind her, she also got spooked at one of her many photo shoots. *Entertainment Weekly* had named Gidget the "It Bitch" of 1998, and they set up a photo shoot with the famous animal photographer William Wegman, who does those iconic shots of his Weimaraners.

He had his dog Chip on the set, and we posed Gidget next to him, so the shot would be mainly Gidget but you'd also see Chip's leg, giving an interesting size reference in the photo. William was shooting with a rare, oversize Polaroid camera that spit out twenty-by-twenty-four-inch photos. He also worked with strobes for his flash, and in test shots with Chip I was amazed to see just how calm the dog appeared to be. I suppose it's pretty logical, seeing as William shoots his dogs all the time. Weimaraners are hunting animals who tend to have wild personalities, but these big gray beauties just stood there like statues.

We set Gidget up for the first shot and the strobe made a sudden pop, startling her, and she jumped aside. I was surprised too.

"Oh, wow, that was a lot louder than I thought it was going to be," I said.

I quickly went over to Gidget and asked her for a "speak." Just the act of barking is a happy, outgoing behavior, so I hoped it would distract her from being startled by the strobe and get her back to her happy look for the photo.

But Gidget was too smart for that. She barked when I asked her to, but I could see her eyes scanning William and his equipment at the same time.

Yeah, I don't know. I'm not quite sure about this whole deal.

It's one thing at a typical shoot where the photographer snaps picture after picture. But with this particular camera and the way it needed to be reloaded after each shot, it took about ten minutes before we could shoot the next one. That gave Gidget plenty of time to contemplate her next move, so I gave her a toy and tried to get her to be relaxed and playful. When it came time for the next shot I moved to the camera and positioned myself next to it. But as soon as William took his position, Gidget's ears went back as she anticipated the pop, giving her a sad, defeated expression that I can't imagine the magazine editors would have wanted for the layout.

"Gidget, look!" I called to her, holding a bait stick above the camera.

Yeah, yeah, it's all fun and games until that thing goes off again. What, do you think I'm stupid?

So for the next twelve pictures, we had to come up with a way to take the shots without looking like that was what we were doing. So we would start off just standing there, having a casual conversation, and then I'd say, "Hey, Gidget!" Then William would release the shutter and we'd get the shot. Of course, by photo number three, she knew that scenario, so we had to come up with yet another way to trick her into thinking that we weren't taking a photo. Holding her treats over the camera worked for one shot, but that was it. For the next shot, Gidget didn't even pretend to be interested in the treats.

Nuh-uh, I'm not getting sold on that trick again. Last time you held a bag of chicken over the camera, that flash went off! I'll just sit here with my ears back, thanks.

Gidget wasn't going to be ruined forever from the fear of this strobe—it was more a matter of getting a pleasant expression from her, rather than the slightly concerned one she put on when she knew the sound was coming (kind of like the way a person might look anticipating construction sounds in the apartment next door). And it was actually a lot of fun to come up with eleven creative diversionary tactics for William to get his shots. He was as patient as could be and a joy to work with.

A month later, I sent him a thank-you note and asked if it might be possible to get a copy of one of the photos. I didn't really think it would happen, since there were only twelve Polaroids from that day, but sure enough, he sent me one—autographed, to boot—that I have proudly displayed in my home ever since.

But the mother of all scares came when we flew to New York for a special appearance. Gidget had been invited to the New York Stock Exchange to ring the opening bell when the stock for Yum! (the company that included Taco Bell, KFC, and others) went public. She was used to crowds, and she knew the "foot" command well, in which the trainer indicates a spot for the dog to place her paw. So I wasn't too concerned about the job.

We flew to New York City on the KFC corporate jet, and even Gidget seemed impressed with our plush amenities, taking her time to check out the plane and gaze out the window before settling in for a nap. We had told the folks at Taco Bell that we needed a prop podium with a button rigged up to the actual button that rings the bell. But when we got there (delayed a bit by the bomb-sniffing dogs outside who all wanted to meet Gidget), things weren't exactly as we'd expected.

As the traders flooded the exchange floor, I noticed that instead of a protruding button that Gidget could press with her paw, the button was actually flush with the podium, so she'd have to press it in, which was different from what we'd practiced at home. I also didn't count on just how noisy it would be, and when we walked out to the podium I could tell immediately that Gidget was distracted.

So, unlike on a set, I could—and had to—cheat things a little bit. I held Gidget lightly while she stood on the podium and, when we got the signal, we mimicked her pressing the button with a little help from me.

Then the bell went off.

Hearing it on TV does not begin to do this bell justice. It was so loud and so sudden (not to mention covered by a sign, so I didn't even know that it was directly behind us on the wall). Without warning, Gidget surged forward to get away from the bell. It scared the hell out of me, so I can't imagine how much louder and scarier it was for her. Luckily, I had my hands on her, so she wasn't going anywhere. Had the setup been the way we'd imagined, however—with a raised button that she could literally step on—I might not have been standing right behind her and holding her, and one of the traders could have had a projectile Chihuahua on his hands!

Once Gidget settled down (with the help of a quick romp with Mrs. Hedgehog), they had a nice surprise in store for us. Everyone who rings the bell at the New York Stock Exchange gets to sign a book. It's hundreds of years old and all the presidents sign it.

And on that day in New York City, Gidget proudly added her paw print.

Lounging in the sun with Moonie

CHAPTER 10

Kindred Spirits

It's fascinating to watch Sue work. She is so focused on set. She has such a connection and understanding of the animals, and when she's on, she's just in the zone. Sue had the whole set trained, because normally you're done with a shot and it's, "Okay, cut!" And everyone runs around. But this was always, "Cut! Okay, we're gonna remain quiet and take care of the duck." I remember we were downtown and the ducks had their little heated trailer, and our human star, Philip Baker Hall, was like, "Hey, hey! What about me?" I think our ducks enjoyed their work with Sue. They were in a safe, fun place in which they could explore their duckhood, doing things they could—and wanted to—do.

—Nic Bettauer, writer/director, *Duck*

During the course of filming *Legally Blonde 2*, I actually got a moment in the spotlight myself.

In the opening scene, Elle Woods's friends are flipping through a photo album, pausing when they come upon a photo of Elle as a child, holding a bunch of fancy shopping bags. That's me! We were in a production meeting one morning before we started shooting and the art department asked if anyone had a dated photo of a blond child. The next day, I brought in a snapshot of myself at around four years old. Through the magic of postproduction, they digitally added the shopping bags, and voilà! I made it into the movie.

The thrill of my "cameo" aside, we had a slew of other fun scenes and details to film in the sequel (not the least of which was Moonie in his pink pillbox hat, which he did not care for all that much—it took quite a bit of chicken to keep him from swiping it away). For the scene with the Million Dog March, we had about a hundred extras in the background who brought their own dogs, and Reese even brought along her bulldog, Frank Sinatra. Where Moonie was the sole canine star of the first film, he definitely had company in the second, including Leslie, a rottweiler (and love interest) in the movie, who was played by our dog Bubba. He was one of the rotties in *The Fan* years earlier, and he's an absolute sweetheart. I had no qualms at all about having pint-size Moonie interact so closely with him. In fact, for one scene we choreographed a sequence of behaviors to make it look like the two of them were playing together. It was quite funny to watch this big rottweiler lie on the ground while a six-pound Chihuahua jumped all over him!

At home, Gidget and Moonie grew even closer, napping daily in the sun outside on the deck and aimlessly following each other around the house. Their friendship worked to our advantage on the movie too, for one of the final scenes.

The end of the movie called for a reunion between Bruiser and his mom, played by Gidget, so the dogs needed to act excited to see each other. Clearly, this wouldn't be a problem, given how happy they were to be reunited at home after just a few hours apart. Getting Gidget the job was no problem either. The casting process was like any other job, but what sold the director on Gidget was that she already had a relationship with Moonie, so they'd interact very naturally with each other. Plus, she looked like she could be his parent, since she was bigger than him. We brought Gidget down for a little show-and-tell with the director, who liked her, and that was it.

A few days before we were set to shoot their scene, I asked another trainer to keep Moonie at her house until we were ready to go. I kept Gidget at home and didn't bring her to set. Gidget was never the type of dog who absolutely had to have the stimulation of set visits, but now, as she got older, she seemed to care even less about going on adventures outside the house. Napping in the sun was more appealing than ever.

But when the director signaled the start of shooting on the reunion scene a few days later, she perked right up. The actors placed both dogs down on the ground and Moonie and Gidget did their thing as if the cameras and crew weren't even there.

Hi, buddy! Where ya been? Oh, this is exciting; I'm so happy to see you! And you smell good too; what have you been doing, anyway? Wow, I'm so glad you're back!

It was our own little piece of movie magic.

During the course of shooting the sequel, Reese had talked about wanting a French bulldog—a brindle one, to be exact—to join her English bulldog, Frank Sinatra. She had been casually looking, but thus far had been unsuccessful. Reese would have preferred to adopt an animal from a rescue, but this was years before the breed became popular, so there was a shortage of French bulldogs to be rescued.

Reese was so hell-bent on getting this very specific dog that I had to smile. After all, I could relate. So I sought out her assistant and told her that I knew some good breeders and we could probably get Reese a really nice French bulldog. Her assistant thought it was a great idea, so I called a breeder in Oklahoma—one of the best Frenchie breeders out there. She had an adult female on her property whom she was looking to sell as a pet. Oftentimes, breeders will keep their pick of the litter for breeding or showing, but if it doesn't work out because the dog isn't quite the right size, for example, the dog will be sold. Such was the case with this dog, so it was time to find her a home.

After a brief consultation with my bosses, Studio Animal Services bought the dog for Reese and she was shipped to the set a few days before Christmas, just in time for the last day of filming. I put a big bow around her neck and hid her in Reese's trailer. Shelly, the other trainer on the movie, and I camped out in the trailer with a radio and waited for word of Reese's return.

After a good half hour of our hanging out with the young dog inside, the first notice came.

"She's heading back to the trailer!" one of the production

assistants (a.k.a. our spy) announced over the crackling radio. Shelly and I smiled at each other, stupid, giddy looks on our faces. The Frenchie let out a big yawn. The next notice came a moment later.

"She's just a few yards from the door!"

I placed the dog right in front of the door and Shelly and I giggled as we hurried into the trailer bedroom to hide. The trailer door opened and there was just half a second of silence before the big reveal.

"Oh, my God!" we heard Reese yell to the crew who was with her as she slammed the door—without entering—as though there were an apparition standing before her. "There's a French bulldog in there!"

She was absolutely thrilled. Reese named the dog Coco Chanel, and has her to this day. Since the dog was a surprise and Reese was going away for Christmas, I kept Coco over the holiday week. And promptly fell in love with her. She was incredibly cute and very adaptable. The breed wasn't very well-known at the time, but I was intrigued by them. I'd never entertained the idea of a French bulldog (I actually hadn't even seen one before her), but all of a sudden I had to have one. So I called the breeder to ask about the next time Coco's mom would expect a litter. Some Frenchies can get really big, but I loved Coco's small size and hoped to get one just like her. I was in luck—a litter was expected that summer, so I'd be able to get one then.

My Frenchie, Tula, was born on July 4. Like Coco, she was brindle, which is too dark for studio work. When dogs are that dark in color, they don't really show up on-screen. (We'll get calls for black Labs occasionally, but the rule of thumb is that very dark-colored dogs don't work for our business.) But her color didn't matter to me, since I only wanted her to be my pet. Deb and I went to the airport to pick her up. It was a real testament to her personality that, at nine weeks of age and after a flight from

Oklahoma, she was as even-keeled and happy as a puppy could be when we took her out of the crate.

After I clipped a long leash on her new collar, she ran around the airport parking lot, completely cheery and unfazed by the entire process. Deb and I looked at each other and then at the puppy incredulously.

"Really? You don't even care that you were just put in a crate and flew on a plane for the first time in your short little life?"

But that's Tula: always unflappable and totally fearless.

When I got her home a couple hours later, she immediately brought out something in Hank. Mr. Little Personality suddenly had a ton of it around Tula. The new puppy would roll around on the floor with him and he'd lie on his back with his mouth open, making all sorts of strange noises, playing with Tula non-stop until *she* got tuckered out. This wasn't the Hank I knew! But she sparked something in him that brought out his puppy side. It was nice to see him acting so carefree and silly. Pretty soon, they were great buddies. I'd even catch them curled up in a doggy bed together at times.

As far as I can tell, there's no real rhyme or reason as to why certain dogs become friends. It's probably similar to the reason that certain people might be attracted to one another—something to do with their energy and that elusive "click."

After filming wrapped on *Legally Blonde 2*, Moonie continued to book plenty of jobs. He did a Cher music video and several commercials, and he guest-starred on an episode of the TV series *Three Sisters*.

That finished product, however, didn't look a whole lot like what the writers had initially envisioned. I went to a production meeting before Moonie was needed on set, and sat down at a long table with about thirty people to do a table read. As everyone went through the script, I needed to find out why I was there. I had only just been handed a script, so I was frantically trying to skip ahead of everyone and get to the part about the dog. Then someone beat me to the punch and read the scripted dog action out loud.

"And the dog does a backflip."

I'm sorry . . . *what*? A backflip? Moonie? I wanted to ask what planet they were from, thinking that I could train a dog to do a backflip in four days, but I had thirty pairs of curious eyes on me, quietly waiting for confirmation that we could do the scripted action.

I felt like asking, "Did you all go see the movie *Cats and Dogs* this weekend?" Maybe they didn't realize that movies like that are made with a combination of live action, CGI, and puppeteer work. I felt the need to educate.

"When you work with an animal and you're not including CGI or puppets, there's a limit to what you can do. Yes, some animals in this business can do a backflip. But that's because those particular dogs showed signs of agility and the ability to be trained to do such a radical behavior. There's a Jack Russell in Valencia who does backflips, and a poodle who lives at a ranch close by. That's it. Maybe they learned it from doing a twisting leap in the air while catching a Frisbee. Who knows? However they started it, it takes a long time to train. There's just no training it on another dog, unfortunately. If you've got a lot of time, I can try to get one of those two dogs whom I mentioned. But to do it by Friday? With *this Chihuahua*? I wish I could say yes, but it just can't be done."

The room silently processed my little speech on studio animal training. Luckily, they understood—at least enough to rewrite the script and not fire the dog who couldn't do a backflip! They completely changed the story line, and the most complicated thing that Moonie had to do was sit inside a desk drawer in someone's office.

Though I continued to work with Moonie on the jobs he

booked, after the movie he went back to live at the fellow trainer's house where he'd previously stayed . . . so Gidget lost her buddy. She was settling into the routine of an older person, though—kind of set in her ways, and without the patience to deal with a peppy little youngster for hours on end. Besides, she still had Mrs. Hedgehog to keep her company. After several years of being completely and utterly enthralled with that little thing, she never wavered in her love for her stuffed animal. I let her have Mrs. Hedgehog pretty much all the time after the campaign ended, but she still loved it dearly, tossing it around during the day and bringing it with her to bed at night.

As the Taco Bell campaign wrapped up in 2000, Gidget's transition to retirement happened faster than most. Fortunately, she didn't seem to mind.

Gidget did book one more job, right in time for the start of the new decade. She was part of a Trivial Pursuit question and answer in their nineties-edition game, and they did a commercial for it with several of the nineties icons who were featured in the game, including Dennis Rodman, Olympic gymnast Kerri Strug, and the killer from the *Scream* movies. In the ad, they all come out of a buried time capsule, and Gidget just appears at the end, popping out of a little hole in the ground and going to her mark. Kid stuff for this dog, but it was nice to see her book one more job after the Taco Bell campaign was over. Like an actor who gets typecast from an iconic role, Gidget became known as "the Taco Bell dog," so it was hard for her to get work after the campaign ended. But she was very happy to lounge around at home, as much as she enjoyed going out on jobs with me, so I wasn't worried about her early retirement.

Years later, she had another fun TV moment, appearing as a question on *Jeopardy* in 2010. They got her name wrong, unfortunately, but it was still pretty amazing that she made it on the show, in an $800 "pop culture" answer, no less: "Sadly, in 2009, the bell tolled for fifteen-year-old Gigi, a dog of this breed, who gained fame starring in Taco Bell commercials."

After we shot Gidget's Trivial Pursuit commercial, I had to drop some things off at the ranch, so I took her with me for a rare visit in those days. The other trainers were thrilled to see her, even if she seemed more interested in cautiously sniffing Dan, our life-size dummy.

As trainers popped by the training house, wrapping up their days, everyone was delighted to see Gidget, who was hanging out in a pen and would allow them to make a momentary fuss over her before going back to sleep out in her sunny spot in her pen on the porch.

When I'd finished things up at the ranch I called Gidget to head out. She leaped up as I opened the gate to the pen and hurried after me, swiveling her little head around as a few dogs barked their farewell chorus.

I came home that evening to find Beans standing next to the toy bin, looking victorious among the tattered remains of the stuffed toys I'd accidentally left out (fortunately, Mrs. Hedgehog was safe in Gidget's bed on the armchair). I sighed as I bent down to clean up the carnage while Hank and Tula made their way over to say hello. Tula was practically standing under Hank as they stood watching me, tails wagging—a perfect little odd couple. After throwing away the remnants of the toys, I wandered into the bedroom, where I saw Gidget patiently sitting at attention in front of her armchair, gazing up at Mrs. Hedgehog. I laughed and picked up the toy.

"Did you want *this*?"

Gidget wiggled her butt and lifted a paw in the air.

Yes, please!

I dropped her favorite toy at her feet and she hurried off to the living room, stretching out underneath the window with her little friend.

Soon after getting Tula settled in at home, I got a job working on a new movie with Dustin Hoffman, Susan Sarandon, and Jake Gyllenhaal called *Babies in Black*. That was the working title—the film would eventually be called *Moonlight Mile*.

As viewers can tell, it wasn't a particularly animal-heavy movie, but there were a fair amount of scenes for our dog Lady, a yellow Labrador, and our cats. One of the first things we were asked to do was to go to a photo studio in L.A. The plan was to take some pictures with the dog and the actress cast as Dustin and Susan's characters' daughter. Those photos would later be placed in picture frames on the set in the movie.

The director, Brad Silberling, introduced me to the young leading man, who was at the studio for a meeting.

"Sue, this is Jake," he said, and I shook the actor's hand, stifling a grin as he bounded around the set.

"Hi, nice to meet you; I'm Jake. I am *so* excited to be in this movie!"

It was a great sign for the working environment to come—Jake was just as nice as could be and apparently very happy to be there. I'd soon find out that I could say the same for another star of the film, Dustin Hoffman.

The most complicated animal scene we had to film on the movie was with Susan and Dustin's old Lab. The actors played a married couple and their senior-citizen dog has ongoing digestive problems, so they give him his food with Pepto-Bismol. Then, at their home after their daughter's funeral, in a scene where everyone's very solemn, the dog is walking around and the next thing you know, he starts throwing up right in the middle of the mourners.

To make this happen, the special-effects team made a rig that would run parallel to Lady while she stood completely still. I'd ask her to hold a bite stick in her mouth so it stayed propped open, and they made this nasty concoction of soup and mashed peas to use as the vomit. We did a test run with Lady first, and she was a real trouper about standing absolutely still on her mark and holding her bite stick until the "vomiting" next to her subsided.

The other big scene that we filmed was the fight between the cat and the dog, although, like most fight scenes in the movies, there wasn't any actual fighting going on at all. Basically, to make it look like a fight, we trained one of our cats (we had four in the team, all doubling one another) to jump on Lady and stay on her back while Lady spun around in a circle. The latter is a relatively easy behavior to train on a dog—and one that Lady particularly enjoyed. They also had a cat puppet that we strapped onto Lady for her faster spins and shimmies, and they cut between the two in postproduction. Lady didn't mind having the cat on her back whatsoever, because we had plenty of time to train the behavior, so it was fairly smooth sailing when it came time to shoot it.

Little did I know that Dustin Hoffman was carefully watching all of my interactions with Lady and the cats. During a break from shooting one day toward the end of production, he came up to me and said he'd been studying all of the dog and cat action, and noticed that after every cut I would go over to the dog or cat and pay her. (He'd even picked up on our lingo—paying the animal with a food reward.)

"So I was thinking that I should get paid after every take too," he said, and my fellow trainer and I laughed.

But Dustin was serious. He asked his assistant to bring him the tin of Altoids that was sitting on his chair.

"Here," he said, handing me the tin. "I want you to take this tin of Altoids, and every time they call, 'Cut,' I want you to come over and say, 'Good Dustin,' and give me an Altoid. Okay?"

I couldn't help but smile.

"But I'm going to be paying the dog and I won't be able to wash my hands, so do you really want me touching your mints?"

"No, it's okay," he responded with a twinkle in his eye. "Give me the Altoid."

So the next time the director called, "Cut," I did just as he asked.

"Good, Dustin!" I said in a tone far peppier than I use with my dogs. He smiled eagerly and tipped his head back for me to drop in the mint.

Of all the actors I've worked with, I'd definitely say Dustin was one of the nicest. Not to mention the humblest and most entertaining. When we had stand-ins on set while the lighting was being set up, Dustin would sit in his chair and tell great stories. Everyone who wasn't lighting or setting up the shot would gravitate toward him, so he'd be surrounded by twenty crew members while he told fascinating anecdotes.

"So I worked on this movie years ago—you might have heard of it, *The Graduate*?" But he wasn't being cute or conceited; he was just that cool and laid-back. Everyone was mesmerized.

When we had two days left of shooting before we wrapped, I was getting ready to go home to England for my mom and dad's wedding anniversary. Since both of my parents are endlessly fascinated by my job, I decided to put together a video from the set, complete with behind-the-scenes action and some of the training we did with the animals. I was getting a shot of the crew outside of the prop truck and craft services when I noticed Dustin walking to his trailer.

"Hey, Dustin," I called out to him. He turned to face me. Suddenly I worried that, nice as he was, this giant movie star might not want to bother sending his congrats to a seventysomething couple from the English countryside. But I pressed on.

"I'm going home for my parents' fiftieth wedding anniversary.

Is there any way you would say hi to them on video?" I asked hopefully.

"Absolutely!" Dustin replied, and my stress melted away. After asking me for their names, he proceeded.

"Hi, Beryl, hi, John. I understand you're celebrating your fiftieth wedding anniversary. I, for one—just another member of the troops here at *Babies in Black*—would like to wish you a most happy anniversary. And all of us here at the soundstage at L.A. Center Studios, on the last day of shooting, hope with all our hearts . . . that you get a little tonight." Then he winked into the camera and strolled away.

I was pleasantly shocked, as were my parents, who have proudly shown off the video dozens of times to the entire village where they live on the border of England and Wales. The funniest part is that while Dustin is talking, you can see a producer walking behind him with a look on her face like, *What is the dog trainer doing now?* Priceless.

Shortly after *Moonlight Mile* wrapped, I got more heavily involved in a unique area in my career: training animals other than dogs and cats. I found myself routinely training ducks for TV commercials, and, on occasion, a squirrel or two. Tucked away behind the large dog runs at Studio Animal Services are our squirrel cages. They're about seven feet tall, with lots of room for the animals to climb around inside. We have a team of matching squirrels, all hybrid red fox squirrels with big, reddish brown tails that look better suited to a fox than a rodent.

The ducks live nearby in their own run, with a pond that flows through each separate stall. Each duck is housed by himself, since ducks tend to fight when they reach maturity if they're kept in the same enclosed area. And all of our ducks are male—I've found over the years that I prefer to train male dogs (Gidget and Beans notwithstanding, of course—there are exceptions to every rule!); male cats tend to be nicer to work with than females;

and now I have a pond full of male ducks. I also know that horse folk tend to prefer geldings to mares. Seems like a trend to me.

It's pretty incredible what you can get a duck or a squirrel to do on-camera. Over the years, Studio Animal Services has trained squirrels for many a Post-it commercial, plenty of Clusters cereal commercials, and even a "running of the squirrels" commercial that looked just like it sounds.

Training animals like squirrels and ducks sounds like a relative impossibility to most people, but it really is a whole lot like training dogs. Obviously, with any animal, it's easiest to train if you start when he's a baby. But we've had both baby and adult ducks and squirrels at the ranch, and it is still possible to teach an old duck new tricks. Just like dogs, when we're working with these animals, we're using positive reinforcement and a clicker to bridge a behavior to let them know when they've done something right.

But before you can establish what the clicker is, you need to make the clicker mean something, and that requires the introduction of food. So the very first step in this type of training is getting the animal to take food from you. If an animal is too scared to take food from a trainer, then the trainer can't reward him for something he's done right and the training process would be dead on arrival. If I reach in to pay a duck who's done a behavior correctly and he runs away from me, that's obviously not going to work.

When we flew to Japan to do a duck commercial, we couldn't bring our already trained ducks. This was during the avian flu scare, so there were very strict regulations about flying any bird into or out of the country. So instead, we had to train new ones from scratch. These ducks weren't like ours—they'd never had a single training session and were basically wild. So we separated them out into small groups and literally sat with them for a week. We didn't allow them to be free-fed: The only food they could eat would come from us. The other trainer and I simply sat there on little stools in front of the ducks for six hours a day. We each had a cup on a stick with the food inside. Let me tell you, it is mind-numbingly boring to wait for a duck to take a piece of kibble out of a cup so that you can click to reinforce him! For hours on end we just sat, and sat, and sat. If I were at the ranch back home, I could sit there for a while, then go do a few other things and come back and try again. But five thousand miles from home, we had nothing to do but sit. And wait. And we were on a tight schedule—we needed to get these ducks trained! When the ducks finally decided to eat from the cup, we clicked, and they caught on faster than we'd anticipated. It usually happens that way. The proverbial lightbulb goes off in the animal's head and he gets it from that point on. As simple as a duck's brain may seem, they do have the capacity to understand the association between a behavior and the clicker.

I've actually been really surprised with some of our ducks who are a lot smarter than others. One in particular just totally gets it and will do everything you ask. When we shoot, we interchange about ten different ducks, and while some are cross-trained (meaning they do a bit of everything), they all tend to excel at something different. Many of them just do the basic stuff, but the smart ones totally grasp it. As with any other animal, you're just going to have some who are more intelligent than others. The basics for a duck include training him to go to and stay on a mark, and getting him to focus on his bait cup (filled with food) so that when the director wants the duck to look left or right, we have a way to get him to do that. The same basics apply to lots of other animals, like cows, goats, and chickens.

We can also put this kind of training on squirrels—something that shocks most people. We can train our smarter squirrels to come out on a mark and stay, stand up, and do all sorts of behaviors based on our verbal cues and body language. The big difference between squirrels and other animals is that they're not hands-on when you're training them. They can actually be quite snippy. They'll jump on you and bite you at the drop of a hat, so their training is very controlled and precise. We use two trainers at a time, so it might be Deb working the squirrel, with me behind it, holding a catch box.

As soon as we take a squirrel out of the large cage, we put him in a catch box and work him using that tool. If we're prepping a squirrel at the training house, for example, and we want him to go to a mark, stand up, and hold something in his hands, I'd open the catch box. Then another trainer would have a buzzer and a spoon with something tasty like peanut butter and sunflower seeds on it, and we'd bait the squirrel to his mark. The very first thing you do in squirrel training is teach him to eat off a spoon. You can imagine this proposition at first with a wild squirrel.

Yeah, okay, how about I just attack you first?

So when we begin, we put a long spoon through the cage with the peanut butter on it and a clicker on the end. Then we'll lead the squirrels around to different areas, so we get them used to eating from us first, and we click. It's the same thing with a duck—he eats a kibble, we click. And it's usually not long after he's done that the first time that the lightbulb goes off and the duck or the squirrel puts it together. You almost see them think, *Well, this isn't so bad; I just sit here and eat!* In the process, they come to understand what the clicker means. You're clicking at the same time they're eating. Clicking means good, and good means they get a treat.

Next we work on buzzer training, which calls the animal toward a certain spot, where he'll then be rewarded with food. This is used strictly for forward motion. The animal's response to buzzer training is sort of like when you've got a cat at home who's dead asleep in the living room, but the minute you open a can of cat food he runs into the kitchen, because he knows the sound of the opener means that food is coming. It's a conditioned response, and it works the same way with a squirrel as it would with a cat. The squirrel knows when he goes to the buzzer that the food will follow, so we always use buzzers when action is called for. I've used buzzer training with all types of animals, from dogs and cats to rats, ducks, and mice.

After we're finished with a squirrel training session, we send the squirrel back into the box using another buzzer. He gets another little treat for going inside, and then he goes back to his big outdoor run. Training is, of course, a lot slower with these animals than with dogs or cats, because they're animals you can't leash or contain in any way. So you break things down to the basics, like having him go to a big mark—maybe a piece of wood or a box—that he physically has to step on.

With a duck, the process goes as follows: I bait the duck with a cup of the food so he's following the cup (because that's where the food's going). As soon as he steps on that mark, I click, then step in and pay him. My next objective is to teach the animal to *stay* on the mark. With the ducks, to establish a "stay" I hold the cup of food up high, at about shoulder level. It's not very tempting for him to get off the mark to try to reach it the way he might if I were holding the cup at waist level. At the same time, I also take a step toward the duck, since it gets him to pay attention. This works well when I want a duck to stay from a distance. He sees me take a step toward him, and then he stops moving forward. At the same time, I'll hold my hand out in front of me, like I would do to teach a dog to stay. Then I step back, and if the duck stays on the mark, I'll click, then pay. It's really the same with all animals: Once they understand what the clicker means, you're on your way. I'm sure there are numerous ways to teach a duck to stay, but this method has worked pretty well for me over the years.

Another big difference between dogs and wild animals is that wild animals have to be at least a little bit hungry to work. They're working purely for their daily meals, unlike a dog, who might be striving for your praise. For a wild animal, though, it's generally food and food alone. If I've got a big fat squirrel out and I'm trying to get him into a box with a treat, that squirrel is not going to be too agreeable.

I'm not going in that box! I don't care if you've got a walnut in there. I'm going to go explore instead, 'kay?

The misconception, however, is that we starve wild animals in order to train them. The truth is, we just don't feed them breakfast before taking them to set. We very regularly weigh the squirrels and their food, and we monitor the nutrition content of what they're eating to make sure it's got the healthy fat content they need. They end up eating the same amount that they would while being free-fed on the ranch; they're just working for it. It's the same thing with studio dogs—if we're taking a dog to set on a Monday morning and we give him three cups of dog food before we leave, he would want to go to sleep a lot sooner than wanting to work. Placing the dog on a really warm soundstage doesn't help either. It's as if somebody gave you five hundred dollars before going to your job every day and said, "Okay, get to work." Chances are you might lose your motivation to be productive if you were handed that money at the *start* of each day.

And ducks are just the same. While they're working, our birds are weighed on a daily basis to make sure they stay at a working weight instead of just being full and fat. So when I'm working a duck for a commercial I'll take a week before shooting to slowly bring her down to her working weight so that she's motivated to do her job.

My biggest duck challenge came in 2004, when we shot a movie titled, aptly, *Duck*. Shot for shot, it was probably the most labor-intensive project I've worked on, since we had a duck in nearly every single scene of the movie. It's one that I recommend too: a quirky, interesting film about a recently widowed man (played by Philip Baker Hall) who forges an unlikely but poignant relationship with a duckling named Joe.

The writer and director, Nic Bettauer, didn't want any CGI or puppetry, so the movie would be all live duck. It was important to her that the man and the duck relate to each other in real time too—it wasn't through the trickery of editing that the movie came to be.

About twenty ducks played Joe in the movie (starting with little ducklings going all the way up to adult ducks), and we had a great time shooting it. Nic had a bunch of actions she wanted to see, but also totally understood that we'd get the duck to do what we could, and then we'd have to just kind of wing it from there. Our trained ducks can go from point A to point B, and they can stay, but there were also more complicated scenes where we were unsure about how it would all happen. In one, the script calls for Philip Baker Hall and his duck to walk down Hollywood Boulevard together, and it's supposed to look like the duck is picking up trash along the way. So we started off with a plastic six-pack soda-can ring around his foot. When he tolerated that, we attached toilet paper to the ring, and then more and more stuff after that. We had no idea what the duck would do, but he just walked toward me, dragging all this garbage behind him! Since ducks are social animals, if we had one walking from point A to point B, we'd often put the walking duck's buddy outside of the camera range at point B to lure him toward his mark. The saying "birds of a feather flock together" rings especially true here. When we're filming with ducks and we release one to walk somewhere, if he sees another duck, he's going to be inclined to walk in that direction. Like horses, chickens, and goats, ducks are herd animals, so they stick together.

Nic was pleasantly surprised at how much we got out of the ducks. She had initially asked that the duck always follow Philip in whatever scene we were shooting. When I told her on the first day of shooting that it would be easier to have Philip follow the duck instead (with us calling the duck and Philip walking behind him, since that helped us "herd" the duck in the right direction), she quickly adapted and reworked the scenes that way. One of the things that made the movie such a great experience was that Nic was so flexible and willing to accept whatever actions or behaviors the ducks offered up.

Of course, a duck is not a dog, so we had to fudge certain things. Ducks aren't natural retrievers—even less so than Chihuahuas. So with the amount of time we had, if it needed to look like the duck was carrying dollar bills in his mouth, instead of actually training that, we would put the money underneath the duck's beak and attach it with an elastic mouthpiece. Then it's a matter of rewarding the duck for not shaking his head when the money is attached. To get the ducks to travel, I'd use the buzzer to get the movement (and maybe the buddy duck for extra motivation), then click and reward him with a treat.

The real key turned out to be swapping out the ducks for different duties. A duck's stomach is very small, so when they get full and don't want to work anymore, we switch them out. We fine-tuned it even more by identifying the ducks who were very good at staying on a mark, despite whatever distractions might be going on around them. We also found that other ducks were better with more action-heavy scenes. One of the ducks in particular loved to be carried, one was a terrific listener who would really react to Philip, and one was a bit of a wild card. We never really knew what we'd get from him! The crew was an integral part of the process as well, since we were working with flight animals. Anytime a piece of the set or a light was moved, the ducks would want to take off much more than a dog ever would. But I had to ask the crew only once to let me know if they'd be moving anything so I could take the duck off set. After the Taco

Bell campaign, I'd have to give my award for best work environment for studio animals to the *Duck* set.

When we wrapped and I had a few days off to just hang out at home, my dogs were thrilled as could be. I took them for long hikes through the creeks and hills, and they lapped up the attention. By the time I had to get back to the ranch, they were so pooped from all our playtime that they happily slept through my morning exit.

Back at work, my fellow trainer Chrissie had just been to the shelter and found a dog who was about to go up for adoption and she was going to try to get him for us. Everyone at work knew that I was looking for a dog like this one. Years back, I had trained a dog named Scraps who was a little short-haired terrier mix, kind of pit bull–looking in appearance. She was a great dog, supersmart, but she died suddenly at a young age. It turned out that all the organs in her body were either the wrong size or in the wrong place. She wasn't destined to live a very long life, and she passed really quickly without anyone knowing what was going on inside of her. It was very sad to lose her, especially since her passing was such a shock. It was totally unexpected, so there was no way to prepare for it. Since then, I'd told the other trainers that I was looking for another dog who fit the Scraps "mold," in case they were ever out at shelters and saw a prospect who fit the description.

When I returned to work, Chrissie told me about this new dog she'd found, named Reggie. He was an American pit bull mix, probably seven or eight months old, and he had that Scraps look about him. He was thin and looked like he'd been through the ringer, but he was sweet, and Chrissie knew we could fix him up and get some weight on him.

At this particular shelter, people who are interested in a dog will show up the morning that he's set to go up for adoption, and there's an auction of sorts where people bid on the animal.

Sometimes one person shows up, sometimes no one does, but if it's a popular breed or a really special dog, you can get twenty people standing there vying for him. Not all shelters are like that, but I've always thought it's a good idea. The auction proceeds go to the shelter itself and make a better life for the dogs who live there.

Turned out Reggie didn't have any other bidders, so Chrissie got to adopt him and bring him back to the ranch. We cleaned him up, gave him a bath, and took him to the vet to have him checked out. Even though he was being treated for worms, he was gaining weight and things were starting to look up for our Reggie.

When a new dog comes to live at the ranch, we separate him from the other dogs for about ten days, but when it was time for Reggie to join some new friends in a dog run, he took a turn for the worse. He didn't seem to have a ton of energy or want to interact with other dogs—not your typical puppy behavior. This normally high-energy young dog was starting to look very sorrowful and pathetic. I was worried about him, so I decided to take him home for the weekend. That Friday night, I set up a dog bed right at my feet by the couch. I popped in a movie but I kept looking at him and thinking something didn't seem quite right. He hadn't done anything during the day but he was out cold, sleeping really hard for a dog who had not been exercised. I'd pet him and he would barely react. I finally checked his gums and they were very pale, which can be a sign of illness. I even opened up his eyes with my finger but he wouldn't lift his head.

So we piled in the car for the hour-long drive down the mountain to the twenty-four-hour vet. She did X-rays and it turned out that Reggie had a bad case of pneumonia. When the vet saw his X-rays she didn't expect him to live. She told me she'd never seen such bad lungs on a dog, and not to get my hopes up for a recovery.

I drove home that night asking myself a million questions.

Should I have brought him to the vet sooner? Did I see any signs of this a week ago? What else could I have done?

After a fitful night's sleep I woke up and immediately dialed the vet's number.

"He's still alive," the vet told me. "We'll update you with any changes."

After a day of worrying and several more check-in phone calls, my phone rang the next morning.

"Sue? I have some good news for you," the vet began. "We did another X-ray and it actually looks like Reggie's showing some improvement. And his attitude is improving as well. To be honest with you, I am totally shocked. But I think if he was gonna go, he'd have gone by now."

She was right. By Monday, this little miracle puppy continued improving, and the vet suggested I take him home, since he might do even better out of the animal hospital. So that afternoon I left work and picked up Reggie and brought him home. For the next week, I moved around the sleeping arrangements in the house and had Reggie on a bed right next to mine. I'd bring him his food each day and hope that he'd get up, but he didn't. For an eight-month-old puppy to just lie there calmly and not show any interest in his new surroundings was pretty surprising.

But then, slowly but surely, he started to become more alert. A couple of days later I was on my computer in the living room when I saw Reggie quietly walk through the room.

Hey, there. I think I'm gonna get up and go check out the kitchen. . . .

For the next several days, Reggie became more and more curious and adventurous in the house. A week later, he'd almost fully recovered. A few weeks after that, once he was back to his normal self, I tried some basic training with him, but he didn't seem to enjoy the training process. It appeared that he would make a better pet than a studio dog. So I contacted an American bulldog rescue and said I had a mixed-breed. They let me put a courtesy listing on their message board, along with a photo I'd sent in. Just one week later, a woman adopted him.

We still get an annual photo of Reggie at Studio Animal Services every Christmas. Year after year, he looks content and happy—almost like he's smiling for the camera—with his central California family and another bulldog to keep him company.

A retired Gidget gazing out the window

CHAPTER 11

The Golden Years

I remember being excited about photographing Gidget, the Taco Bell Chihuahua, at the height of her popularity. She was megafamous. My dogs were pretty well known too and the thought of bringing them together was sure to be a blockbuster. I would photograph her with the giant Polaroid 20 x 24 camera in Soho. Tiny Gidget would appear within a forest of Weimaraner legs, a kind of homage to Elliott Erwitt. This would be the easiest photo of a non-Wegman dog I ever took. First, the set: A pale backdrop of set paper rolled out over an eight-foot table and brought up to the height of camera, strobe lights above and on either side, providing a safe little cocooned arena for my tableau starring Gidget. The first shot, as is typical with this beast of a camera, did not go so well. The second was bad, too. Gidget had the uncanny ability to anticipate the flash and to move laterally with lighting speed. I got Weimaraner legs but no Gidget. I tried sneaking up on the cable release. I tried having my assistant snap the shutter. I tried every conceivable trick but could not get it. Finally I did get something like the picture I had imagined. It involved an age-old trick . . . which I am not at liberty to divulge.

—William Wegman, photographer

As Gidget happily settled further into retirement, I was settling into yet another new home. After living up in beautiful, far-from-civilization Lake Hughes, I wanted to be closer to work, closer to the city, and mostly not in my truck for three to four hours a day.

Not that my new neighborhood was in Los Angeles proper or anything. My new house—just the second I'd ever bought—was in the Santa Clarita Valley in California in a small neighborhood nestled in a canyon that felt like the perfect hideaway. It was both worlds away from Hollywood and just a five-minute drive to work. My three-bedroom ranch-style home was built in 1953. It was funky and cool, and the vibe really suited me (even if my neighbors had a penchant for throwing all-night parties in their garages). The fenced-in backyard was perfect for the dogs. Plus, the doggy door that led to the secure yard complete with a shallow, inground doggy pool meant free rein for the crew while I was out of the house.

I made the move in August 2007, and by October I felt totally settled in. It ended up being the perfect time to move closer to work for a pretty unfortunate reason: Our area was being threatened by wildfires.

October is the most common month for fires to start. It's been baking hot all summer, and come fall, the dry Santa Ana winds kick up from the desert and blow up to seventy miles per hour in our direction. Everyone who lives in southern California gets nervous when the weather is hot, dry, and windy. The staff at work is on especially high alert, because we have over two hundred animals to evacuate if there's a fire.

Wildfires are such a viable possibility in the fall that every year we load all of our horse trailers with enough crates to transport each animal if need be. To complicate matters, there are days when all the trainers are working on set or on location, so there might be only one office worker at the ranch. We keep the trailers loaded so that anyone can show up (we have a list of friends and trainers who live close by if no one's working at the ranch) and methodically go around putting animals in crates and then drive them off the property.

For the previous few days, we'd been watching a wildfire that was burning north of us slowly head in our direction. So on Sunday morning, several trainers came out to the ranch to put all the water bowls, dog food, leashes, and other supplies into the trailers. The possibility of an evacuation was becoming likelier by the day. The last time we were evacuated from the area we were gone for three days, so we had to prepare for that again.

As we moved supplies from the office to the trailer, I went to check on Frankie and Vito, the two English bulldogs I was still training at the time. The smoke from the hills was making their eyes red, so I decided to take them home for the night for them to be more comfortable. They didn't get along well with my dogs at all, so I'd have to keep them in crates for part of the day, but it was better than risking their accidentally scratching an eye due to the irritation.

Once I got home I put Frankie and Vito in their crates in the kitchen to sleep, and my dogs settled into their beds in the living room, I went to sleep myself. I got the call from my boss shortly after midnight.

"Sue, it's Paul. We're going to evacuate."

That was all I needed to hear to jump out of bed and get dressed in a flash. Having been through a ranch evacuation before and figuring I'd be back in a few hours, I left Frankie and Vito snoring in their crates and my dogs loose in the house. Gidget and Hank opened their sleepy eyes as I walked out the door. Beans didn't wake up, and Tula cocked her head quizzically.

"Be right back, guys," I whispered as I closed the door softly behind me.

Just three minutes later, I reached the end of the road that leads to my neighborhood at the base of the canyon. There was a cop sitting in his patrol car front of me, stopping traffic from coming in. I slowed down behind him and he pulled over to let me through. I drove past him about ten yards when a horrible thought crossed my mind.

What if he won't let me back in?

I reversed, opened my window, and leaned out.

"If I leave, can I get back in?" I asked. The cop replied with a sneer.

"I don't care who you are, where you came from, or where you want to go. You are *not* going back in there!"

I was stunned—not only by his nasty attitude, but also at the thought of my dogs stuck at the house by themselves for who knew how long.

I drove another twenty yards or so and pulled over onto the side of the road to get my bearings and figure out what to do.

Maybe we wouldn't be evacuated for more than just the night, I thought. But what if we weren't allowed back for days? Then, without warning, the cop shined his patrol car spotlight into my truck and got on the loudspeaker.

"I've told you once to move; now *move!*"

Totally astounded—boy, was *he* having a bad day—but with no other choice, I drove out to the ranch and I joined the ten other people working to get all our animals loaded onto the trailers. The fire wasn't imminent (the last time it had literally been a race against the clock to get out of there), but it was definitely heading in our direction. I felt like I was in a fog as I loaded the dogs. Still in shock that I couldn't get home, I felt my mind racing as I mentally went over all sorts of scenarios. But there was really just one option for me: Get back to my dogs.

Once it was clear that things were under control at the ranch, I decided I was going to try to get home through the oil fields. I took my friend and fellow trainer Marissa with me for moral support. I didn't know what that nasty cop might do to me if we got caught, but I couldn't risk leaving my dogs alone for days on end. I simply had to get back.

Just as we were ready to leave, a team of local sheriffs pulled up at the ranch to make sure we were evacuating. I tried to appeal to their soft side, telling them about the mean cop at the end of my road, and how I'd left my home to help evacuate more than two hundred animals, then made my plea.

"Is there *any* way you could drive me the four minutes that it takes to get to my road and get me back in to my dogs?"

No dice. They were nice, but said they were under strict orders to keep everyone out of the canyons. Marissa and I were going to be on our own.

The silver lining, if you looked at the scenario with unabashed optimism, was that I knew these hills and oil fields very well from hiking and horseback riding through them. But what would happen to us if we got caught? Marissa and I sat in my truck in the two a.m. darkness and contemplated our choices. Maybe we could plead temporary insanity if we got caught, I joked to Marissa. I asked her if she thought we should go, and, crazy girl that she is, she answered without hesitation.

"Let's *do* it."

We drove along cautiously, trying not to use the headlights much, except for when we feared we might fall off the road. Marissa and I barely spoke as we strained to make out what was in front of us on the dark road, holding our breath, as though that would make our illegal journey more covert.

Thirty tense, dark, scary minutes later, we finally pulled off the fire road and onto my street with a sense of accomplishment and exuberance. I had promised Marissa she could have whatever alcohol I had in my fridge in exchange for joining me on our treacherous mission. So as soon as we walked in, she made her way to the kitchen and proceeded to drink the rest of my Coronas and then a bottle of wine.

Meanwhile, I was going around the house gathering stuff to pack in case we had to evacuate the neighborhood. Marissa walked outside to the middle of the street in her socks, every hour on the hour, and looked toward the direction of the fire—which now was in the hills on the other side of town, about a mile away. With a bottle of beer in hand, she made her hourly observation.

"Well, I'm no expert . . . but it doesn't look good."

This went on all night until the sun came up. As much as I enjoyed Marissa's hourly proclamations, I figured maybe she was needed with the other trainers to help with all the animals they'd just evacuated. I called Chrissie, who ran the ranch evacuation, and asked if they needed Marissa back. They did.

So we prepared ourselves for one last undercover operation. The main road outside of town had now been closed, and Chrissie and the other trainers were camped out with all the animals in trailers at the end of the ranch road, waiting for the fire to pass. Chrissie would have to drive along this road toward mine (with the mean cop parked at the end) and pick up Marissa, whom I was going to drop off around the corner from the cop. Then my partner in crime was going to have to hike it across some fields to get to the road (that was technically closed) where Chrissie was stationed.

When I dropped her off, I issued one last warning, feeling quite like a character in an action-adventure movie.

"Run, Marissa! And if he shoots . . . just keep on running!"

A tad overdramatic, perhaps, but our traumatic evening and lack of sleep heightened the already tense situation.

Turned out, the fire never got close enough to my area to pose a serious threat, so I was able to stick it out at home. But the people who had left the area weren't allowed back in their homes for over three days as a precaution. So I would have had six dogs—two of them in crates—stuck inside with no food or water for three whole days! If I couldn't have driven through the hills to get home I probably would have hiked the three or four miles back to my house for my dogs. Many people in my area ended up doing just that.

After we settled back in to work postevacuation, I kept busy working on a string of commercials and TV shows. Things were pretty much status quo at home. Gidget slept for about twenty-three hours a day (at times, I've joked, it felt like looking after a plant: She just needed food, water, and sun), but she remained pretty agile and feisty as she got older. Nothing changed all that much about Gidget outwardly, except that her rich tan color lightened up a bit around her face and eyes.

I had been hired to assist a couple of other trainers from another animal company for one week on the set of *Monster-in-Law*, starring Jennifer Lopez and Jane Fonda. We were shooting a beach scene where Jennifer is walking a few dogs, and she has to fall and get tangled up in the leashes. There wasn't much to prep on our part, really. We had the dogs do a "go with" next to Jennifer and run in a circle around her as she yelled and carried on (which would inevitably up the dogs' energy level, adding to the hurried comedy of the scene).

The scene started off well, with the dogs behaving themselves and Jennifer doing her staged trip-and-fall in the sand. But then, as she flailed around, one of the dogs' leashes stretched tightly across her neck as she thrashed her arms. The leash seemed to get tighter under her chin as she let out a gulping sound that sounded more like reality than comedy to me.

"Help!" she shouted in a raspy voice to no one in particular. "Helllp! *Help me!*"

I looked around at the other trainers but no one budged. Why wasn't anyone helping her? I gave it another couple of seconds before deciding that this couldn't possibly be part of the scene— these dogs were inadvertently choking Jennifer Lopez!

I dropped the water bottle I had been holding and unabashedly threw myself in the sand and ripped the leash off her neck before grabbing the dogs by their collars. Crunching on grains of sand between my teeth, I stood up and brushed myself off.

"Cut!" called the director while choking back a laugh, and Jennifer stood to face me.

"Oh, honey," she said with a kind smile as she touched my arm. "I was *acting.*"

Half-embarrassed, half-annoyed, I briskly wiped my hands on my jeans.

"Well, we need to come up with a safe word then, because *help* isn't going to help you if you're really in trouble!"

Shortly thereafter, I was due to work on a set with another big star: Katherine Heigl. For this job, I was working with cats for about ten days on set. Director Rob Luketic, whom I'd worked with on *Legally Blonde*, had contacted Studio Animal Services because he needed a cat for this new movie, *The Ugly Truth*. After we read the script, we suggested a few different cats and he chose our brown tabby team. There were a few tricky things to train in the movie. In one scene, the cat needs to run out of the apartment and up a tree, where he sits until Katherine's character runs out and climbs the tree to rescue him. At that point, the tree branch snaps and they both fall to the ground.

We had a couple weeks of prep to get our team trained, and a wonderful stunt team to help us. Katherine's stunt double, Cheyenne Ellis, enabled us to prep the cat over and over again until we felt comfortable with the action. The cat who made the final cut running up the tree in the movie was named Albert, a fantastic animal whom Deb had adopted from a shelter just three weeks prior. We also had another member of our brown tabby team named Arthur who was very affectionate, so we used him to rub on an actor's leg. Rounding out the team were Sasha and Sebastian, whom we trained to look like they were trying to scoop a goldfish out of its bowl. After some trial and error, we finally settled on placing a thin, empty glass vase inside the bowl with a piece of chicken inside of it. Then the cat (Sasha and Sebastian doubled each other in the scene) would do one of two things: Either he would press his head into the top of the vase so it looked like he was putting his head inside the bowl, or he would put his whole paw inside the vase, trying to fish out the chicken. Either way, it looked like he was up to no good, and Robert loved it.

I've worked on several movies with a small amount of animal action. The biggest movie I've ever been a part of—period—was one such project. The animals are barely noticeable in the final cut, but it was one of the coolest jobs I've ever had. Right when I had started at Studio Animal Services in 1995, they lent me out to another animal company to work on a massive production down in Mexico for a little movie called *Titanic*.

I made three trips down to Rosarito Beach, Mexico, totaling ten wonderful weeks. I spent days on end marveling at the incredible set down there. Fox Studios had built a half *Titanic*, literally. It was nearly to scale, and the details—all the way down to the bolts on the ship's exterior—were one hundred percent accurate. There I was, sitting on a fake dock with two border collies, looking up at the *Titanic*. Amazing.

Unlike most productions, this film was shot pretty much in sequence. We began with the boarding scene, with horses and carriages and people with their dogs milling around on the dock. The assistant directors wanted a few dogs running around through people's legs, so you didn't really see them in the final cut, but those dogs were my charges on the set. Because it was a film by the perfectionist filmmaker James Cameron, the assistant directors insisted that the other trainer, Shelly, and I both be in wardrobe so that we'd blend into the crowd of extras as we called the dogs back and forth. There were not many blondes back then, so they put me in a brown wig to go with my big felt dress and hat. I have a great photo of me with the dogs and the ship in the background—pretty neat stuff for a new job.

And I was told that the dogs they hired for the movie matched the ones who were on the actual *Titanic*: an Afghan hound, a French bulldog, and a fox terrier, among others. There is a scene in the final version where you can catch a quick glimpse of Shelly leading one of the dogs onto the ship.

Later on in the film, in the scene where Billy Zane's character fires a gun, mayhem ensues on the boat, so we trained the dogs to respond to a silent dog whistle and run toward us through the crowd. It wasn't a difficult job, by any means. Our most important duty, really, was making sure the dogs didn't fly off the ship, since there were giant sections missing on the side of the set when the lifeboats had been lowered. It was about a two-story drop down to either very cold water or on top of a lifeboat, so we had to make sure we didn't get too close to the edge with the dogs. Again, this called for Shelly and me to be in wardrobe. Although this time we were made up to look like we were from the steerage section of the ship. Entirely unglamorous! And quite a downgrade, considering that we were dressed as higher-class passengers in earlier scenes.

We also trained the rats that ran up the ship's corridor as it was sinking and the water was rising. We spent days down in a soundstage that was capable of filling with water, training about thirty rats to run from point A to point B. It was a great time and an epic job to be involved in—one that I'll never forget.

Rounding out my busy movie and TV stint in the late 2000s was our work on NBC's *Heroes*. Studio Animal Services did the animal work for the third through fifth seasons, providing and training all of the dogs and other animals on the show. Those animals included our Pomeranian, Lestat (who also did a Canon commercial with tennis star Maria Sharapova), and a tortoise named Elvis who appeared in three episodes.

It was pretty funny for *me* to work on this particular series, since I was such a big fan. I would go on set after watching the first or second episode of the season, but given the shooting schedule on a weekly show, they'd already be filming the thirteenth or fourteenth episode. Once, during rehearsal, I couldn't help myself and actually asked out loud, "He's *dead*?!"

After my Jennifer Lopez gaffe and my plotline surprise on *Heroes*, I sort of knew I was due for a third embarrassing moment (these things happen in threes, right?). We were shooting the story line where they're in Africa and Greg Grunberg is sunburned and facedown in the sand in the desert. Then he's supposed to wake up and see a tortoise sitting in front of him while he has a bunch of flashbacks and flash-forwards. So I'm placing

Elvis the tortoise in front of Greg at the top of the scene, which they were shooting with two cameras. I'm pretty good about asking where the frame line is so I can get off and on the set without appearing in the scene—after all, it is part of my job to figure these things out and not pop up on film!

After placing the tortoise down on his mark, I moved back behind the two cameras. Then, when I saw the camera leave the tortoise, I moved back in to pick him up. It was a really long scene, and I didn't want him wandering back in and getting stepped on. Since he didn't like to be held, I walked over a few yards and put him down, as I'd done for the previous five takes. It's not like he was going to run away, after all. I placed him on the ground, stood up, brushed some dirt off my hands, adjusted my baseball cap, and rested my hands on my hips, waiting for the scene to end.

"Cuuut! Um, Sue? You're in the shot."

There I was, with my blond braids and bright white T-shirt, blending into the background of Africa real well. Seemed they had moved the cameras after the last take and my frame lines had changed. Oops.

"What? Oh, no, I'm sorry!" I yelled as the crew laughed.

"We'll get your close-up later, okay, Sue?" joked Jim, the first AD.

It was probably the first time that I'd ever walked slap-bang into a shot and just stood there! It was almost too funny to be embarrassing, and luckily I knew most of the crew—they were an extremely nice bunch—so no harm was done.

Aside from my flurry of set activity, I was keeping busy in March of 2009 scouting for a new dog. I had recently placed Frankie, one of our two English bulldogs, who wasn't suitable for studio work, in a new home, so I was on the lookout for a new bulldog. I didn't want to get a puppy—the plan was for me to keep the new dog at home, and I didn't have the time for housebreaking and other fun puppy-training adventures. Plus, you get a better idea of a dog's personality when he's older. So I looked around a bit online for an adult bulldog, but it's pretty much impossible to find a purebred in a shelter. If a purebred does show up, the shelters usually call breed rescues to come pick them up to make room for new animals who come through. This is why the average pet seeker will rarely come across a purebred dog in a shelter—the breed rescues (of which there are many) tend to scoop them all up. This is a relatively new phenomenon. I remember walking through shelters years ago and seeing everything from German shepherds to pointers. So the change meant I had to branch out in my search for a bulldog.

After I'd exhausted all the rescue avenues, I turned to the breeders. Occasionally, they will keep an adult dog if they think she'll be good for breeding or a good show dog, and if the dog doesn't grow up exactly the way they thought she was going to, she can end up as someone's pet (like Reese's Frenchie, Coco). I called a bunch of breeders and explained what I was looking for. Since we'd decided that our new bulldog would live with me, I was especially excited to find just the right one.

After several phone calls, I found a breeder named Sue out in Palm Springs who had a few adult dogs. I went out to see them and immediately fell in love with a brindle-and-white male named Serious. He had a great look—totally befitting his name—and a sweet disposition, but he would get so excited that his breathing became really labored. That's pretty typical of the bulldog breed, but it presents a problem in studio work.

"I really like him, but I can't imagine taking him on set," I told Sue. "He's going to get so excited and start panting like crazy and have a heart attack or something!"

Serious looked up at me and stuck his tongue out over his top lip. This was a tough dog to walk away from. He had a smaller, more compact body than most English bulldogs, but a head that was larger than most. And there was something about the way he just sat at my feet, happily looking up at me, almost like he was studying me, that drew me in.

"You can take him for thirty days and try him out," Sue suggested. I took her up on her offer.

Serious got along well with my gang at home, but he never really calmed down. He was so excited every time any of my dogs wandered into the room (or even if I wandered in after all of two minutes being away) that he'd get totally worked up, wearing himself out without doing much of anything.

I called Sue to tell her I didn't think it would work out. I made arrangements to meet her in a couple of days to return the dog. The next day, though, I took Serious to work and decided to try out a bit of training with him, just for the heck of it. I'd been only observing him and obsessing about his breathing, so I never thought to see how focused he was when I had a treat in hand.

I quickly learned that Serious wasn't really an English bulldog after all. He was a German shepherd trapped in a bulldog's body. This dog was so smart and driven to learn that I had to convince him to relax after a training session. To this day, after two hours of working on behaviors, Serious will sit at my feet, gazing up at me, eagerly waiting for direction. I canceled that dropoff with Sue and kept Serious, who settled down at home after his initial excitement at being in a new place, and regulated his breathing and panting. I still have to be careful on set, and we don't submit him for jobs that would have him do anything highly physical outdoors in a hundred-degree summer, but other than that he's worked out really well.

Shortly after Serious's arrival, I got a call from Karin about doing an interview with a local news station featuring Moondoggie. It was about animal trainers in Hollywood and the dogs we train. I already had him at my house for a few days while prepping for a job, so the crew decided to set up the shot with me and

Moonie out in my garden. Then they saw Serious and wanted to include him too, so they got some footage of me with the "new dog in town."

When we shot Moonie's segment outside, Gidget wandered out through the doggy door to check out the scene. Now fifteen, she was almost completely deaf, but there was enough commotion with the film crew's presence that she had decided to come outside to investigate.

As I put Moonie through his behaviors in the sunny garden— spinning, speaking, lifting a paw, jumping into a handbag— Gidget walked right up to us and started dancing around. First she'd sit, then bow, then lift her right paw, then her left. It was as if all her studio behaviors came back to her in an instant.

Oh, yeah, this is familiar. Hey, guys, I can do it too!

She may have been an old, deaf Chihuahua, but Gidget hadn't forgotten all the tricks she once knew, and she was eager to join in with her buddy.

After a rousing twenty minutes of shooting with Moonie and Gidget—who pretty much insisted on being in the segment as well—the film crew wrapped. I saw them out and spent the rest of the afternoon at home with the dogs.

The next morning, I experienced the first of many Serious moments of madness, as I like to call them. He gets quite excited when I'm getting ready to leave. As soon as I sit down at the end of my bed to tie my shoes, that's his cue to do something crazy. He may pick up my shoe and take off with it, or slobber all over my cell phone, or pick up a toy from the bin and shake it like crazy for a solid five minutes.

Fairly soon after I got him, Serious booked his first job—a small part in a Travelers Insurance commercial. The larger part belonged to Chopper, a big, shaggy mixed-breed dog owned by Boone's Animals for Hollywood. Over time, he would become pretty well-known for this spot, as well as for his role in *Pirates of the Caribbean*. Busy guy.

The concept of the ad, featuring the Ray LaMontagne song "Trouble," was that a sweet dog wants to protect a prized possession: his bone. After trying to stow it in the couch cushions, under a rug, in a hole that he digs in the backyard, and even in a safety-deposit box at the bank, the dog just can't seem to relax in the knowledge that his beloved bone is safe (until he purchases Travelers Insurance, naturally). We also subcontracted another dog, Harrison, to be his backup. I was hired as the head coordinator for the commercial, and we had a week of prep time at home. Then my colleague Shelly, Chopper's trainer Mark, and I all headed to San Francisco to shoot.

In prepping the behaviors, we found out what each dog was good at. It turned out that the two things that weren't quite Chopper's forte were behaviors that Harrison excelled at: rolling around on his back and frantic digging. So for the part of the commercial where the dog is rolling around in his dog bed, dreaming about the bone, that's Harrison. The nighttime digging scenes are also Harrison, since he happened to dig with a lot more gusto than Chopper. (The sleeping part is the only piece of that commercial that was digitally enhanced: Harrison's eyes were "closed" digitally in postproduction. We can do a lot of amazing things with studio dogs, but training them to hold their eyes shut *while* rolling around isn't one of them!) For such an action-heavy ad, it's important to have a backup to give your hero dog a break to "save" him, as we say. Harrison fit that mold perfectly.

In the sixty-second version of the commercial (commercials sometimes have a thirty-second and a sixty-second version that both air on TV), Serious makes his debut. In the part where Chopper is riding the bus to the bank, he looks out the window and sees Serious being walked on leash down the sidewalk. It just so happened that Serious licked his lips during the scene, which was perfect for the plot, since Chopper is worried about someone taking his bone. It was almost like Serious knew his role could use a little something extra, so he licked his lips as he lustfully gazed at the bone. He also appeared in the dream sequence. All three dogs were total stars on the set, doing everything that was asked of them in very few takes.

I could tell while we were shooting that it was going to turn out to be a really cute commercial, and I'm so happy that ended up to be true. In addition to getting tons of airtime, the commercial also showed up on YouTube, where it got serious praise from the normally critical commenting crowd—not to mention well over half a million hits.

On the drive back home to L.A. from San Francisco, our motivated little bulldog stood or sat at attention in his crate, very rarely lying down to take a nap. This was a dog who wanted to do nothing but work.

And work he did, very regularly. Serious shot an industrial ad for Toby Keith that aired at the country star's concerts, a Walmart commercial, a Target commercial, and a Pup-Peroni ad, all in a matter of months. The Pup-Peroni photo shoot was probably the cutest, as far as I'm concerned. He and a little girl sit next to each other, both wearing pink tutus, and Serious is holding a sign in his mouth that reads, NO, YOU LOOK THE BEST. His four-year-old colleague on the shoot absolutely loved him—and the feeling was mutual. On breaks, the little girl would throw her arms around him in a big bear hug, and he was as sweet as could be with her. You could see his bulldog wheels turning as he became accustomed to studio work.

Oh, this is fun! I like this job!

Sometime later, Serious made another new friend while sitting with me at an outdoor café near my house. A little girl came over and asked if she could pet him. After a mutual love fest between the two of them—lots of hugging (her) and kissing (him)—Serious sat for the rest of the afternoon staring lovingly at his new friend as she ate dinner with her family at a nearby table. After my ups and downs with Frankie and Vito, I was thrilled to find that this bulldog didn't have a bad bone in his body. And unlike Gidget early on, who I just thought was totally stinkin' cute, I had a real sense that Serious could be a star.

Soon after, I developed a fun rivalry with a trainer from another animal company who also had an English bulldog. Every time I saw her, I'd ask, "So, what has *your* dog done? Because mine just did another commercial—he's got two airing at the same time right now!"

Serious quickly became a favorite among clients too. If they see his picture, they'll usually say, "Oh, he's cute," but if he goes into a casting where he actually meets the client, he gets the job. Every time. For one Target commercial, in which the client wanted a Boston terrier, I brought Serious along to the set as well. As soon as the clients saw him sitting in his crate, they said, "Oh, wait, we want *him*!" Luckily, unlike with actors, no one's feelings (or egos) get hurt in this scenario.

I would easily put Serious among my top dogs of all time to train—right up there with Gidget. The really unbelievable thing is that he's an English bulldog. They're not exactly a breed known for their work ethic.

Back at home, my oldest dog, Beans, was starting to show the telltale signs of aging. She was deaf to the point that a gentle pat on the head could make her jump with surprise, and hikes through the woods were too labor-intensive for my sweet girl. Even after a long walk, she'd sleep for longer than usual and even be a little sore the next day.

While these signs of old age can be hard for pet owners to cope with, in my line of work they're a pretty standard part of the job. I wouldn't say I'm jaded—losing a dog is gut-wrenchingly difficult no matter what—but by this stage in life, the average person may have put to sleep one or two dogs. In my seventeen years of working at Studio Animal Services, however, I've seen dozens of dogs pass away. It's always heartbreakingly sad in the moment (especially when it's a dog who's always lived with me), but after I've lost so many, the aging process isn't debilitating for me. I've had to come to accept it.

Now that she was fifteen, I had prepared myself for the end of Beans's life. I really wasn't sure how much longer she had—other than being deaf and having less than stellar eyesight, she was in good shape. One day I came home and all the dogs greeted me at the door except for Beans. I walked right up to her and she didn't even lift her head. Her breathing was shallow too, and she didn't want to eat dinner. *This is it*, I thought to myself. I put a big blanket on my bed that night and put her on top of it, falling asleep with my hand on her side so I'd know if she was still breathing.

Around three in the morning, I felt Beans stir beside me. Then she stood up, jumped off the bed, got a drink of water in the kitchen, and jumped right back up on the bed. I was thrilled, of course, to see that she was okay. When her last day did come, in the spring of 2010, as awful as it was, I took comfort in knowing that she'd led such a full, amazing life.

Gidget, meanwhile, had also celebrated her fifteenth birthday, but since Chihuahuas can live to be eighteen, nineteen, or even twenty years old, her own passing was far from my mind. She was in great health, never got sick, and hadn't even been to the vet, save for routine checkups and to have her teeth fixed. So I wasn't on the lookout for anything.

One night, around ten o'clock, while I was watching TV, I heard a strange noise in my living room. I wondered if it might be Gidget, doing what vets usually refer to as a "reverse sneeze." It's an odd squeaking sound that some dogs make, but it's pretty common. And I swear, Gidget was so smart that she actually could fake it and use it to her advantage. There were times on set toward the end of the day where she would be like, *I don't want to do this anymore; I've been working all day*, and like a kid who can induce an asthma attack to get out of gym class, she'd do her little reverse sneezing. To which I'd say, "Gidget, knock it off," and we'd go on with our shoot.

So when I heard the sound coming from my living room, I thought, *Huh. Who is that?* though I wasn't too concerned. But the sound didn't stop. I got up and did a quick body check. Hank was in the large dog bed in the living room, Beans was in the bedroom, and Tula and Serious were curled up by my feet. But I still couldn't tell where the sound was coming from.

"Where's Gidget?" I wondered aloud. I walked across the room to the small dog bed tucked between the TV stand and the chair. That's when I saw her. She was lying down with her head twisted at an odd angle, staring off into the distance. I just stood there for a moment, unable to even take in what was happening.

"Gidget!" I shouted. She barely responded to me, just moved her head at a funny angle. I picked her up and brought her to the couch, but the little dog couldn't even hold up her head. She just kept making that odd sneezing sound while staring off into space. That was when I lost it.

All I could think to do was call a friend to pick us up to take us to the vet. I feared the worst—that I was watching Gidget die—but I'd never actually seen a dog pass away before unless he was being put to sleep at a vet's office. I couldn't reach my friend, so I called Karin at home. The call went to her answering machine, so after I got the outgoing message, I started shouting.

"Karin! Pick up the phone! Karin, you've got to pick up the phone!"

After what felt like an eternity, her son Andy picked up.

"What? What's happening?" he asked in a panic.

"Your mom has to come pick me up," I replied. "I think Gidget's dying."

About ten minutes later, Karin was on my doorstep, and she drove us to the twenty-four-hour vet. Karin had seen this before and gently told me what was wrong with Gidget.

"Sue, she had a stroke."

She went on to tell me that when dogs suffer a stroke, they become paralyzed, which explained why Gidget couldn't hold her head up when I found her.

By the time we arrived at the vet, another thirty-five minutes away, my head felt empty. I held my sweet little companion wrapped in her favorite cashmere blanket in my lap. The unusually large Chihuahua felt incredibly slight in my arms as I carried her inside.

Despite my best efforts hoping for the contrary, the vet confirmed Karin's diagnosis. After a few tests to be sure, she delivered the news.

"Gidget is completely paralyzed. We'll have to put her to sleep."

The little dog in my lap made some soft whimpering sounds and I squeezed my eyes shut. I was glad that she was so peaceful and there was very little stress. And I was thankful that I was home when this all happened and could be with her.

When the vet administered the injection, I held Gidget close to me, whispering in her ear. Karin was crying, I was crying, and then Gidget was gone. She was so tiny and frail-looking that I wrapped her tighter in her blanket and asked that she be kept in it, even though she didn't really need it anymore.

Gidget had done well, I thought as I stroked her ear. She made a whole nation laugh and became a pop-culture icon—everyone in America had known who she was. That's pretty big . . . for such a little dog.

Sprig perched on a rock along the California coast in 2010

CHAPTER 12

From Heartache to Hope

It's an awesome talent that Sue shares with all her animals. I have fallen in love time after time with Sue's animals, and I delight in her rapport with them. She just gets it when it comes to studio animals, and I have only seen smiles and coaxing from her during training. No wonder they all do what she wants! Great acting coaches often make a good actor better. A great animal trainer likewise brings the absolute best out of any beast. Sue is a champion for all the dogs.

—Missy Stewart, production designer, *Moonlight Mile,*
Legally Blonde 2, and *Win a Date with Tad Hamilton!*

I sat in the stifling silence of the vet's office, mentally retracing the last few weeks. Gidget had been completely normal. Just her usual self: sleeping, eating, and strolling around the house with the other dogs. She didn't show a single sign of illness, and then suddenly, without warning or any time at all for me to prepare, she was gone. Running my fingers across her collar, I reminded myself of how grateful I was to have been with her when it happened. I could have been on set for a sixteen-hour day while Gidget just lay there, paralyzed and helpless. Or I could have been on location and a dog sitter would have had to deal with the whole thing.

But above all else, I felt so thankful that it was fast. The last thing you want is for your animal to have a long, drawn-out, miserable illness. I felt like I'd lost a best friend, and the pain was excruciating, but I still knew this was the most ideal scenario I could have hoped for.

After everything was wrapped up at the vet's office, we drove all the way back to Valencia in silence. I gazed out the window, thinking about the big, full life that Gidget had lived, even smiling a little through teary eyes as we drove along.

When we pulled up at my house, I thanked Karin and opened my gate. Just as her car disappeared down the road, I realized I'd left my keys in the house when we rushed out to get Gidget to the vet. Karin was gone, and I didn't have my cell phone on me, so I rooted around in the yard a bit, trying to remember where I'd left my spare key.

The other dogs had convened in the window, watching me search. Serious danced in place, clearly ready to dive into a training session, while Tula and Beans gazed longingly at me. Hank let out one low, gruff bark.

Are you gonna come in or what?

Finally, I found my spare key and let myself in. The dogs swirled around me, leaping and licking and welcoming me back home. I wondered what they had thought of Gidget's last moments.

I fell into bed, exhausted, and let sleep take over. In the morning, I glanced over at the chair with the dog bed—Gidget's dog bed. Gidget's dog bed that was now empty and cold. I could have stayed in my room and cried for hours.

Still, I had to get up and go to a TV show job with Serious. We had been hired by another animal company to do an episode of the Disney Channel series *The Suite Life of Zack & Cody*, and I was due on set that day. I didn't really want to go to work, but I knew it was probably the best thing to do. If anything could lighten my mood a bit it would be a funny, entertaining, incredibly smart bulldog.

I walked into the kitchen to get the coffee started and the dogs scrambled and climbed over one another to get to their bowls, more than ready for breakfast. I scraped my hair up into a ponytail, and as I reached for the bag of dog food, I found four—not five—dogs gathered together. I swallowed hard as I took out the bag, feeling a sharp stab of pain now that I could physically see that Gidget was gone.

After everyone was fed, I sat down and e-mailed a friend at a celebrity Web site to see if she could post a little tribute to Gidget online. Within an hour, the story was up.

"She charmed millions without ever saying a word," the story began, and I felt myself tearing up again. But before I could really get going or even keep reading, the phone rang.

"Saved by the bell," I said to no one in particular as Serious rested his big head on my foot.

That phone call, and the next several calls after that, were all from reporters from newspapers, magazines, and Web sites, wanting to do interviews with me about Gidget. I was shocked. She hadn't been on TV in several years, but the world seemed to be reaching out to me, wanting to memorialize Gidget in print.

By the end of the day, the Associated Press had picked up that first online story, and the Gidget tributes were piling up online. I went to bed early that night, having been up for most of the night before. My dogs all seemed to go to sleep as usual, and I was happy that they weren't feeling Gidget's loss the way I was. I think that when just two dogs live together and one of them passes away, the surviving dog might feel the absence and look around the house for his friend. It's a heartbreaking effort for the owner to see. But with my lifestyle and the revolving door of dogs who come in, plus all the full-time residents, my crew didn't seem overly upset by Gidget's absence.

The next morning, I fed the dogs breakfast, still feeling that ache of loss deep in my chest for the dog who should have been with us in the kitchen. Then I sat down at the computer again and did a search for Gidget. I was shocked by the results. CNN, ABC, NBC, and all the other major networks had done a story on her, as did countless newspapers and blogs. I clicked and clicked and clicked through the Google results, thinking after each page that it couldn't go on much longer. But it did. By lunchtime, I was on the twentieth page of results, and I was getting hits on people's personal blogs, which really amazed me. One wrote, "The Taco Bell dog died! I loved that dog." And a story would follow about this person's memories of Gidget. I knew people liked her, but I couldn't believe that so many cared this much.

In the days that followed, tributes popped up everywhere from Letterman's and Leno's shows to *The View*. And all at once, I felt compelled to put my own memories of Gidget out there too. The American Humane Association wanted to post a first-person story from me about her life. So I took to my laptop and just wrote and wrote. And with every recollection that I shared, my smile grew wider and wider. I wanted people to remember everything about Gidget that I did. I started it simply, with my own personal estimation of the little Chihuahua with the very big presence.

Gidget was a star. She truly enjoyed being in front of the camera; that's where she came alive. She was a consummate professional on the set, and she won the hearts of her directors and crew. During her days on the Taco Bell shoots, no one was allowed to talk, move equipment, or walk around. You could hear a pin drop when Gidget walked, off leash, onto the soundstage. She would trot over to the raised set, move through the crew, and find the camera—and nine times out of ten, she'd be sitting or standing in front of the camera before I caught up with her! She commanded attention, and everyone who met her fell in love with her.

One of the reasons Gidget was so comfortable and confident on set was that I treated her like a big dog from the very start. It's so easy when you work with small dogs to just pick them up and carry them around, but I made sure Gidget walked everywhere. She definitely had a big-dog attitude.

Gidget loved Moondoggie, the Chihuahua who played Bruiser in *Legally Blonde 1 & 2*, so it was a fun shoot on *LB2* when they both worked together, especially at the end of the movie, when they reunited. We kept them apart for a couple of days so they would greet each other and play naturally. It was a sweet scene, and you could totally see how happy she was to see him.

The most challenging aspect of working with Gidget was cold weather. Chihuahuas need warmth, and this was a dog who could sunbathe in hundred-degree heat and not pant! Working with her on the Taco Bell/*Godzilla* campaign on Wall Street in Manhattan when it was two a.m. with snow flurries was the absolute worst. She had sweaters and jackets and booties and microwave-heated disks that went inside a fleece sleeve she lay on, and we had huge jet-engine-type heaters that blasted heat in her direction, and of course she had her own heated trailer, but we made sure that the time she spent outside was very limited. Her "look" was very important to the campaign, so if her ears were slightly back or to the side, the shot wouldn't work; having her ears perked up and forward was the ideal, and for that she had to be happy!

Gidget's life was full of adventure, from riding in limos to flying on Taco Bell's private jet and staying at the finest hotels (where she loved to scoot at lightning speed up and down the long hallways) to gracing the red carpet at movie premieres. She rang the opening bell for the New York Stock Exchange and added her paw print to the hundred-year-old book that has been signed by U.S. presidents, dignitaries, and thousands of celebrities who have also rung the bell. At one Taco Bell convention, Gidget walked onto a vast stage in a huge stadium all by herself to meet R2-D2 from *Star Wars*. She hit her mark perfectly, stayed there while the robot talked, then exited on cue while thousands of people cheered and applauded. Gidget also held her own when she was set adrift in a Chihuahua-size remote-controlled boat on Lake Powell for a Taco Bell shoot. It was all fun to her, and she loved every minute of it. Gidget's fame extended to articles in *People* magazine, *Entertainment Weekly*, *USA Today*, *Advertising Age*, and many other publications. She was photographed by the best:

The directors of photography on her Taco Bell shoots included Jeffrey Kimball (*Top Gun, Mission Impossible II*) and Guillermo Navarro (*Pan's Labyrinth*), and her still photographers included William Wegman, who shot her alongside one of his famous Weimaraners. She was featured in a question in the 1990s version of Trivial Pursuit, and celebrities . . . were just as excited to meet her as their own fans are to meet them.

There will never be another Gidget. Everywhere she went, she stole hearts and made people smile. Her star will shine forever. . . .

When I returned to the ranch a couple days after Gidget's passing, I was hoping for some distraction. But the shocked faces and condolences from my fellow trainers made it hard to think about anything else.

Serious had done a good job on the *Zack & Cody* shoot for Disney over the past couple days, which was a nice focal point for me. He shot one funny scene in which a bunch of people are changing into different things, so one of the kids in the episode actually changes into a bulldog. He had a lot of action to do too. He would run to a mark, travel from point A to point B behind some scenery, and do a beg up (standing on his hind legs with his front paws in the air, which most bulldogs can't do, thanks to their anatomy), so it was a perfect job for me at that time. Serious is such a fun and funny dog to work with that it helped lighten the mood for me a bit. And it made me excited for his prospects too. By nature, bulldogs tend to be bossy and dominant, but this German shepherd–slash-bulldog was anything but.

Trying to get Serious to cock his head on this particular job was really quite amusing. To get a dog to do this, we use a noisemaker or whistle like hunters use—one that actually sounds like certain birds or deer—and we use them behind the camera so the dog will look in the direction of the sound. Since they don't really know what the sound is and they're trying to figure it out, many dogs will just naturally cock their head to the side.

Some dogs do this quite well and it gives them that cute look on a job. Chrissie has two Dobermans and she's trained them to do the head tilt when she says, "Do you wanna go to PETCO?" At this point, all she has to say is, "Do you wanna" and their heads snap to the side! But what many people (and directors) don't realize is that this behavior is not always something you can train. Either an animal will do the head tilt or he won't. Whenever a director wants a dog to look cute, he'll say, "Oh, get him to cock his head!" But if a dog doesn't do it, there's nothing we can do. It's sort of like people rolling their tongues—they can either do it or they can't. There's no training or practicing; it's very black-and-white. And it's the one thing that Serious cannot do. But no one holds it against him. He's so good at so many other things.

When we wrapped the *Zack & Cody* job, I brought Serious home, checked in on the other dogs, and sat down on the couch to call my sister and catch up. I hadn't dialed the first few numbers before Serious reappeared at my feet. He looked up at me, then sat down definitively, like he was tucking in for a training session.

Okay, I'm here. What's next?

I put down the phone.

"Relax!" I said, taking his face in my hands. "Go lie down."

But Serious just licked at his nose and shifted his weight, intent on being productive.

"You're not on right now; we're not working," I said with a laugh. After Gidget finished a job, she'd look around like, *Where's my dog bed? When can I sleep?* But not this guy. Serious wants to work *all* the time.

So I made my phone call, and eventually Serious gave up and went to find someone to play with him. That someone was usually

Tula. Serious and Tula quickly established a brother-sister type of rapport. There's a lot of competition between them, and they often feel the need to play with the same toy at the same time.

As I chatted with my sister, I watched out of the corner of my eye as Serious and Tula eyed a bright blue squeaky toy in my bedroom, then each other, then the toy again. A moment later, they both went for it, each grabbing an end, and took off running into the living room. The bedroom is the only room in my house that's fully carpeted, and they seem to know they can get good traction in there. So this silly little caravan of bulldog–squeaky toy–French bulldog would come careening toward the couch, then rebound off of it to run back toward the bedroom, the dogs shuffling in place for a moment on the slippery wood floor before getting their paws under them to bound back onto the carpet.

Meanwhile, Hank was completely oblivious to their antics, lying stretched out on his side by the front door, gazing outside and letting out a big, contented sigh every now and again. Beans was equally unconcerned with the ruckus in the house, snoozing in the corner where Gidget used to sleep.

When my sister and I hung up, I walked over to Serious and Tula, who were now lying on the wood floor, both still holding the prized squeaky in their mouths. (Okay, I guess Serious *can* be a little bossy from time to time!)

"Hey, Tula . . ." I said, and she jumped to her feet. Serious, suddenly overcome by the urge for water, scrambled to his feet as well and trotted into the kitchen. He's a fairly small bulldog, but when he trots by you, you can actually feel the floor shake a bit under his sturdy body. And he loves to barrel through the doggy door headfirst—my boss Paul says it's like someone throwing a bowling ball through the doggy door.

"Tula," I said again, and she gazed up at me. "Tula, shake it up!" This is my little girl's top trick. Give her that command and she'll pick up the nearest toy and shake it mightily, tossing her head around furiously while making her signature grunting and oinking sounds. She's even got one noise that sounds like a dolphin call that tends to come out when she roughhouses with Serious!

I walked into the kitchen for a glass of water and heard the clatter of bulldog paws on linoleum behind me. And there Serious was, looking at me, then at the doggy treats, then at me again.

Is it my turn now? Are we gonna work?

I laughed, thinking about how much this dog was aware of my every little move. For her whole life, Gidget never really had any sense of whether I was in the kitchen or somewhere else in the house, unless it was mealtime. *Who cares?* I imagined her thinking. *I'm sleeping in the sun.*

Since he was here and focused, I decided to put Serious through a quick round of his behaviors. I asked him to beg up on his hind legs, spin in a circle in both directions, and hike his leg up like he was peeing.

I watched Serious's brain working overtime on the last one. He'd practiced this move with a prop, since dogs use this behavior in studio work to mock peeing *on* something, not just into the air. So I signaled him over to the leg of the table and he happily hiked up a hind leg.

Ah, yes, this'll do just fine.

We finished up working on his retrieve. I had him hold a dog bowl, some keys, and even a bag of dog treats. He eagerly grasped each one in his teeth, breathing noisily through his nose and gently holding his mouth closed as he looked to me for the next move. He even showed off for me a bit, hiking up one leg toward the coffee table while doing his retrieve, and then raising a front paw in the air like he was waving. When this overachieving dog works, his whole demeanor changes. It's like he's Business Serious, sitting at attention like a round little soldier, forehead wrinkled in thought.

As I straightened up the living room, the scratched-up coffee table caught my eye. Serious likes to wash his paws at least once a week (the only body part he can reach, thanks to his stout build!), and he methodically props each leg up on the table to lick them, one by one, as if his alarm had just gone off to remind him of the weekly practice.

It's time to clean my feet!

The constant propping scratches the table slightly, but he's such a good dog that I figured any minor coffee-table damage was just the price I'd have to pay.

As much as Serious loves working, he tends to be a little con-flicted in the mornings when I get up early for a job. Sometimes I'll try to gauge whether I should bring him to work with me. I'll be dressed and ready to go before the sun comes up, and say, "C'mon, let's go!" But on some days he won't move a muscle. I think I'd be a little concerned about this workaholic bulldog if he didn't ever want his downtime too. It's nice to have that balance of *I'm working* and *I think I'll sleep a little longer, thanks.*

After a full day on set, while Serious and the rest of the crew stayed home, I returned to find an all-out massacre in the living room. Every corner of the coffee table had been gnawed beyond recognition, and Serious, who'd clearly forgotten about his handi-work earlier in the day, happily greeted me at the door. I was beside myself. It was as if he said, *Today is the day I'm gonna eat the coffee table.* And that was that. It had been a year since I had found him in Palm Springs, and we never had a single chewing incident. Then, suddenly, the coffee table was gone!

The next morning, I tossed four leashes into the car and took the dogs out for a long walk to burn off any excess table-eating energy. It had been a while since I'd been up in Lake Hughes, so I set off on the drive to take advantage of the nice day. I walked the dogs down a ravine into the small, shallow river that crops up in the fall. Even at a slightly wobbly sixteen years old, Beans was happy as could be to traipse knee-deep through the water. Not a care in the world. Tula, meanwhile, launched her own one-dog lizard-hunting excursion, while Hank proudly forged ahead in front of the others through the rippling water.

And Serious? This was his first time ever seeing something like a river, and he eagerly dunked his big head into the water with the same abandon with which he barrels headfirst through the doggy door at home. I pointed to a big rock and called him.

"Serious, go to your mark!"

Then, in a move that most other bulldogs could only dream of performing, Serious leaped out of the water and onto the rock, paws sliding a bit on the slippery surface as he bravely arranged himself on the perch. Whether it's having them land on a mark or just retrieve a stick, I always try to engage my dogs (the studio ones as well as the pets) in this kind of play while we're out and about. It stimulates them in a way that plain old walking never will, and it's fun for all involved.

Back at work that Monday, I got a couple pieces of good news: I'd be working for another animal company with a Studio Animal Services dog on an episode of *Ghost Whisperer*, guest starring Cesar Millan. And, the Jack Russell puppies I'd chosen for studio work were just about ready to be picked up from the breeder.

On the set of *Ghost Whisperer*, I was pretty excited to meet Cesar Millan. I truly believe that people across the country are walking their dogs a whole lot more because of him. It's a simple, ingrained concept to me that dogs need to be walked—after all, that's what dogs do—but this simply isn't the case with many pet owners. People tend to just think, *I have a big backyard; the dog can run around in there.* Of course, as Cesar has shown us, they couldn't be more mistaken. I think it's great that he's helped pet owners to see that their dogs need to get out of the yard and get walking on a leash.

For his scene in the show, Cesar plays himself, autographing books for fans. The dog in the scene plays a ghost that belongs to Jennifer Love Hewitt's character. We used Dallas, a black-and-white border collie mix, and he had to enter, hit one mark, and stay. Then, minutes later, he had to get up off his mark and walk behind Cesar to another mark without my jumping into the scene—pretty standard stuff. Dallas did all his behaviors perfectly. I paid him and snapped on his leash to walk him through the crowded back set to the crate room. On my way, Cesar stopped me.

"What you did was *really* hard!" he said with an admiring smile. I grinned in response and thanked him. I think that was the first time in all my years of training that someone truly appreciated how much work goes into training a studio dog to do those types of simple behaviors. And it was coming from the Dog Whisperer, no less!

A few days later, I worked a job in Mammoth, a ski resort about five hours outside of L.A. This was a particularly fun job because it involved something I'd never done before—training a goat to slide backward down a very small bunny slope on skis for a Capital One commercial. We prepped for the commercial in L.A. first, which was a true work in progress. The first thing we realized was that the skis had to be attached to each other, because it would be too difficult for the goat to balance on two skis. So we attached the skis with a bar that viewers wouldn't be able to see in the final commercial. Then we built ski boots around the goat's hooves so that his center of gravity stayed low, right over the skis themselves. And to prep the goat for what was to come, we built a ramp with Astroturf and a pulley system to lower him down, mimicking what he would do on an actual ski slope. Our goat knew how to stay on his mark (the skis) while we pulled him, and I was stationed at the bottom of the ramp with his food bucket. That way, he was focused on the food, and not on the skis, so all he had to do was stand still. Once we arrived in

Mammoth we prepped him again on the actual snow and he was just as good as he'd been back in L.A., and the commercial turned out to be really funny.

Since I was halfway up the state for the Capital One job, I decided to leave Mammoth once we were wrapped and head over to Yreka, California, to pick up the Jack Russell puppies I'd selected from a breeder for Studio Animal Services. Jack Russells can be tricky in terms of getting the look and temperament that you want, and without any solid breed-rescue options, I decided to go the breeder route.

I got them at about eight weeks old and they were just too cute for words: brown and white, tiny, with smooth coats and sweet, loving personalities. I figured that at least one of them would end up living with a different trainer. For now, though, I wanted to keep both of them with me for the first four or five months so I could monitor their behavior.

By the time the puppies—whom I'd named Sprig and Decoy—turned twelve weeks old, they were pretty much hell on wheels. Nothing tired these two out. I would take them out hiking for miles and it did nothing but build their endurance, like I was conditioning them for a marathon or something. I'd get home after a big, two-hour hike and think, *They're going to just pass out, they'll be so tired.* Instead, they'd be like, *Wheeee!*, running around the house with such enthusiasm that Serious and Tula looked worn-out just watching them. I could hardly believe they were still awake, let alone tearing around my living room.

Before long, their exuberance turned to puppy play-fighting, and when that became part of their daily routine, I decided it was time to split them up. Rather than have them become enemies, we had Decoy live with another trainer while Sprig stayed with me. I couldn't help myself—he was my favorite.

As I continued taking him on long walks through the canyons, I noticed what a personal connection this puppy had with me. Whereas Decoy would happily trot on ahead, making his own way, if Sprig got more than ten feet in front of me, he'd always turn back and look in my direction to check in. He wanted to be with me and interact. Sprig engaged with me in a way that almost reminded me of Gidget.

But unlike my other dogs, Sprig has a way of making me throw my rules for dogs out the window. I have a white couch in my living room—*white!*—and simply because he's so cute, I let Sprig nap on it all the time. His favorite spot to fall asleep as a little puppy was burrowed between the couch frame and the pillows, upside down, with all four paws in the air.

He quickly showed me how smart he was for studio work too. At home one night, I was doing the dishes and watching from a distance as he got up and grabbed his tail, like he had an itch.

"Goooooood!" I praised him, thinking of the behavior "get your tail" that I would train him to do at some point. He froze immediately, stopped what he was doing, and looked at me. It was as if he was retracing his steps and thinking, *What did I last do?* Without dropping his eye contact with me, he slowly moved his head back toward his tail, as if to ask, *Was this what you praised me for?* I couldn't believe it. Was this dog *that* smart?

A quick, fun, ten-minute training session later, and I had Sprig getting his tail and circling on command. Other trainers would stop by at the ranch and marvel, "*How* old is this puppy?" It was really exciting, and I got my hopes way up for him. It also gave me a good kick in the pants. Training animals day in and day out can, at times, get a little repetitive. But a dog like Sprig comes along and all of a sudden all you want to do is train. So just like I would take Gidget with me everywhere when I wanted to get her used to all sorts of people and environments, I began taking Sprig with me in my travels. I brought him along on one Friskies commercial that I worked, and put him and Decoy on a chair between takes to keep them from wandering off. I smiled to myself, seeing just how intent they were.

Ohhh, we're gonna do something! She's got food!

Since Sprig was acting pretty excitable, I decided to try to work on his "speak." At one point, I blew lightly on Sprig's face and he looked at me and barked. I clicked right when he barked and paid him.

Hmmm, what did I just do? Whatever it was, I got a treat for it . . . so I'll try it again.

"Good!" I said, and rewarded him when he barked again. Then his stature changed and he sat up proudly.

I can do this!

And thus, Sprig's "speak" was born.

It was the perfect example of a lightbulb learning moment. Even at just a few months old, Sprig understood that the clicker meant he'd done something right. A few days later, I trained him to do the "hide your eyes" behavior with a piece of tape on his head. It took all of five minutes.

On another job, I took Sprig onto the set for a lighting setup. I figured it would make a good training session. Since I knew the crew and the director, I also felt confident that it would be a good experience for the puppy overall. As the crew adjusted the lights, Sprig just calmly took it all in. The production had a huge piece of material that made crinkly noises, which they were setting up to create a softer light. This might have been disconcerting to some dogs, but Sprig just gazed at it happily. His tail didn't stop wagging the whole time. Every now and again he would get excited and want to stand up to check something out, but Karin, who was the other trainer on set with me, would walk over and sit him back down. Still, his focus and work ethic on that set were like a glimpse of Gidget all over again.

As of this writing, Sprig is still a puppy and has just started booking jobs. There might not be a way to tell for sure whether a dog will be a star, but I think he's got as much of a chance as any dog.

Not that I think he'll be the next Gidget. I hope he'll get a big feature film or a TV show or something. He's got Decoy too, so the dogs can easily double each other. Sprig's face is a little darker, but there's a powdery "dog makeup" we can use and they'll look almost identical.

But no dog since Gidget has truly reminded me of her; nor do I think there can be another phenomenon quite like Gidget. Not since the Taco Bell dog commercials has an ad campaign risen to those levels of pop-culture phenomenon. And personality-wise, no dog since Gidget has been as relaxed and mellow as she was, but equally focused when it came time to work.

I admit it would be nice to have another dog who's as special and iconic as she was. Still, the Taco Bell dog was a truly unique result of creativity and personality, and I'm not sure it will happen again. At least, not with the same magic that Gidget brought to the camera.

The Christmas after she passed away, I brought her ashes to Las Vegas to my sister's house. She has a jewelry-making hobby, and she put together a unique fused-glass pendant for me. We put a tiny piece of bone from Gidget's ashes between pieces of glass and then put the whole thing into the kiln, fusing them together. Then she melted some ash in another piece of glass and strung both onto a necklace.

I wear the necklace often, and I think about Gidget even more. On sets, at the ranch, at home, when I'm with my dogs—she's never too far from memory. Every time I put on that necklace, I know that I'll always carry that little star with me, wherever I go.

ACKNOWLEDGMENTS

Mom and Dad, thank you for encouraging me and supporting me every step of the way, while I'm sure you were wishing I'd stayed a little closer to home. Sunday afternoons with you were country drives with picnics, visiting stately homes with their magnificent gardens, and even local garden centers became amusement parks—I didn't need Disneyland. I had gardens, forests and woods—usually with our dog. Because of this, I am sure I have a better appreciation of every beautiful thing that has ever come into my life.

My sisters, Pamela and Julie, my biggest supporters and cheerleaders: You paved the way for me taking off to the States when I was nineteen! Thank you for believing in everything I do.

My best friend, Deborah Dellosso: We started this journey together, and seventeen years later we stand strong! Well, we're standing, not sure how strong we are anymore! I don't know if I would have lasted this long without you. To the Dellosso family, thank you for always welcoming me into your homes.

To Kim Bonham, for all those years of powering out our visions.

Thanks for believing in mine; now it's your turn. And let's find a home for those sweaters! www.terrahues.com.

Victoria Vopni, your opinions are always refreshingly funny and honest: You make me laugh, even at the most inappropriate of times, like on set, when you are telling the director that you think the shot looks just fine and he doesn't! You know which job I am talking about!

Paul Calabria, thanks for taking me on as a volunteer all those years ago, and to Karin for training me and making me stand in the way on set for all these years so they can't put a flag or light where I need to work. Seventeen years later I still refer back to all the little things you taught me in those first few years at Studio Animal Services.

To Doris Hall, thank you for having that little brown puppy in your office.

Thanks to the Ashcroft family, where my real adventure began, and the reason this all has happened. My life would have been very different without every single one of you.

To Rennie Dyball, thanks for suffering through my edits. I'm so glad you had the opportunity to meet Gidget. This union was definitely meant to be.

To Mollie Glick, my literary agent, thanks for being the one person other than myself who saw a great story about a wonderful little dog.

To Danielle Perez at NAL, a big thank-you for your expertise and for being as much of a dog lover as I am! And to your entire team that has worked so hard to make this happen.

To all my favorite directors, producers, actors, and trainers: Working with you is just like Oprah said: Find something you love and get paid for doing it. I am doing it.

To all the directors, producers, actors, and trainers who are not such a joy to work with: It still beats working in an office.

Thanks to Reese Witherspoon, Steve Loguidice, Patty Grubman, Jami Lavullo, Gina Johnson, Alan Ball, David Alan Basche, Nic Bettauer, Buzzy Cancilla, Charles Herman-Wurmfeld, Rob Lorenz, Kristina Rivera, Chrissie Tomas, David Meyers, Megan Valinote, Missy Stewart, Jeanine Barry, Marissa "Slacker" Schwierjohn, the boys at Jet Sets, Brian Lee: Dog trainer extraordinaire, Ken Kalin, Barry Boxall, Matt Edwards, Travis Bauer, Rachel Bati, Margo Keeping, Jackie Sparke—one day we'll get back on that damn boat, Val Treanor and John Hollitz.

To all the freelance animal trainers, and trainers from other companies: Thanks for that jolt of inspiration and renewed desire to train from being around fresh blood. I try to soak up all your knowledge and different approaches to training every time I'm around you guys.

Thanks to Oliver Wilson, Lauren Duda, and Alex Duda. Bryce Carroll-Coe, you made me change my "list," and damn it, "I know your mom" (Gail Carroll-Coe).

Jane, Fergus, Joseph and Ellie Ahern: miss you, love you. To Sue Rhodes Calhoun, thanks for Serious. To Hans and Nancy Aberg, thanks for Sprig and Decoy. To George Boucher, thanks for finally agreeing to hire me at Ocean World.

I feel very lucky to have walked on the sets of so many talented directors: Tony Scott, Clint Eastwood, Joe Pytka, Adrian Lynne, James Cameron, John Woo, Kevin Costner, Steve Chase, Rob Luketic, Brad Silberling, Jeff Gorman and David Ellis to name a few. And the wonderful photographers: Norman Parkinson, Herb Ritts, William Wegman, and Bruce Weber. And thanks to Stephen Vaughn for being a part of Sue Chipperton, Phase III.

To my dogs: Tula the clown. Hank, you big Spank, hang in there, buddy. And to Beans, who passed away during the writing of this book: I pulled you out of the shelter to train you and teach you and you ended up teaching me. Thank you x.

★ ★ ★

Rennie Dyball would like to thank Danielle Perez and the team at NAL and superagent Mollie Glick for everything. You made it such a pleasure. Thanks to Sue for sharing your amazing story and trusting me to put it all down on paper. To John, for all the loving support, encouragement, and trips to George's as needed. Every ounce of my gratitude to my mom, for the tireless reading of drafts, endless patience, and for being my champion. Thanks to Berner for the tough love back in the day, and to Alex, for all your help and expertise along the way. This book and those to follow are for my dad. I wouldn't be the writer I am without you.

Sue Chipperton started her career in Florida, working with dolphins, and has been a studio animal trainer for nearly two decades. She has worked with such notable Hollywood figures as Brad Pitt, Clint Eastwood, and Jennifer Lopez, and has worked at Studio Animal Services in Los Angeles for seventeen years. Visit her Web site at www.afamousdogslife.com, and check out her blog at check-the gate.blogspot.com.

Rennie Dyball is a *People* magazine writer and coauthor of Christian Siriano's style guide/memoir, *Fierce Style*. She lives in New York City.